VIKING SPITFIRE

THE STORY OF FINN THORSAGER

TOR IDAR LARSEN

FONTHILL

A Norwegian Spitfire V over Catterick. (*Wilhelm Mohr*)

FONTHILL MEDIA
www.fonthillmedia.com

First published by Fonthill Media 2012

A CIP catalogue record for this book is available from the British Library

Typeset in 11pt on 13pt Bembo
Typesetting by Fonthill Media
Printed in the UK

ISBN 978-1-78155-043-4 (print)
ISBN 978-1-78155-134-9 (e-book)

Connect with us
 facebook.com/fonthillmedia twitter.com/fonthillmedia

This book is dedicated to Gurli Thorsager who so sadly passed away on 9 January 2011, on a beautiful winter's day in Norway. This book would never have been written if it wasn't for her. Thank you.

332 Squadron over the English countryside, *c.* 1942. (*Finn Thorsager*)

Contents

Finn at home with his family after getting his wings, 1938. (*Finn Thorsager*)

Acknowledgements

I would like to express my gratitude to the Thorsager family for the support and encouragement they have given me throughout this entire project. They are all such wonderful and kind people. My wife Noorit and I will never forget the gathering in Ellen's garden in the summer of 2010; it was such a wonderful ending to this project. Gurli's enthusiasm and support for the original Norwegian version of this book was followed by the same reaction from her daughter Ellen when I first told her about my intentions of translating the book into English. I am forever grateful.

I would also like to give my thanks to Edgar Brooks and John Clifford for their work on this book. My English is far from perfect, and I was truly lucky to have them both. Especially thanks to John for doing such a superb job of correcting my embarrassing mistakes. I promise I will never ever again write 'grass'! John has become a good friend of mine, and we had a great time at the Spring Airshow at Duxford in 2011. It was quite fitting to see 332 Squadron's ML407 in the air that day.

I would like to offer my thanks to Lieutenant General Wilhelm Mohr who so kindly invited me to his home in Oslo in 2008. He offered pictures and stories of his dear friend Finn Thorsager, and without him, this book would have suffered greatly. Also thanks to Rolf M. Kolling who telephoned me after receiving the book. He was full of praise and invited me to become a member of RAFA Norway.

I am also very grateful for Kaare Nevdal's approval and support regarding the missions he flew with Finn which are retold in the Stockholmsroute chapter. I also want to give my thanks to Gunnar Støltun who so kindly introduced me to two legends in aviation: Gladiator veteran Per Waaler and Lancaster crew member Anton Wang in March 2011.

The forum members at Key should not be forgotten; my thanks to everyone who helped out. Many thanks to my father Tore Erling Larsen, who introduced me to historic aviation by reading me comic books about Spitfires, Mosquitos and Hurricanes, taking me to airshows, and watching *The Battle of Britain* with me more than once on video. I am grateful for his belief and support in my work. Last, but certainly not least, I want to thank my wife Noorit Larsen for letting me fill up our apartment with aviation books, and for encouraging me to write and follow my dreams and crazy ideas.

A-flight, 332 Squadron, 1942. Detail from picture on p. 101. (*Finn Thorsager*)

Prologue

May 2010

I get off at Epping tube station in blistering hot sunshine. Summer has definitely arrived in England. I have flown down from Norway to attend an event called 'Gathering of Warbirds and Veterans' at RAF North Weald. This trip is paid for with royalties from *Gladiator*, the Norwegian version of this book about Finn Thorsager. It was only fitting I spent it on a trip to North Weald were Finn was based with 332 Squadron in 1942-43.

Coming up the main street, I easily spot the famous Thatched House pub, a favourite of the Norwegian pilots based at North Weald during the Second World War. However, there's no pub on the first floor any longer, and the hotel upstairs has sadly seen better days. It sets the right mood though; this little trip is to be done with Finn in mind, and in his honour. In my little suitcase I have a few copies of my book; one of them ready to be signed by the veterans attending the event.

I unpack and decide to walk to North Weald by foot. With no food in my belly since the flight, it's clearly not one of my better ideas, but I want to do it, and I start walking. The forest separating Epping and North Weald hasn't changed much since 1942, but the traffic certainly has!

Hungry and tired, I finally reach North Weald. 'Norway House', the old officers' mess, appears on my right. I take a breather in front of the North Weald Museum gazing at its lovely memorial, and then stroll down to the King's Head for a pint of Spitfire Ale and a well-deserved steak dinner.

The next morning I arrive at North Weald early. A member of the Key forum has invited me for a tour of the airfield. Later on, I'm given a special treat: I get to fly! After a couple of hours reading magazines and watching life go by from The Squadron, the famous North Weald clubhouse, we make our way to the plane. I instantly regret that pint I had right before take-off, but it will have to do.

With North Weald somewhere behind us, I wonder how many Norwegians have seen the airfield from the sky since 1945. A few perhaps, but it can't be many. Circling over Epping, we're told over the radio that three warbirds are inbound North Weald. I spot them in the haze, coming from the north. Two Spitfires and a Hurricane in close formation. We circle while the fighters prepare to land. I set my eyes on the Hurricane and follow it closely while we get in line behind it. Minutes later, we touch down; second down after a Hurricane! I can't believe it. How many Norwegians since the War have shared the sky with Spitfires and Hurricanes, and how many have landed after a Hurricane? It can't be many. I feel grateful, but first and foremost I am in total awe over of having witnessed and experienced such a thing. It feels like I have something in common with Finn, who I so sadly never got to meet.

Two hours later I have given away my other copy of *Gladiator* to the pilot in charge of my little sightseeing tour over North Weald to express my gratitude. I am in The Squadron again, now talking with pilots and people connected to North Weald, who seem to be doing their best to get me drunk. With another pint in hand, I remember reading that Wing Commander Wilfrid Duncan Smith said the Norwegians at North Weald were always ready for a party, so I decide not to be rude, and to follow in the footsteps of heroes.

The next morning, with a surprisingly small headache, I take a taxi up to North Weald. My contact from Key lets me come as close as possible to the Spitfires and Hurricanes. I shoot wildly with my camera.

By noon, most of the veterans have arrived, and I stand in line to get my own book signed. They are all larger than life. Tom Neill, Peter Ayerst, Hans Ekkehard-Bob – what a sight.

'Aaaahh, *Gladiator!*' says one of them, and grabs my book to have a look through. He glances up at me with a puzzled expression before looking down again. He goes through another couple of pages and then gives up. It's certainly not in English.

'Did you read this?' he asks, still puzzled with the book in his hand.

'No,' I reply. 'I wrote it.'

With everything winding down, I grab a soft drink and take a seat outside, close to Spitfire TA805. This is the spot where 331 Squadron had their base of operations. It's historic ground. I grab the signed copy of my own book and look at a few pictures of Finn. It has been a superb trip, all in his memory. He was never far from my thoughts.

I never knew Finn Thorsager personally, but I feel like I did. I never met him either, but somehow, on that day, among the Spitfires of North Weald, I felt he was with me.

Finn revisits Kjeller, 1990s. (*Finn Thorsager*)

A famous photo of a Gloster Gladiator during the winter of 1940. (*Finn Thorsager*)

Chapter 1

Last Flight

Travellers are rushing by Finn with their briefcases and travel bags. He can see the constant flow of people from the cockpit of the DC-9 he's flying. Just a quick turn-around and he will be back in Oslo by tonight.

Dusk is starting to descend over Hamburg Flughafen by the time the first passengers board the Scandinavian Airlines flight. Finn can see the passengers from his window. Plenty of businessmen, some tourists as well, all in good spirits. Tomorrow is a holiday, Norway's National Day. Finn has had this date in his head for a long time. 16 May 1976, the day it all will end. This will be his last flight, and then no more.

Finn's mind wanders back forty years, back to those days when he was introduced to flying. The enthusiasm he had for it, the feeling of freedom that enveloped him when he first took to the skies. It's a majestic feeling, and he will sorely miss it. Even during the dark days of the Second World War, he felt it, flying back over the coast of England, seeing the white cliffs of Dover rushing by underneath. He can clearly remember that feeling of freedom, the joy of simply being alive. Even after all those years, the memories can still rush in on him. But today, it will all be over. He feels it's a fitting day, one day before that special day they all place so highly, Norway's day of freedom.

Finn allows his imagination to take over; he feels that tomorrow will be extra special. The thought of Gurli back home baking a cake for the big day fills him with excitement and joy.

The last passenger boards, and Finn and his co-pilot finish off their pre-flight checks. He lets his thoughts rest and focuses on the job at hand. The co-pilot is strapped firmly to his seat, looking at the check list. Every now and then he holds his gaze on Finn. But Finn doesn't want any fuss; he ignores it, and keeps working. He was always modest about his own achievements, why change now?

They finish off the checks, and the two Pratt & Whitney JT8D turbo jet engines come roaring into life. The memories flow back to him once again. It feels as though his whole life has progressed through his years of flying; the navigation, the instruments, the force of the engines. To be back in a Spitfire, to throw it around over the English countryside, in and out of the clouds without the fear of being shot out of the sky. If only for just five minutes.

The DC-9 gathers speed down the Hamburg runway. Finn pulls the controls towards him, and the big nose of the passenger jet rises majestically up. They are airborne.

The stewardesses start their rounds just after they reach the right altitude for Finn to level out at cruising speed. He is offered a cup of coffee, and accepts with warm thanks. His co-pilot says nothing; he has sensed that Finn does not want to talk about this being his last flight. However, sometimes Finn can still notice him take quick glances in his direction, as if he's trying to say something. He can't deny that it's getting to him as well. The whole atmosphere in the cockpit is different to normal.

They soon leave the German coast behind, and Finn starts his normal speech to his passengers.

'This is Captain Thorsager speaking. Fornebu reports 15 degrees Celsius, calm winds and scattered clouds. We will land as scheduled in about forty-five minutes. Thank you.'

That's it. Just a normal message. He doesn't want any attention. Just like he told Gurli before he left this morning; he wants to keep things quiet, the way he likes it. She simply smiled, gave him a hug and watched him leave for his last day as a captain for Scandinavian Airlines.

They slowly descend over a peaceful Norway. Even though it's late, Finn can still clearly see all the landmarks that he knows. Again, he is taken back to 1940 and that dark day when he flew his Gladiator to engage the Luftwaffe's invasion fleet just south of Fornebu airport. It all happened in these skies, but it seems like a world away.

The wheels of the DC-9 touch down, giving off their normal whiny sound. The engines are put in reverse, and they break before exiting the runway. Two fire trucks have placed themselves strategically on each side of the DC-9 when it rolls into the gate. He won't be able to get out of this one, but he knew that. It's normal custom for a pilot's last flight before retirement.

The water splashes over the aircraft. Some of it runs down his window; the sign that it's all over. Finn turns off the engines at the gate, and the sound of them quickly dies. He's parked his last DC-9.

A Scandinavian Airlines DC-9 'Dan Viking', *c.* 1975. (*SAS Museum*)

A nice line-up of SAS DC-8s at Fornebu, 1970s. (*SAS Museum*)

Several of his old friends have shown up; they shake his hand, reeling off the normal banter when he arrives in the terminal. Finn puts on a brave smile and thanks them for coming. He wants to get it over with quick and go home to Gurli. He stays for an appropriate amount of time, and then excuses himself and drives home alone.

In the car, he feels a little bit guilty about his quick departure. Guilty also because he did not want his family on the flight to Hamburg and back, even though they were invited. He pushes the thoughts to the back of his mind. He did not want any big celebrations. Just a normal day.

Finn feels extremely tired when he finally sits down in the living room at home. It's past eleven at night. Gurli noticed it too, how tired he was when he came through the door. The day had taken its toll; he couldn't help his mind trying to wander back to old times. Gurli gives him a glass of water and kisses him on his cheek, leaving him to his own nostalgic thoughts. The radio is on, giving him the last news headlines before the day is over for good. He doesn't pay attention. All kinds of memories keep returning and he finally lets them encompass his mind, having kept them at bay for the entire day.

Finishing his water, Finn turns off the radio and leaves a single light in the living room on for the night. Gurli has already gone upstairs, preparing for a long day tomorrow with parades in Oslo and then their family over for dinner.

Finally, Finn stumbles into bed. He is asleep before his head meets the pillow.

Chapter 2

A Norwegian Legend

July 1931

Finn Thorsager sits in his dad's rowing boat out on the Oslofjord. He is together with his father, Conrad, and older brother, Carl Fredrik. Finn looks upwards to the brilliant blue sky and enjoys the hot weather while the water gently laps against the sides of the small boat. He looks over at Carl Fredrik. Finn is proud of his older brother. He feels that he's just how older brothers should be.

Conrad takes a good grip on the oars and rows slowly forward. They go around Bygdøy and Finn spots a large number of boats all around the inner parts of the fjord. Using his hand to shade his eyes, he can see most of them, gently floating on the water.

He knows there's something going on; there are more boats than normal, even on a beautiful sunny July day. They are all waiting for something, something exciting.

Conrad suddenly stops rowing. The boys turn around and look at their father with questioning eyes, but before they can say anything, they hear an engine sound, somewhere far away. It is getting louder and louder. The boys turn frantically back and forth to find out where the sound is coming from. Finn stops moving and scans the horizon.

'There!'

He points to a spot in the distance. There is something coming low over the fjord, landing on the water. A flying boat! The majestic aeroplane takes the water perfectly, making a gigantic white valley in the water. Everyone is waving and shouting. It is not just an aeroplane, it is the arctic explorer Roald Amundsen's aeroplane, a Dornier Do J 'Wal', registration number N-25; the flying boat that has been way up to the North Pole.

The boys look with excitement while N-25 slowly reduces its speed across the water. Not far away from their small rowing boat, the flying machine

Finn's older brother Carl Fredrik, out sailing sometime in the 1930s. (*Finn Thorsager*)

Left: Finn out rowing with his mother and brother, 1921. (*Finn Thorsager*)
Right: Finn with the house cat on his lap in 1931. (*Finn Thorsager*)

comes to a halt. Conrad grins at his two boys, takes a grip on the oars, and rows towards it. They get so close that Conrad grabs Finn, lifts him up and puts him on one of the aeroplane's floats. So there he sits, the little boy with a huge smile on his face. His father laughs and takes him down again. It had only lasted a moment, but Finn had been there, sitting on one of the floats of N-25!

A couple of days later I was at Killingen where we used to swim. N-25 had been tied up there, and now it was about to start its engines. The plane came roaring towards me, and suddenly it took to the air. Those of us who were standing a bit higher up on the island could look down on it when it flew past us. I will never forget that sight.

The years went by with school, scouting, skiing, ski jumping, RC flying and long fishing trips in the woods. Our 'special area' stretched from Bogstadvannet, Østernvannet, Abbortjern [small lakes around Oslo] and further inland. To get there, we had to walk through Ullernåsen [suburban area of Oslo], which at that time was completely uninhabited. The fact is that I have always been a man of nature, and this has given me huge pleasure and joy through the years. Maybe sometimes there's been a bit too much of it!

At Røa, in Oslo, there used to be a grocery store called Brødrene Randklev [Randklev Brothers], where we used to buy our essential food, like bread and margarine, and matches and the like. How we got money for this, I don't remember. A can of fishcakes, which were the cheapest, was really popular. We used to be in the woods for weeks at a time without any connection with home.

We had it quite good in our childhood years, even if the economy was pretty bad. It was normal in those days of the early '30s. Our father also sent the two of us, Carl Fredrik and me, to a boxing course at Halling Skole [school]. He probably felt it would be good for us to get kicked about so we could defend ourselves in years to come. Throughout that time, I was also really interested in aviation. I used to buy American aviation magazines and made models of aeroplanes.

I really wanted some kind of technical education, but I wasn't among the very brightest students at school, and those technical schools in Germany were really expensive. To be prepared for a technical education in those days, you needed mechanical experience. Therefore, my father got me hired at Lindviks Carshop at Thune, an area in Oslo, as a trainee. I had a really good time there. I was 16 years old, and worked gratefully without pay from 7 a.m. to 5 p.m. After a while, I started to get really good at it, and I took on work which I should have been paid for. The other workers wanted me to join the union and get on the payroll. When the boss got to know about this, he told me that if I joined the union, he would fire me. So I quit on my own and got a place in a school for ironworkers in Elvegaten [street] with technical lectures during the afternoon.

Finn on a mountain trek in the 1960s. Finn was always a man of nature, loving his time in the great outdoors to the fullest. (*Finn Thorsager*)

Chapter 3

Airborne

The wheels of the bike quickly stop turning when Finn notices something unusual down at Maritim, Oslo's harbour. Something interesting is tied to the small pier. He gets back on his bike so he can get closer. He passes a few boats on the way, but he doesn't spare them even one thought. Finn has something else in his view beyond the ordinary. It is a small seaplane. He stares at it. It has two sets of wings, stags between them on both sides. He examines it down to the tiniest detail. The front is angular in shape, while the body of the plane becomes gradually narrower the further back it goes. The tail is big compared to the rest of the plane, while the wings are thick and covered in fabric.

Finn puts down the bike and walks over to a man who is standing next to the seaplane, gently cleaning one of the wings. The man hears Finn approaching, and looks up.

'I'm flying pleasure rides,' the man says calmly. 'Would you like one?'

Finn looks at the aeroplane with big eyes.

'Hey, it will only cost you 10 kroner.' He grins. He sees that Finn really wants the trip, even if it would cost him a year's income.

Finn starts to mess around in his pockets. He pulls up a few coins and starts counting them. His heart skips a beat when he discovers that he's a little short. Maybe he won't get the trip.

'I have almost 10 kroner.' Finn looks at the coins in the palm of his hand. He really wants that trip!

The man straightens his hat and smiles calmly. 'That will have to do then. Hop on board.'

Finn Thorsager is not someone who needs to be told twice.

'By the way, the name is Halvor Bjørneby.' Finn, already halfway down into the front cockpit, puts his hand out and shakes Bjørneby's.

'Finn Thorsager. Nice to meet you.'

Finn on one of his lucky trips with Widerøe, early-mid 1930s. (*Finn Thorsager*)

A quick handshake and Bjørneby gets ready to start the engine. Finn's hands are moist with sweat. He will finally get to fly. Excited as never before, he sits and listens to the engine starting up. The sound is spectacular for the young boy.

Bjørneby gives it full throttle when they reach Bestumkilen, a small bay north-west of Bygdøy. Before Finn knows it, they're airborne. The pilot takes the small aeroplane into a turn towards Oslo and Bygdøy. Finn looks up, left, right and straight ahead. He can hardly sit still. Behind him, the pilot chuckles. Bjørneby pulls the plane upwards and into a stall-turn while Finn sits there as if it was Christmas Eve, National Day, and his birthday all in the same day.

Bjørneby puts the plane into a deep dive and then into a hard turn that pins Finn into the seat. The wind is screaming, the engine is roaring, and Bjørneby suddenly throws the plane into an opposite turn; suddenly, the plane is on its side and Finn can see directly down beneath him. He gasps at the amazing view. Never before has he seen such a glorious sight.

After a couple more minutes, time is up. Bjørneby reduces throttle and prepares to land on the fjord. The aeroplane gently rocks in the wind before they touch down.

Bjørneby ties the aeroplane to the pier again while Finn gets out of the cockpit. His legs are a bit shaken when he takes his first step back on land.

With the biggest smile he can produce, he gets on his bike again and says goodbye to Bjørneby, thanking him again and again for the ride. Going home, he cycles faster than ever; it would be quite something to tell his mother and father, and especially Carl Fredrik.

Later on, I got in touch with the pilots at Widerøe [a Norwegian airline company] and I helped them out selling tickets and such at airshows held around the south of Norway. In Sandefjord and Drammen I used to sit in the front seat going to different airshows, and sometimes I was even allowed to fly the plane. These events could also take place during the winter, and frozen lakes were normally used as airports and runways.

In between all this, I lived a normal life with school and everything else. However, my future goal started to appear in my mind. I wanted to be admitted into the Army Air Force at Kjeller [an airfield in Oslo, close to the town of Lillestrøm], so I started school at St Hanshaugen to get the necessary qualifications. Unfortunately, I didn't pass the exam, and thought I could try again next time, but when I saw an ad in the newspaper recruiting new students for the Army Air Force, I sent in an application and added my mid-term grades. I was lucky and got accepted as the final reserve added to the course in June 1936. This was the turning point that was to decide my future once and for all.

I enjoyed the training; it was a great challenge for young boys with lots of written work, exercise and discipline. We were toughened and learned how to handle being shouted at, even if we didn't deserve it. Ole Reistad was our teacher, and that was purely a good thing. He was a great advocate of sports, and during the winter we were out on skis. As trainee pilots we were paid 50 kroner per month, minus 2 kroner in taxes.

Throughout the autumn I learned about engines, navigation, meteorology and military strategy. We practiced flying in de Havilland Standard Moths and Tiger Moths, common aeroplanes during the 1930s. I also flew more advanced types, such as Fokkers, which had more powerful engines and bigger frames than the Moths. All of the aeroplanes were 'open' – no enclosed cockpits – which meant our faces were exposed to frostbite. We used wheels during the summer and skis during the winter.

Viking Spitfire

Group photo at Kjeller, possibly 1936. Finn Thorsager can be seen in the middle of the group, with Wilhelm Mohr further to his left. (*Finn Thorsager*)

Pupils at Kjeller during a funny moment, 1937. (*Finn Thorsager*)

Another view of Kjeller Aerodrome, 1937. (*Finn Thorsager*)

Chapter 4

An Eventful Journey

Twelve Tiger Moths stand ready for take-off at Kjeller airfield. The students are standing in groups discussing today's trip. It is a task they have yet to experience. Finn is feeling stirred up; he is nervous and excited. Formation flying all the way to Sola airport to participate in its official opening is rather beyond their normal training routine at Kjeller. Sola is near Stavanger, a long way over to the west of Norway.

Some nervous laughter can be heard from some of the pilots; a few jokes are told while others grin back, even though they're not really paying attention. Their thoughts are elsewhere. To fly all the way to Sola is a difficult task, especially in planes that have no radios or navigational aids.

The leader of the formation stands ready beside his Tiger Moth.

'Alright fellows,' he shouts, 'everyone ready? Let's go!'

One by one, the engines start up. They're ready to go.

Finn takes his Tiger Moth gently into the air. Soon, he has enough altitude to turn gradually right with the others. Beneath him, houses and trees slowly become smaller and smaller the higher he climbs. Minutes later, all the twelve planes are in formation behind their leader.

The Moths fly over large Norwegian forests, little lakes and tiny gravel roads. Finn is sitting alert in his cockpit. He adjusts his plane's position just a tad; he knows the formation needs to look perfect.

In another Moth not far away is Finn's friend Wilhelm Mohr. Mohr holds a steady grip on the controls while they fly south-west over Norway, through the mid-summer skies.

The leader turns his head and notices that a few students aren't holding their place in the formation correctly. He makes a mental note to make sure they're told when they land at Sola. With the exception of a few clouds scattered around, everything is set for a nice trip.

Finn's aeroplane rocks in the wind. He reacts quickly and straightens it

A Tiger Moth is coming in for a landing, Kjeller, 1937. (*Finn Thorsager*)

up again and onto the correct course. Turbulence. Finn feels that he isn't fully comfortable with it just yet. It doesn't bother him, but all the bumping and shaking is truly something to get used to. It requires a lot of work to hold the plane steady. He likes to fly the plane and to have something to work with, but it's too shaky for him to feel relaxed.

Again, Finn's aeroplane meets heavy turbulence and gets thrown about. He tries to stretch his neck out of the cockpit and gets hit by the strong wind. In the distance, thick, heavy clouds are closing in. Finn's plane makes another jump. The turbulence is definitely getting worse. The formation leader has also seen the dark clouds, but decides to press on.

The formation flies straight into the thick clouds and is suddenly completely surrounded by darkness. This weather has come too quickly upon them. Finn knows there will be trouble now. The formation was not prepared for such conditions, and they were not forecast either.

Half the aeroplanes in the formation have absolutely no instruments to handle the situation, and they don't have any sort of maps. Finn's grip tightens on the stick while the Tiger Moth is violently buffeted by the wind. A loud crack breaks through the regular sound of the engine – thunder. Holding the plane on a steady course is getting harder and harder; Finn is getting desperate. He tries to focus his vision forward, but he can only see a dark sea of grey. The rest of the formation has completely disappeared. Suddenly, to his left, a Moth comes into view. It looks like Wilhelm Mohr with his passenger, Hørlock, sitting in front of him. Finn hopes that Mohr can spot him, but it seems he is using all his concentration to control his

Students at Kjeller, watching a Tiger Moth landing, 1937. (*Finn Thorsager*)

aeroplane. Finn can see Mohr stretching out of the aeroplane, trying to look for anything that might help him know how to keep the plane level. Then he disappears into the fog, and visibility returns to zero.

The formation has come to pieces in the clouds. One student loses control of his aeroplane and comes spinning down towards earth. Some take the chance to go lower to see where they are. Another takes no chances, makes sure his parachute is fastened correctly, and steps out of his doomed Tiger Moth. He releases the 'chute while the sound of his aircraft disappears in the clouds.

Per Egge, another student, hesitates in making a decision. He pushes the stick forward and tries to break through the bottom of the clouds. Frantically, he looks for anything that can help him, but there is nothing to be seen. He is drenched in sweat beneath his flyingsuit. The clouds give out another large bang while the aeroplane, for a fraction of a second, is completely lit up by the lightning.

Egge does what others have already done; he checks his equipment and jumps out of his plane. Per is falling down in a thick soup of black and grey. He pulls the ripcord, but too late. From the skies above, the boy drops through the clouds and hits Lake Ekeren with a huge splash. Nobody can survive such a fall.

Finn still flies steadily on. He looks down at the few instruments he's got and tries to keep a level heading. In quick movements he looks ahead and to the sides to try and figure out where he is. The dark surroundings and the terrible turbulence are racking his nerves, but his Moth's engine fights

A Gloster Gladiator at Kjeller in 1938. From left to right: Per Waaler, Dag Krohn, Per Schiøts, unknown English mechanic, Birger Motzfeldt, Arve Braathen, Hans Jacob Fredriksen, Finn Thorsager and Per Smith. (*Finn Thorsager*)

the weather bravely. Finn points the plane in a south-westerly direction and hopes to emerge from the cloud somewhere over the sea. He doesn't know what else he can do.

Time passes and the clouds begin to thin out. Finn has held the same course and expects to see water rushing underneath him any second now.

When the ground finally comes into view, it's not the ocean Finn's flying over, but a little lake. He descends further and flies low over a little river connected to the small body of water, running in between the hills of Telemark. And then, in the distance to his left, he spots another Moth. The two planes meet up and wave their wings at each other.

Finn can now see it's Wilhelm Mohr at the controls. Mohr waves and wags his wings. It can't be anyone else but him, with Hørlock, his passenger, in the front seat. They try to communicate with each other through hand signals and waves. Wilhelm tries to get Finn to look at a specific field under them. He wants them to land there.

Wilhelm breaks off from the formation and goes in for a landing. Finn sees his friend turn sharply into the final stages. They haven't noticed an electricity line stretching out at the end of the little field – Mohr just manages to fly underneath it. From Finn's position in the sky, they look to be alright. They have come to a full stop on the small field.

Wilhelm Mohr, Mohr's passenger Hørlock, and Finn Thorsager after their now famous emergency landing at Bamble when their formation broke up due to bad weather, 1937. (*Wilhelm Mohr*)

Now it's Finn's turn. He makes a sharp turn and heads straight towards the field. He passes the electricity line just barely – it feels as though he brushes it as he glides underneath. And then his wheels touch the earth, bumping heavily over the rough terrain.

Finn pulls off his flying helmet. His forehead is covered in sweat. It was a close shave – far too close – but he's ok. On the ground, spectators are flocking around the two planes. It's not every day that visitors drop in out of the sky.

Wilhelm and I were invited for specially bought boiled mackerel for dinner, and, when the weather improved later that day, we flew back to Kjeller.

But Wilhelm decides to leave Hørlock behind. Taking off from a field with two people in the plane is not something he wants to do. Hørlock will have to get home by some other means.

In those days, there were lots of discussions in the press about where the main airport should be located. A man wrote in a newspaper with the opinion that it should be absolutely no problem when two students could make do with just a small field!

27 May was a serious day with lots of angry opinions in the newspapers concerning the ill-fated trip. The conclusion was that the formation

Finn at work on the boat
Arne Kjøde, late 1930s.
(*Finn Thorsager*)

Finn on his way to Antarctica on *Arne Kjøde*, late 1930s. (*Finn Thorsager*)

Finally, the wind settles and *Arne Kjøde* can be manoeuvred close to the big whaling ships and anchor up beside them. *Arne Kjøde* gives them plenty of oil and, in return, gets whale oil bound for Germany. The boat bounces gently against three dead blue whales, which act as massive fenders. They hang helplessly down from the sides of the ship as people work around them. From one of them, a dead offspring is sticking halfway out of its mother's womb.

With the trade about to be done, *Arne Kjøde* leaves the big ship and turns round to complete its journey towards Germany. This voyage is Finn's first aboard such a great ship.

We got a grand view of the drama of harpooning whales, and I got to see, first hand, how tough this life could be. Our oil was taken to Germany and I left the boat there; Carl Fredrik had received notice about a possible job that could be a step towards working for DNL. When I finally got home, I got in touch with a telepraphist called Knut Skavhaugen who was working aboard *Black Watch*. He had been offered a job as a co-pilot for DNL. Sadly, he was shot down in a Mosquito during the War, and was killed in the crash.

Knut suggested that I took his job on *Black Watch*, which was a great way into a future job at DNL. He would then take up a new job at DNL at once. At the same time, he would move in with me at Bestun.

'Alright,' I said, and that's how it went. It was really superb of my mum and dad to accept Knut as a housemate!

Black Watch was an elegant passenger ship that sailed the route between Oslo, Kristiansand and Newcastle. It was owned by Fred Olsen. It had radiophones onboard, with five 'kiosks'. The telegraphist always had to fine-tune the signal while a conversation was going on. I got to hear a lot of tear-jerking stories, but obviously I was under contract not to tell anyone about any conversation. Both *Arne Kjøde* and *Black Watch* were sunk during the War.

The work I did on *Black Watch* was really interesting, but during the summer of 1939, I was called up for service with the Air Force, a service that would last for forty days. The war in Europe had begun.

Black Watch, the passenger ship Finn got a job on as a telegraphist, trading places with Knut Skavhaugen. The ship was sunk during the War. (*Finn Thorsager*)

Chapter 6

Battle in a Gladiator

The days [at Fornebu with the Royal Norwegian Air Force] went by with practice of different types. Because the telephone radio wasn't very reliable, we communicated predominantly by Morse code. Flying-wise, we were quite well trained, even if our politicians didn't give us the back-up we wanted. For some time, some of us were put off duty due to national economic reasons. Those of us who were not off duty applied to use their free time and weekends for practice. It was denied.

The pilots lived in double rooms at Oksenøen Bruk [farm houses close to Fornebu], while the ground personnel lived in a greenhouse with planks over the earth floor. They slept where the plants should have been. Pilots on duty rested on the floor in the old restaurant.

To be prepared in the best possible way for what could happen, we were sent out on several orientation trips around the area to find useful places for alternative take-off and landing runways. The reports were delivered to our commanding officer. We were all in high spirits.

On the morning of 9 April, we were woken at around 1 a.m. The alarm had gone off at one of the Oslofjord's outer fortresses, but because of our pitiful communication conditions, we got no exact information about what was going on. So, having been up at Fornebu airport, where we did our preparations to the best of our ability, we got sent back down again to Oksenøen Bruk and continued to sleep.

Many people who were not in the military got better information that morning than we did. They received it through normal broadcasts. Our commanders got their incomplete information from their superiors, and had no radios to listen in on.

Finn shrugs the sleep off himself with a couple of shakes and remembers the night's strange events. The alarms, the conversations, the discussions and

Pilots and ground crew in front of a Gloster Gladiator, possibly 1939. (*Finn Thorsager*)

the strange atmosphere that had started to develop. A surreal feeling that something was going on, but what?

He crawls out of his uncomfortable bed and looks towards the door where there's a man talking loudly. Lieutenant Tradin[1] stands in the entrance to the restaurant in front of all the pilots on duty. It must have been the same person that woke him up just now. He has a serious face and speaks with a shiver in his voice.

'Second Lieutenant Thorsager, you're on duty from 5 a.m. We have reports coming in that say something serious is going on. All pilots have to meet at the airport. We're on full alert!'

Finn tries to shake the feeling of sleep from his body. It's not easy to get the brain going after just a few hours' sleep. He looks at his watch. It's 4.30 a.m. He had better get going. No point in dwelling on what's happened. It will only create uncertainty.

He curses when he can't find his flying jacket and other necessary equipment. He's not the only one a bit worked up. They all are. Everyone is rushing around, causing chaos.

Finn looks at his equipment, trying to remember what he needs to bring. He concludes that a thick sweater under his uniform could be wise. He grabs a high-necked one, plus his goggles and flying helmet. He puts all the layers on. He feels a bit stiff and awkward but at least he won't freeze if he goes up this morning. It's still early April and the winter is not quite over.

Finn stumbles out the front door of the airport restaurant, the pilots' makeshift bedroom; they were sent there when things started to happen so they could be on readiness close by. He knows he is not feeling his best; in fact, he hasn't been feeling well for several days. Finn feels his forehead with his right hand. It's warmer than it should be, and he fears he might have a case of fever.

It's still dark outside. The low cloudbase doesn't help. Once the sun comes up, the weather will warm up and the cloud will disappear.

Finn gathers with the rest of the pilots before they are taken by car down to the airport. On arrival they are told by Captain Erling Munte-Dahl, commanding officer of the Gladiators at Fornebu, that unknown aircraft are coming from the south, heading north. They've heard several flying over Fornebu already. Munthe-Dahl turns to Finn and Second Lieutenant Arve Braathen.[2]

'Take off immediately to gather information and report back over the radio,' he says, with a firm but friendly voice.

They wander over to their Gladiators. Finn's is easy to spot among the others; it's the only camouflaged one they have. The rest are silver-white in colour with Norwegian markings stretching over each wing and the rudder as well. Even if his Gladiator isn't one of the better looking ones, Finn feels confident that it will 'do the business' in the air. The camouflage might even make it harder for enemy planes to spot him. The thought of the unknown makes his pulse quicken. A few butterflies flutter in his stomach – not the friendly sort.

Finn is surprised to see his Gladiator's 840-h.p. Bristol Mercury engine already running. Everything is prepped and ready for take-off. It really must be serious this time. Last night the Gladiators were separated, but now they are all lined up together.

Finn climbs into the cockpit with ease. He's done it so many times before. It hits him for a moment that, even though the aeroplane is almost brand new, it's construction already seems out-dated. It is pretty manoeuvrable though, and that should work in his favour if he gets into combat with an aircraft faster than his.

He leaves the hood open while he pushes the throttle slowly forward and taxis out to the end of runway 15. He will take off eastwards. Finn places the Gladiator perfectly on the runway's centreline and checks his magnetos. All good. He pulls the hood into the locked position, then puts the fuel mixture to 'normal' and turns the carburettor heating to the 'off' position. Finn selects the correct fuel tank and corrects the gyro, altitude meter and compass. Finally, he moves the stick to its full extent to check the rudder. The Gladiator is ready to be taken up.

Braathen is approaching behind him in his Gladiator, and places himself at Finn's tail, out on the runway. Throttle forward. Finn's Gladiator roars with power as it picks up speed down the runway. He can feel the cold wind hit his face. Braathen disappears somewhere behind him.

> Lieutenant Braathen took-off right after me, but what I did not know was that he was supposed to listen for messages I transmitted. Because of some misunderstanding we were on different frequencies, and he never heard my transmissions.

It's only half an hour since Finn was woken up, but now he feels strangely calm. The uneasiness and tension is still there, but after getting into the cockpit, his nerves have subsided and he feels a growing sense of confidence flow through his body. It is something a fighter pilot needs more than anything, and he's pleased with his training.

Finn looks up and sees the thick cloud floating quietly above. But there are gaps in it, and he is confident there should be no difficulty in getting above the fog.

The sun is beginning to rise and the sky is becoming much brighter. The Gladiator climbs well, and Finn anticipates achieving a good speed above the fog.

The thought of firing his guns comes to mind; should he open fire if he spots unfamiliar aircraft? The idea feels a bit unclear when he thinks about it, but if the situation arises, he is confident he will make the right decision.

Another quick check of the instruments. Everything seems to be alright. Fuel for another two and a half hours of flying and plenty of ammunition for his two Browning machine guns out on the lower wings. The firepower is synchronised and he's well equipped if something should happen.

Finn puts his left hand on the throttle. He can feel his knuckles tighten underneath his thick gloves. He pushes the throttle a little forward. His right

Norwegian Gladiators lined up at Fornebu, winter 1940. (*Finn Thorsager*)

leg is ready at the rudder pedal to balance the torque of the engine and the plane's 3.2 m-long propeller. Best speed for climbing is 168 kph.

Finn maintains his speed and breaks through the fog, but where is Braathen? Finn looks behind – no Gladiator is to be seen. There had been some trouble with the magnetos on Braathen's plane; Finn satisfies himself that that must be the answer. The task still stands; look for strangers. He will do it alone.

The sky feels peaceful when Finn sees the cloud stretched out underneath him; the sun beams through the gaps towards the earth. It's hard for him to imagine enemy aircraft in such quiet and serene surroundings. It just feels too peaceful.

Finn turns left and then right to be able to see downwards from his cockpit. He can spot Kolsåstoppen and Holmenkollen, two small mountains on the outskirts of Oslo. The Gladiator doesn't feel in perfect shape and it takes some effort to see well enough, but he spots nothing out of the ordinary. He would have felt even more confident if he had been flying one of the new Curtiss Hawk planes the Norwegian Government has just bought from the USA. Not that the new monoplane is any more manoeuvrable than the Gladiator, but its speed is a lot more impressive. It would have meant being able to catch up with an unidentified aircraft a lot quicker. However, in a dive Finn could get his Gladiator up to 400 kph. The thought of the dive calms him down again.

Finn is at 2,000 feet and well above the cloud when he spots something black underneath him. A sense of confusion comes over him – is it something on the ground, or in the air? The black object looks to be moving below him. He can clearly see it down to the left, about a kilometre away flying on a 40-degree course. Finn glances at the unknown object. It has double tail fins. Several German aircraft types have double tail fins – that much he knows.

Finn does not know for sure what the plane is and where it's from, but he's certain it's not Norwegian and that it should not be there. It must be an intruder.

He pushes the throttle all the way forward and puts his Gladiator into a shallow dive. Serious thoughts fill his head while he closes in on the stranger. Will he be opening fire on the unknown aircraft? There are people on board after all. Probably young men like himself.

He pushes the thoughts away. The plane is breaking Norwegian neutrality, it has no right to fly over here. Finn pushes away the safety guard over the button for his machine guns. He wonders if they have spotted him yet. It doesn't look like it; the stranger is still flying steady. It dawns on him that, with the speed he is now carrying, he will be within range to fire very soon.

Once more, thoughts appear in his mind. Dark thoughts. He's closing in. Someone might be killed because of what he's about to do. Again he ignores his feelings and readies his thumb on the firing button.

The black and grey plane with double tail fins grows bigger and bigger by the second. Finn is rapidly catching up. The wind is increasing in strength the faster he goes. He can't believe it's happening. It seems unreal. He's about the engage the unknown plane, and will shoot it down if he can.

Finn manoeuvres into firing position, lining the intruder up in the Gladiator's gun sights. He needs more speed, and pushes the Gladiator further down into a dive. And then it's happening. His thumb holds down the button on his stick and the Gladiator sends of it's deadly load.

If only he had tracers in. He can't see where his bullets are going. He pulls away from the aircraft, unsure if he fired at the right distance to cause damage. Did he forget to calculate drift? It's impossible to see whether he hit his target or not.

Then he sees it, up close for the first time. The symbols, the colour, the design are German. The stranger banks to the right and dives down into the fog. It must be German, and he won't stay in that cloud for long. Finn flies above. The German can't have any idea where he is; he might fly into a mountain top at any moment. Finn tries to anticipate his next move, and manoeuvres his Gladiator to where he thinks the German will appear. He keeps his safety off and his thumb hovering over the fire button.

Seconds later, the German breaks up through the cloud, just as Finn expected. His plane seems be to be a twin-engined Dornier of some kind, but he can't be sure. The swastikas are starkly visible on the plane's tailfins.

Finn dives down on the intruder once again, and opens fire when he senses that he's within range. Again, it's impossible to see if he's hitting his target or not. He can't even see if the German is returning fire. Then it's over for a second time. The Dornier disappears below and into the fog. Again, Finn tries to anticipate the German's movements and outmanoeuvre him.

The German is trapped; he emerges from the cloud, Finn fires, and he disappears again. The same thing happens again and again, every time Finn is waiting for the German above the clouds. Finn is almost getting used to the routine until finally, the Dornier disappears for good. Maybe Finn's bullets really did hit the Dornier and its engines have caught fire. He hopes the people on board survive; he's not a brutal warrior.

The adrenaline rush slows down gradually, and it makes him think a bit clearer. How long has he been in the air? It must be over an hour? To the left and below of him, Finn observes thick, black smoke rising up from underneath. The cloud covers where it is coming from but it looks to be somewhere around Drøbak, by the Oslofjord.

> Below me I saw a huge plume of black smoke rising up through the fog. This was *Blücher's*[3] last position before it sank, but I didn't know it at the time.

Finn receives a radio message to set course straight for Fornebu. He reluctantly turns back towards the airfield. He's been in the air for a good while and has used up half of his fuel. The fight took place not far home, but the cloud is still thick and it makes it hard to navigate. Over Drammen, he can finally spot landmarks, and from there, it's easy to fly into Fornebu.

The Gladiator sinks slowly through the cloud and levels out under it. The rest is easy. He puts the plane nicely down on the tarmac and taxis towards the restaurant where several people are waiting for him. In the corner of his eye he notices that several Gladiators are missing. They must have taken off later to get a clear view of the situation. Almost before the engine cuts out, he's being questioned by the people waiting.

'Did you see any planes?'

'What happened?'

'There must be something going on. Right?'

It's quite a show, and Finn is at the centre of it all. They all want to have their questions answered. It's understandable. One of them sees that Finn has used his machine guns. He looks at Finn with big blue eyes and a gasping mouth. Finn answers the questions as best he can. He tries to act calm. He doesn't want to show everyone how excited he is.

'Our neutrality has been breached by German aircraft.'

It's the first thing Finn manages to say while he's standing by his Gladiator, fishing out a 'smoke' from his pocket. He tells everyone nearby about the black smoke coming up from Drøbak, and they all understand that something serious must have been taken place. On the other hand, they all have a hard time comprehending that Norway might be at war with Germany.

It suddenly dawns on Finn that he could have been killed during that battle, or at least shot down.

Captain Munte-Dahl makes his way through the little crowd of people around Finn's Gladiator. His face is serious and his lips are tightly pressed.

'You have to write a report immediately,' he orders.

Finn's camouflaged Gladiator is taken by the ground personnel for refuelling and reloading of ammunition while Finn gets himself indoors to write his report. Before he starts writing, he takes a deep breath and wonders how the day will end.

Just before seven in the morning, he's approached by three other pilots who have just come back from a patrol; Dag Krohn, Per Waaler and Kristian Fredrik Schye. They tell of how they did not see anything out of the ordinary, but Finn can tell them in return that at least one German intruder has breached Norwegian neutrality. They look at him with serious faces. The thought starts to creep up on them that this is more than just a breach of neutrality. Just a few minutes later, their talk is interrupted by orders to take off for another patrol. This time, there will be five Gladiators in the air – all the serviceable Gladiators they have.

On the way out to his Gladiator, Finn spots another three Gladiators being worked on, with the hope of getting them into the air. Rolf Torbjørn Tradin will, as usual, lead the formation. Finn spots him getting into Waaler's Gladiator, but doesn't dwell on it any further. Finn is helped into his Gladiator for the second time that morning; again, he feels calmer once he's buckled in. The orders are simple: form up at 3,000 feet and await further instructions. Finn's place in the formation will be at number 4, at the back and to the left.

Tradin powers up his Gladiator's engine and it speeds off down the southern runway. Pebbles and dirt fly up behind him as he collects speed and takes off. Finn follows close behind and climbs up into the sky. Over

Sandvika, just outside Oslo, they join up in formation. Gladiator 425 is the closest to him. It's Per Waaler; he's number two on the left side after Tradin, and to the right of Finn.

The formation flies south, and they can easily spot the heavy black smoke arising at Drøbak, just like Finn had seen it earlier that morning. It is a bizarre sight for the young pilots. Tradin turns the formation north again.

In a short while, the Norwegians spot a formation of six German planes under them. There are no doubts any longer. This is real and it's happening. The Germans planes are Messerschmitt 110s. Finn can easily see the type this time around. He thinks about the 110's manoeuvrability, tensing up a little in the small cockpit. Is it really superior or will their small Gladiators have a chance in out-turning them? The 110 has two engines and it is much larger than the Gladiator. Maybe that will really make a difference here.

Below the Norwegians, the sun flashes against the cockpits of the Messerschmitts, and their wings, painted with swastikas and German crosses, shine bright. To the right, Finn glances at the Norwegian markings on the Gladiators; red, white and blue stand out in stark contrast to the black and white German markings on their camouflaged planes.

Finn looks below again at the German formation and then, just for a second, he glances at his instruments. When his eyes return below, the sight almost takes his breath away. Formation upon formation of German planes have emerged, seemingly from nowhere. There are so many he can't even begin to count them all. What an armada they are now facing! His whole body tightens up. They are hopelessly outnumbered.

'Break formation,' orders Tradin on the radio. 'Every man for himself. Good luck!'

Finn kicks his left rudder and almost rolls the Gladiator on its back, diving down towards the armada. He can hear the roar of the wind through the noise of the engine. The Gladiator picks up speed. A Heinkel 111 appears straight ahead of him. This time around, Finn waits until he's closer before firing. When he feels he's in range, and the German is right in his sights, he opens fire. The machine guns burst out deadly bullets; the Gladiator shakes with the force of it, and Finn keeps firing. Smoke suddenly gushes out of one of the Heinkel's engines. The enemy plane banks hard right and loses altitude, disappearing somewhere beneath him.

Suddenly Finn's machine guns stop firing. All he can hear is the sound of pressurised air. He makes a quick mental note of the incident, and then decides to go after another plane. They are all around him. He picks one and pushes the firing button. Nothing happens. The disappointment washes

Viking Spitfire

Stein Sem rolling a Gladiator, winter 1940. (*Finn Thorsager*)

over him like a creeping nightmare; the machine guns are jammed! He goes around and attacks a third plane with the same result. He's useless without his machine guns. Finn pulls sharply out of the ongoing battle and makes a decision to head back to Fornebu to fix the problem.

A quick look at the compass and he speeds off in the direction of Fornebu while keeping a sharp look-out for more enemy planes. The sight is overwhelming. The air is full of them. Norwegian Gladiators dive down on them while tracers from the German gunners are flying everywhere. Finn sees a Gladiator barely getting away from a stream of bullets from a Heinkel 111. The tracer actually helps the Norwegian get out of the line of fire.

At the sight of the Gladiators fighting bravely against an overwhelming force of Germans, Finn's disappointment turns to massive frustration. He can't help his comrades in the battle. Finn feels like kicking the rudders in despair, just to be doing something. He bites his lip and dives back towards Fornebu. He needs to be there as quickly as possible, so he can get back in the air.

He's still inexperienced in combat, and he is aware of it, but he knows to keep an eye out. There might be more Germans around, and he mustn't be an easy target. He pushes the Gladiator to the limit going homewards, and it's not long before he's closing in on runway 33. He's just about to put out the flaps when he sees plumes of smoke rising from the airfield. It sends shivers down his spine. Two of the Gladiators which were under service when he left for the mission are now burning on the ground. It can only mean one thing. The Luftwaffe has paid a visit, and they must be close. At that moment, instinct and fear prompt him to look behind. Two Messerschmitt 110s are about to give him a very warm surprise. Finn knows that, with a good hit, their firepower is enough to split his Gladiator in two.

With full power from the engine, Finn turns hard left. The G-force pushes his body into his seat. The Messerschmitts on his tail can't keep up with his tight turn. In fact, his turn has put him behind one of them, within firing range. Finn pushes the button once more, but yet again, there's only air to be heard from the machine guns. Before the German in front knows what is happening, Finn throws his Gladiator on a different course and disappears from Fornebu, leaving the Messerschmitts behind. He heads south for Kjeller.

Finn is tired, disappointed and frustrated, but he still gets behind a few Germans on his way down to Kjeller. He can't miss them. They are everywhere in the sky. Ten minutes later, he sees Kjeller ahead of him. There are several fires on the ground at the small airfield. No chance to land there.

I then tried to go to Fornebu again, but there were so many German planes around, I had no idea what I was going to do. Then a message came from Sergeant Jespersen, who was under fire in his radiohut: 'Land, but not at Fornebu. Land, but not at Fornebu.'

Finn is unsure of what he should do. He ends up on a south-eastern course and spots a small frozen lake below. The decision is quick. He needs to get down and soon. There is no other option.

Exhausted, he still does a circuit and the rest happens automatically. Carburettor heat on, nose up, flaps out, adjust speed for landing. Finn is unsure of the conditions on the frozen lake, but gives it little thought; it seems like a mere detail compared to what has just happened.

The Gladiator comes in low over the pine trees and the wheels touch down on the icy lake. They burrow a little into the ice, weakened by the approaching spring. Finn tries to slow down the aeroplane by braking very gently. Too much it seems, as the Gladiator dangerously tips forward and is about to tip over. But it just holds on and begins to slow down, until finally it comes to a stop. The plane is undamaged and Finn is unhurt.

Just ahead, Finn spots a rocky beach and taxis his Gladiator over to the shore. Not far from there, he can see a farmhouse. The ice can barely hold the aircraft. He realises that a take-off from this lake would be impossible. At the shore, he turns off the ignition and Gladiator 433 gives out its last few puffs before stopping. Only the sounds and smells of nature meet him when he climbs out of his aircraft. It's all quite unreal. The contrast to the events that have just taken place is colossal. He can hardly believe it.

I landed at Lake Mjærvann in Enebakk, south-east of Oslo, and was helped in to the city again by the owner of a farm. I had to sit on a bus, as a paying customer. I did not know anything about the situation unfolding, and was not sure if Norway was at war or not. I had not been speaking to anyone of course, but I did understand that something dramatic and quite catastrophic was happening.

I tried to get myself to Fornebu, but I managed to get over to Akershus Fortress at the harbour of Oslo where I met most of my friends and colleagues. We were bombed by Junkers 87s here, so we had to get away quickly. I was injured from the explosions, and had a bleeding cut from my forehead. My father, who had seen the dramatic happenings over Fornebu, and was totally unaware of the situation. At Lysaker, on his way to Fornebu airfield, he met the rest of our personnel marching towards Akershus. He asked them if anyone knew anything about me, and was told that I had been in combat and was probably killed.

With others, I took the train to Kjeller where we had our newly bought Curtiss fighters in mind, but they were not assembled yet. We got ourselves something to eat and left with another train back to Oslo. We weren't able to get any clear view of the situation. Everything was very chaotic.

I ended up at home instead. I had fever and pleurisy, something which I had had for a good while already. I got into bed and was very sick the whole summer. The country, meanwhile, was in German hands.

The mystery concerning my machine guns was solved at a much later time. A young fellow, Thyvold, had seen my plane after landing, and he told me that there was no more ammunition. I had not used a lot of shots during the main German assault, and my weapons worked well during my first mission. I started my second trip after the Gladiator was refuelled, but the weapons were not reloaded with ammunition.

Chapter 7

Escape from Norway

I had pleurisy throughout the summer of 1940. I had caught it at Fornebu months before and was lucky to be able to stay with my family. I stayed in bed for two months before I was healthy again. I was nearly 24 years old. I heard a lot of rumours in those days, and one that interested me especially – that colleagues in the air force had escaped Norway and gone to Canada where they were starting a new air force to continue the fight.

Several of my flying buddies and I felt that it was our duty to get over to the other side of the North Sea if we could. In England, we could contribute to the ongoing war effort and throw the Nazis out of Norway.

I had my own ideas about how I could get out, and I got in touch with an anonymous group of men. We met in a basement close to Bislett in Oslo, where they were dealing with a project to get a boat over the North Sea from Ålesund, a coastal town north-west of Oslo. The plan was abandoned when it was discovered by the Germans.

The days went by and I got in touch with Dag Krohn, a colleague of mine. We agreed to leave for Sweden. It was all about rumours then, and we heard it was possible to get to England from Sweden, which was still neutral. My brother helped us to get illegal permits to travel by train to the town of Elverum, and further by bus to Nybergsund, a town on the border with Sweden. We kept quiet about our plans, and didn't tell anyone about them before the afternoon of 18 October 1940.

'I have news for you both.' Said Finn, calmly.

His parents are sitting in the living room, drinking coffee. Outside, the trees lurch in the autumn wind. Their few remaining leaves are swept off the branches and swim around in the gusty air. Finn's father, Conrad, folds up his newspaper and looks at his son.

A Curtiss fighter hanging in Finn's bedroom at Bestum, Oslo, in the late 1920s. (*Finn Thorsager*)

'Yes?'

'Listen. Tomorrow, Dag and I will head for Sweden.'

He tells them the entire story. From Sweden they will go on the best possible route to England, either via a plane from Stockholm or perhaps the long way round through the Soviet Union and the USA. Finn is determined to fight on. If the rumours are true, they might end up in Canada, but first of all the goal is to get across the border to Sweden. With a lot of luck, he might eventually end up in Britain where he can continue to fight for a free Norway. It's his duty. It feels right.

His parents are listening to his words. They don't come as a shock, but the news is still hard to bear. Their youngest son is now standing in front of them, telling them he's going to war.

After the German invasion, they have all lost some of their innocence. Young men over the entire country are now standing in front of their parents, their wives and children, telling of their plans to continue the fight, and to risk their lives by trying to escape. The Thorsagers are not alone in facing it.

Finn's parents accept their son's belief. After a good conversation, they understand his plans.

Finn goes to sleep that night at his parent's home for the last time in a very long time. He tucks himself in under his blanket while the cold autumn winds rage on outside. It might be a while before he's lying in a good bed again.

The next morning, he's ready to go. Finn gets out of bed, pulls the curtains aside, and looks out the windows. He feels tense inside. The plans are ready. He doesn't hesitate for even a second. The decision has been made.

He pulls the rucksack onto his back. His father appears behind him and takes his arm gently.

'Will you come with me for a moment, Finn,' he says quietly.

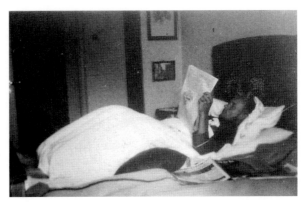

Finn in bed with pleurisy,
a serious illness at the
time, spring 1940.
(*Finn Thorsager*)

Finn follows his father down into the cellar. A bottle of champagne is standing on one of the wooden shelves.

'I have this bottle of champagne here, and I will save it for the day you return. When you come back, we will drink it together.'

'The bottle will be a symbol of my return,' thinks Finn to himself. With the bottle there, he will come back. He will be returning home alive, there's no doubt about that. Finn can't allow himself to think otherwise.

Not long after, goodbyes are said and the door of Finn's loving home has been closed behind him. He arrives at Furulund railway station dressed in good boots, a jacket, and a backpack. He says goodbye to Carl Fredrik who has followed him down to the station. He gets on and the train starts pushing out of the station. A quick look in the window and he sees Carl Fredrik standing there waving.

I took the tram to Østbanen, Oslo's main railway station, where I met Dag Krohn as planned earlier, and we boarded the train to Elverum. We had travel passes with us. If we also had normal passports, I don't remember. At Elverum, we got on the bus to Nybergsund. From Nybergsund, we managed to arrange transport to Østby, the last town before the border, where we spent the night.

The next morning we headed into the woods, towards the Swedish border. We walked partly on narrow gravel roads and partly on small pathways in the forest. We tried to be careful so we wouldn't be caught by the Germans. To be caught would be a disaster.

Huge pine trees are swaying in the wind. Between the big trees are two young men, walking through the forest towards Sweden. They've been heading east for some time. It's been hours since they left Østby, after a good night's sleep in a hotel. From time to time, the two of them speak to each other, quietly and calmly. They speak of plans ahead, their future. Maybe next year, they will be in a fighter plane over the enormous Canadian forests, trying to find their way, practising navigation. Or maybe they will be somewhere over England, in a Spitfire, fighting the Luftwaffe?

In the forest, only the sound of the wind flowing through the trees can be heard. Maybe one or two birds take off from the bushes nearby as they pass. Finn's backpack bumps gently up and down as he walks through the rough terrain. There are still several hours until the sun sets. If they keep up the pace they might make it to the border before it gets too dark to continue. Seeing a route going their way, they exit the forest and continue on the small gravel road.

In an instant, Dag stops. He's standing awkwardly, a little bent forward, just about to put the other leg in front. Finn continues for another two or three steps before he notices that his friend has stopped. He turns his head around towards Dag, just about to ask what is going on, when he hears the sound of an engine approaching. Dag's eyes are unmistakeable. They must get off the road, regardless of what is coming towards them. They don't have to make a plan. Finn just nods to Dag, and they know what to do. They jump into as ditch and hide as best as they can.

Just as Finn covers himself up with a few leaves and branches, the sound appears out of a slight turn ahead. Seconds later, a truck full of German soldiers drive past them. Finn can see the soldiers sitting there, looking very pleased with themselves. They speak, smile, laugh and sing soldiers' songs about Britain; 'Wir fahren gegen Engeland' (We set sail against England). Luckily, not one of them looks in the direction of the ditch. After the truck disappears behind them, Finn and Dag get out of their hiding place, and brush off the dirt from their clothes.

'A bit too close, I would say,' says Dag, with an involuntary quiver in his voice.

Finn agrees in a heartbeat. However, some luck is good on the road to Sweden. Finn can't help but grin a little about those Germans in the truck. Dag can't help doing the same. Maybe they do it out of nervousness, but it helps their mood. Dag is great company. Finn knows he made the right choice by going with him.

When night came, just by the border, we found a little abandoned hut which we entered. We laid down in the hay there, and we were very happy when Dag reached for his small whiskey bottle ... It did wonders.

It is suspiciously quiet in the forest when they reach the border. They can hear a few birds singing, but besides that, not a sound. In front of them, they see an opening in the woods. It stretches out in both directions, about 50 m wide. If they can cross it they will have reached Sweden, safe from German soldiers, quislings and the Luftwaffe. The two boys duck down and take the last step forward. Their ears are pricked for any unusual sound. They lean on a big pine tree while they look both left and right. Things appear to be quiet.

'Do you see anything?' says Finn, as he stares hard into the distance.

'No, I don't see or hear a thing.' Dag whispers so Finn can barely hear him.

What if the Germans are supervising the border? The question is floating around them like a fearful grey mist. They look at each other, knowing that there might be soldiers around. But what are the odds? If only someone could have told them about their experiences of crossing this way.

They decide to go for it. It is the only thing to do. Finn and Dag jump out from their hiding place behind the tree and run across the open space in the forest. Finn doesn't set a foot wrong and runs as fast as he can, but he's still waiting for that shot in the back from a German soldier.

It doesn't come. They were alone after all.

Well hidden by Swedish trees, they stop inside the forest on the other side. Everything on this side seems to be a little brighter and better. The birds are singing a little louder, the weather feels warmer, and the trees looks more beautiful. They are both relieved, but the dangers are not over. It's best to be on the look-out for the wrong type of Swedes, especially the military kind. There had been rumours floating around back home about Swedish military patrols arresting Norwegian refugees and then delivering them straight back to the Germans. They can't take any risks.

Finn pats Dag on his back, and they start to move forward again. Suddenly, there is movement in the forest. Out of nowhere, a Swedish girl appears ahead of them. By the looks of her, she might come from a farm nearby. They don't stop, just say a quick hello and continue forward. She came upon them a too quickly and they had no time to hide. But an ordinary farm girl surely can't be dangerous?

Later on we saw and heard a Swedish military camp. There were a lot of those around at the time. We sneaked around, and got on with it. We heard later from the police that the girl had reported us, and that the military were indeed looking for us.

The darkness is about to cover Sweden. The young men are hiding inside the forest from where they have a view of a small Swedish town. Their legs have taken them far. Their bodies feel the pace they've kept up all day. They both feel immensely tired.

They sit on the stump of a cut tree, left by Swedish workers. Not far from their spot, they see a river and a bridge crossing over it. They both know that the bridge is the key. They have to cross over it.

'Do we cross it now, or do we wait?'

Dag seems unsure. He's letting his legs rest as best he can while he studies their problem. Finn runs his fingers through his hair. His forehead is sweaty. He is tired, just like Dag.

'It's either go now, or wait until its dark. It might be safer to cross it once it's dark and we won't be easily spotted.'

But Finn is in doubt too. They go silent for a few seconds. Neither of them has a complete solution to their dilemma. If they go right away, in daylight, there's a bigger possibility of meeting strangers. They still have no clue as to who they can trust in Sweden and who will deliver them to the Germans. The darkness will indeed cover them well enough to get across, most likely unnoticed.

'Listen, we're both damn tired and sleepy. It's really tempting just to go now and get it over with.'

Finn looks at Dag while he gives his final verdict. They're just so tired. They've sneaked around a Swedish military camp and walked God knows how many miles through the dense forest.

'Let's just get it over with. Alright?' Finn gets to his feet and straightens his backpack.

'I agree. Let's just do it,' Dag replies, and he too gets up.

Finn can hear rumbling sounds coming from his stomach. It's been a while since they last had a decent meal.

Halfway across the bridge, they spot a person coming towards them on a bicycle. Finn observes him from a short distance away. There's no doubt in his mind that the person is wearing some form of uniform. Both of them look away from the person and the bike. Too much staring will raise suspicion. A last quick look and Finn can clearly see that the uniform is not of the military kind.

'Keep the pace up. Don't slow down. Let's just keep walking,' says Dag with a firm but low voice. The man on the bicycle passes them without saying hello or stopping to investigate who these strangers with backpacks are. Finn doesn't dare look back after he passes them. They just keep walking.

His pulse quickens. He suddenly feels like everyone knows they're from occupied Norway. Is it only because he knows they took a chance with the daylight crossing? Are they trying so hard not to raise any suspicion that they are attracting attention to themselves?

The man on the bicycle is several metres behind them now, but Finn hears his brakes squeaking, he is slowing down. He puts a foot down and turns his bike around.

They've done it now. Finn bites his upper lip.

'So, who are you, gentlemen?' calls the Swede.

'We are Norwegians,' replies Dag without hesitation. Finn is impressed. Even in these circumstances, Dag speaks with confidence and authority.

'We are on our way to Stockholm,' adds Finn, but he regrets it instantly. Too much, too eager.

The Swede introduces himself as a policeman. He seems to be very forthcoming and friendly. He stands beside his bicycle, without any suggestion of hostility.

'Stockholm yes? Well...' He makes a face, evidently disapproving of their travel plans. 'I think it would be best if you chaps follow me to the police station.'

Finn and Dag can't think or talk themselves out of this one. They reluctantly follow the police officer to the nearby station. The fact that he seems sympathetic makes it easier to obey his orders.

When we arrived at the station the officer asked about everything imaginable. We had to undress and show him what we had been carrying with us since Norway.

'Listen my good man,' says Dag, trying to maintain his friendly air of authority, 'I would rather not take off my underpants. I've been involved in ground fights in Norway and got hit in my buttocks.'

The Swede is polite, and agrees to Dag's request. Finn tries his best to hide a little grin when Dag thanks the police officer for understanding about his little problem. Dag is bluffing away in a manner that suggests he is much more important than he really is.

After a time of questions and examinations, the officer took us to a hotel and said we were under house arrest. At this hotel, we did not suffer one bit and had a jolly nice time.

I did, however, overhear a conversation between the police officer and his superiors in Stockholm. He told them that he had two Norwegians in custody, but since he got the impression that we were of the prominent type (thanks to Dag) he had not put us in jail, but in the hotel instead. We stayed at the hotel for two or three days before he finally got the message that we could be on our way to Stockholm. The officer had also been in touch with the Norwegian embassy, so they let us go.

We arrived in Stockholm and stayed the night at Blue Cross, before we went over to the embassy. We were received very well, and were told we would be given assistance for further travelling to Toronto. Toronto was the meeting point for escaped Air Force personnel.

From the day we left our homes, we had no contact with our families for several years, and they were not even told we had arrived in Stockholm.

The time in Stockholm was spent applying for visas at the Russian and Japanese embassies. Both of these countries were on the German side in the War, even if they were not allies. With the Russians, we had some contact with the famous Madame Kollontai. Some days we were promised a Russian visa, and denied a Japanese one. On other days, it was the other way around, so it was a bit problematic. In those days, the War was going well for the Germans, so things were far from optimistic.

We used to eat for free at a place called 'The Food Hall'. Most refugees hung around there. It was quite a collection of different people, including spies who gathered whatever information they could. One day, I was asked to participate in the shooting of a traitor, but luckily I didn't have to do it in the end. He was taken care of by the Swedes.

Our papers and visas were finally ready by 6 December 1940. We booked seats with Aeroflot on the 7th, and early that morning we left in a DC-3 for Moscow. Before we left Stockholm, we were given 500 dollars each [by the Norwegian Embassy]. This money was meant to cover all expenses until Toronto.

'Hey, this cannot possibly work,' cries Finn. The seats are hard and the aeroplane jumps heavily in the terrible Russian weather. Dag presses his face to the window and tries to spot landmarks beneath.

'Shouldn't think so, no. I can't see anything outside!'

The plane pushes onwards, shaking and shivering in the wind. The view ahead grows worse and worse; most of the passengers are tense, twisting and turning in their seats, trying to look outside and see the ground below for some sense of comfort.

The DC-3 descends gradually. The captain wants to get below the cloud cover. Soon, they are nearly skimming houses and tall buildings. The captain has already taken a decision to land in Riga and stay there for the night, waiting for better weather.

The plane lands safely and the passengers get out of their seats. Some look very happy to have landed. Dag gets up and brushes a few bits off his clothes. Finn collects their few possessions and they walk out.

> The Baltic countries had just been invaded by the Russians in cooperation with the Germans, so there were Russian soldiers everywhere in Riga. At night, they kept marching with the heaviest footsteps and loud singing. The situation reminded us greatly of Oslo with its German soldiers.

The atmosphere in Riga is dark and sad. The people in the streets look at the marching soldiers with despair. Riga is not a place for two Norwegians with hopes of fighting the Germans. The whole city is under a spell. A good future suddenly ruined by soldiers only waiting for their chance to be sent into battle. Riga is sent into apathy, surrender and darkness.

'I'll be happy once when we get out of here,' Finn remarks. There's nothing to do in Riga, and he wants to be on his way. Dag agrees fully. They both want to move on.

> The next day, we flew onwards with a stopover in Velikie Luki where we had to wait for the weather to improve in Moscow. Finally, we arrived in the capital and checked in at the Metropol Hotel. In Moscow, we bought tickets for the trans-Siberian railway. We had to wait for about four days before we could get on it.
>
> In Moscow, we did some sight-seeing. We stood in line with a few thousand Russians in Red Square to get into the Mausoleum where we had the honour of seeing Lenin. The church with the famous spires was also there. We visited the famous underground system and walked around with ordinary Russians.
>
> One evening, we visited the Bolshoi Theatre and saw the Russian ballet 'Ruslan and Ludmila'. It was very interesting for us Norwegians. It was almost like a parody of the Russian people with lots of officers and soldiers with their shirts hanging out and peasants with sixpenny hats. Everyone was extremely excited about the ballet. We ate at the hotel, but the food was not very good. It was usually Russian soup and black bread.

The Russian band is starting to play their instruments. The ballroom floor of the hotel fills with happy Russians, more than glad to accept invitations for a dance or two.

'What about asking a Russian girl for a dance?' asks Dag, leaning over the table and the empty vodka glasses. 'I mean, we're already here and the music has just started.'

The band plays a Russian waltz, followed by another one. The vodka glasses are raised high and the Russians tap their feet to the music. Finn gets up from his seat and moves through a group of people, seeing a girl behind them sitting down with a glass in her hand. He bows and puts out his hand, smiling. The girl has a pretty face. She smiles and takes his hand. They push a way for themselves through the thick crowd of people, finding a small empty spot on the dance floor.

Finn tries to lead the girl through a couple of easy steps, but gives up. She is far from sober. In fact, Finn is shocked at how drunk she really is. He tries to ignore it when she pinches his buttocks. Then she stumbles and nearly falls heavily to the floor. Luckily, Finn catches her just in time. He lets go of her while she's still on her feet in one piece, and bows and leaves her there to find her own way back to a seat. He hasn't learned a lot about Russians so far, but what he has learned is that they drink a lot more than Norwegians.

'So, how did it go with you then?' asks Dag.

'Not so well. Tried a few steps, but the girl was absolutely dead drunk.'

Dag bursts out in laughter. At least they made a good effort of it. They lean back on their chairs and choose instead to watch a group of Russian folk dancers doing a memorable show.

Finally, the day arrived when we could get on board the train. There were two other Norwegians travelling on the same train, so we got a cabin just for ourselves. This included normal seats which converted into beds at night, so it was alright. We were given food coupons, and the train had its own dining car.

In Stockholm, I had enough foresight to get a Russian-Swedish dictionary, with all kinds of common sentences and conversational phrases. I became good friends with one of the train's Communist conductors. Each coach had its own member of staff, who, among other things, looked after our passports, which we had to hand over to him.

Every day, I had my own 'classes' with my 'supervisor'. We exchanged words and several sentences that would come in handy. After about ten days on the train, I managed to speak enough Russian to order food, count, and ask for prices. Through the loudspeakers, we constantly listened to Russian folksongs. I can still hear them in my head when I feel like remembering.

I also have to mention the meals. We had to pass between several coaches in the bitter cold weather, through lots of steam, before we entered the dining car. It was quite good, and we were served three courses. The other passengers in the diner were mostly Russian officers with their families, and we got to know them well after a while, using bad German as our common language. We got either champagne or vodka with our food. After some time, we started to trade our dessert coupons for vodka.

The train speeds through the flat and deserted Russian landscape. The smoke pours out of the engine in the extreme cold. Cold even for Norwegians. Inside Finn and Dag's cabin, there's a great atmosphere. After several hours of talking, the Russians and the Norwegians have developed a friendship. They're all very keen to enjoy social gatherings, as they go through the vast, empty Russian landscape. The time passes slowly otherwise. The Russians whistle and sing bold Russian soldier songs, followed by thunderous applause and more vodka.

The Norwegians can't fail to match these Russians, and Finn decides to whistle a tune. He presses his lips together and does a version of a Norwegian folksong called 'Solveigs sang'. While he whistles, a quietness sinks in and they are all taken by the sentimental beauty of the tune.

Finn ends his last note, and the cheers break out!

I had to perform this musical masterpiece several times on that trip to Vladivostok. I performed it in my own sentimental way. A Russian officer whistled a quite similar piece in return.

It was cold outside, about -40 to -50 Celsius. The terrain was flat and never ending, with a thick blanket of snow everywhere. In some stations, we saw trains parked. The carts were often freight wagons with no windows. Through small holes, we saw many sad faces peeping out.

'Excuse me, sir,' Finn asks the conductor in broken German, 'how long will the train be standing still in this station?' The conductor stops for a moment, checks his watch and tells Finn that the train will be standing at the platform for about twenty minutes before continuing towards Vladivostok.

Finn decides to get off for a moment to have a look around. It's not every day that one gets an opportunity to examine the people of Siberia. He opens one of the doors and jumps the last step down to the platform. The cold instantly bites his face. Water vapour pours out of everyone passing him.

Finn keeps walking down the platform. Inside the station he sees families, soldiers, the elderly, and mothers breastfeeding their children. They all look poor. He sits down in a small restaurant inside the station hall and orders a glass of vodka. As soon as the waitress places it on his table, Finn grabs the glass and drinks. It burns down his throat. He puts it down again and decides to drink slower. If he's ever going to make it back on board that train again, quick drinking won't help. With his second mouthful, he almost swallows all of it down the wrong way.

In the corner of his eye, he can clearly see the train moving away from the platform. Still spluttering from the vodka, Finn jumps up from the chair, grabs his coat in one movement and runs quickly through the crowds of waiting Russians. He manages to grab on to the train in the last second, and jumps on board.

Breathing heavily, he finds Dag and sits down beside him.

'Didn't expect to see you again, Finn,' he says, laughing.

The train gathers speed, and it's soon continuing eastwards. Finn sighs heavily. It would have been a nice little disaster, being left behind in the middle of freezing Siberia with hardly any money and no passport. Well, at least some poor Russian will have half a glass of vodka to finish.

> We didn't drink as much vodka as you might think, but vodka was, during those times, a very common drink, and it was often served. By Lake Baikal, we were served fresh fish, and it tasted superb.
>
> Among the other passengers on the train were German Jews, trying to reach the USA. I had a visa to enter into the States as a student.
>
> Finally, we arrived in Vladivostok after a journey of ten whole days. Thanks to my new skills in speaking Russian, we could go into any restaurant and order food, even asking for the price with no real problems.

Dag and Finn both agree that Vladivostok is a horrible place. After the ten-day journey, they wander around the streets of the city, but wherever they go it looks to be crowded. No matter what the Russians are doing, a wall of people meets them. Finn keeps his hands well into his pockets, trying to keep warm as best he can.

In front of him, he sees something that makes him take notice. He pulls a little on Dag's jacket, to get his attention.

'What?'

'Look forward, straight ahead.'

Finn nods in the direction he is looking. There, just ahead of them, lies a lifeless man on the street. Everyone just walks around him; the crowd divides in two on reaching the man, and then blends together again on the other side. No one seems to be interested in helping him.

At the hotel, it was a long way to the nearest toilet, which was full of human waste, and there was used toilet paper in the hallway. Dag got food poisoning at this hotel and had to be helped on board our boat, which was called *Amakusa Mara*. This boat was to take us to the west side of Japan, to a place called Tsaruga.

Stern Japanese sailors show Finn and Dag to their cabin, deep in the bowels of the ship. The further down they go, the more moist it gets, and the smell is terrible. There, on the bottom deck, where conditions are at their worst, is where they have to stay.

'So, I guess this is our place.'

Dag's eyes widen in horror. He is still very sick. 'So, we're going to be travelling, sitting on these thin mattresses?'

Now they know what travelling by boat in Asia is all about. Dag shakes his head in despair, but there's no way out of it. This is where they will be staying for the trip to Japan.

A Japanese sailor screams out orders. Some soldiers start to walk around with what look like coupons. A Japanese gives one to Dag and Finn before he quickly continues through the crowd.

They all seem to be getting a coupon each.

'Hey, this is a coupon for apples,' says Finn with surprise.

'Well, it could be a lot worse,' replies Dag, 'they could have decided not to give out any coupons at all, you know.'

They laugh. Dag was right. It could have been a lot worse.

After a couple of days, we arrived in Japan. It was raining heavily and conditions were pretty terrible. Lots of Japanese workers were out in the rain, and they just had thin hats for cover. We bought tickets for a train going to Tokyo. It was Christmas Eve, 1940.

Finn puts his palm on the windows and wipes off the moisture. Somewhere in the distant darkness there is a gigantic city. There's nothing like it back in Norway. It all feels alien to him. They can hardly be further away from their home.

Finn tries to focus on the objects outside his window. From time to time, lights flash past him, not far from the railway line. His face is sometimes lit up by stations rushing past, where the train doesn't stop. Other times, he sees lights far away in the distance. Japan is still at war with China. It is very noticeable. On the train there are plenty of Japanese soldiers; some sleeping in their seats, some walking down the corridors.

'I wonder how they're doing back home tonight,' says Dag. They are both thinking it.

For the two Norwegians, this is a special night. Christmas Eve brings them a feeling of home. Finn wonders about Carl Fredrik and his friends. Maybe they are out on their skis now. It's already the first day of Christmas back home. Maybe they're looking through those presents they got last night. Are they thinking of him? What about the Germans? How are people coping back home? In a few months' time, the Germans will have been in Norway for an entire year.

Dag and Finn go quiet again, thinking about the Germans' hold on their country. It's starting to be a good while since they left. Now that the Germans are there, do they have enough food to make Christmas as special as it should be?

Engulfed by nostalgia and feelings of patriotism, the two young men decide to celebrate in their own way. Finn lights a candle on the table in front of them. It's soon burning nicely in the dimly lit carriage. A little candlelight is enough to make it feel a little bit like Christmas.

Finn stares into the flame and lets his thoughts wander back to happier times. He dreams of snow-covered mountains and the smell of Christmas trees, of putting on skis and going for a trip into the forests around Oslo. Dag suddenly pinches him and he comes back to reality; they hear the footsteps of a Japanese soldier quickly coming their way. The soldier gives them a cold glance before he puts out the candle with two fingers.

'That's it for Christmas, then,' shrugs Dag.

At the station in Tokyo there were many people walking around in their sandals. There were lots of families, all carefully carrying precious urns containing their relatives' ashes from the war against China.

To be closer to the harbour, we took the train out to Yokohama, and checked in at the Grand Hotel. The hotel was wonderful, real luxury. Among other things, they served American 'minute steaks', and the service was just excellent. A few Germans were also living there, and I guess they found out we were Norwegians. They tried in the most stupid way to spy on us and our whereabouts. They even sat down at the next table in the restaurant to try to listen in on our conversations.

We walked around in the harbour by the boats, and luckily we found a Norwegian tanker with the name *Bralanta*. We got on board, and by a stroke of luck, it was going to San Pedro in California. It was the perfect fit. We asked the captain if we could go with them, and we got the trip for 100 dollars each. Great! Departure was set for just before New Year.

With their few belongings, Finn and Dag stand outside their hotel, ready to get a taxi going to the harbour.

'Look over there, Dag.' Finn nods in the direction of the Germans appearing outside the hotel, on their tail, no doubt.

'Oh yes. Here we go again.' Dag is annoyed by their futile attempts at spying. Enough is enough. As soon as they jump into the first taxi that stops, the Germans do the same with the next one. Finn looks back from inside the taxi, looking at the Germans coming 'hell for leather' after them.

'We'd better end this once and for all, wouldn't you say?' says Dag. Finn is sick and tired of them too. After a brief discussion, the plan is ready.

'Take us to the nearest railway station, please,' says Finn to the driver. The Japanese man nods willingly and changes his course.

When the taxi comes to a halt outside the railway station, Finn and Dag pay the driver and get out. They quickly merge with the rest of the people there and walk straight through the building and out on the other side of it. Dag waves his hand in the air, stops the first taxi and they both jump in. As the taxi disappears, Finn catches sight of the Germans, frantically searching for where the Norwegians have gone.

'Now, would you look at that? It worked!' grins Finn.

'Peace at last!'

Minutes later, they set foot on the deck of the boat bound for San Diego. A large part of their task is done now. Next stop is the United States of America. For the first time since leaving Norway, they start to imagine actually arriving in Canada.

We got on board the boat, which also had a Norwegian crew. We had it very well there. After eighteen days, we saw the green hills of California appear. We were well received by US immigration in San Pedro. We checked in at a YMCA in town, which to us was heaven. Great food, plenty of orange juice, eggs and bacon. Even coffee in the morning. After breakfast, we sat in parks and tanned.

Souvenir

Glamorous Earl Carroll Theatre

Hollywood

Finn Thorsager and Dag Krohn having finally arrived on the American continent. Here at the Glamorous Earl Carroll Theatre, Hollywood, summer 1941. (*Finn Thorsager*)

Chapter 8

Little Norway

After a few days on a wonderful train across the States, we arrived in Toronto and could finally report to Ole Reistad, the commanding officer of Little Norway [a training base for Norwegian pilots]. We arrived there in January of 1941.

In Little Norway, it was a great pleasure to meet up with old friends again, among them Wilhelm Mohr, who was the commander of the training unit at Island Airport. Here, Dag and I split up as Mohr wanted us to work in different sections.

'Pilot class number one are already out there at the airfield where they will undertake training in the usage and packing of parachutes. Alright?'

Mohr is standing there fully equipped in military uniform. Compared to Finn, in his civilian clothes, it's quite a contrast. Wilhelm seems to be the complete leader, standing proudly in front of him. There are not that many years between them, but Finn had always felt that Wilhelm was like a big brother to him.

Finn sharpens his senses. So the first class is already out there. He's not sure what Wilhelm is referring to. What's it got to do with him? He's just arrived! Mohr sees the look in Finn's eyes and understands that his friend wants an explanation. Mohr takes a deep breath.

'Unfortunately, we don't have any instructors for this course at the moment.'

'Well, that's regretful,' says Finn.

'Listen, you have to be the instructor.' Mohr gazes at him with a serious look on his face.

'Well, alright then,' says Finn simply, and he heads off in the direction of the students.

Finn must admit things are moving fast here in Canada. It wasn't long ago he and Dag shook hands and congratulated each other with a trip well

Werner Christie, 1941.

From and Thorsager in Canada, 1941.

done. Now he will suddenly instruct pupils in the art of parachuting! After all, the pupils know less about flying than he does; he just has to try his best to teach them and hope for good results.

Still in his civilian outfit, he greets the pupils at the airfield. He grabs his hat and raises it while he introduces himself.

'I am Second Lieutenant Finn Thorsager, and I will be instructing you on parachutes.'

That's how easy it was back then. I didn't know much about parachutes!

I had been told by Reistad that I would be going to England pretty soon, and needed to have a uniform fitted for me as soon as possible. However, I was to stay in Toronto for about five months. The academy needed instructors, and I became one of them. Fourteen days after I had arrived in Toronto, two other friends of mine arrived, Reidar From and Werner Christie. We all stayed on as instructors. Our pupils were the first ones educated during the War, and several of them became some of our most skilled leaders.

When we started out we got five or six boys each and were simply told, 'teach these boys to fly.' This was before any schools were started for educating instructors.

'Ready to fly?'

Finn looks at his young pupil in front of him. The boy can't be more than 17 or 18 years old. He seems very young. Finn isn't among the oldest of the bunch either, but the boy must be at least five years younger. The pupil stands there with rosy red cheeks. He looks like a kid back from school, on his way home to his mother to eat supper. If he wasn't dressed in flying overalls and climbing into the cockpit of the Fairchild Cornell, Finn would never dream of this boy coming to Canada to learn to fly.

Being an instructor is new for Finn. He's already concluded that he'd better just do it in his own way, on his own terms. Just jump in with both feet and see how it goes. The pupils don't seem to be unhappy after a flight with him either. It's reassuring to know he's doing something right with them.

Racing down the runway, the teenager is in front, and pulls the stick back. The Cornell lifts off the runway beautifully. Finn is simply keeping a soft touch on the stick in the rear cockpit, ready to take over if anything happens. First and foremost, he's concentrating on giving the lad a chance to fly on his own.

The teenager lets the aeroplane go into a shallow right turn. Finn puts his foot gently on the rudder pedal, and then a little bit more firmly. The boy notices his pedal disappearing underneath his foot, and reacts quickly to follow Finn's movement. Despite his extremely young age, the boy is flying well. Finn lets him show what he can do, and what he's good at. The boy doesn't let the opportunity pass. The quiet and firm treatment from Finn gives him increased confidence in his abilities. The landing is far from perfect, but well within the range for qualification.

'A little bit too much speed during the landing, but otherwise very good.' Finn gives him a quick pat on the back as they walk away from the parked aeroplane.

'Yes, I'll do better next time. I can feel I'm getting the hang of this now.'

Finn isn't the yelling type. Calmly, he tells the boy what he did badly, and what he did well. Some of the other instructors are far too quick to yell out orders and bad words when the pupils do things wrong. Not Finn. He's calm, firm and very consistent in what he's saying. What is wrong, what is good, and what can be improved on next time.

Over the next few days, the boy does five more landings and Finn is pleased. After an excellent one, Finn jumps out of the aeroplane and walks round to the lad, still strapped in the cockpit.

'You can do it yourself this time, and watch the airspeed, will you?'

The boy grins nervously and gathers his thoughts for his first solo. Finn backs off a little, away from the aeroplane. The boy opens the throttle and the Cornell speeds down the runway. Finn uses his palm to shade his eyes from the sun as he watches the aeroplane fly parallel to the runway. It all looks to be going well.

The aeroplane heads downwind. A little low perhaps, but that's minor. Finn sees he's doing well. Soon enough, both the boy and the aeroplane are safely down on the ground again. Both student and instructor are proud of the achievement.

'Not a problem at all, you see? Well executed!' Finn shakes the boy's hand. The lad has just done his first solo trip, and only after a mere six hours of flying. It looks like Finn has done well with this one. The boy seems to be a natural.

We worked intensively from morning to well into the afternoon. In addition, we were also instructors on the Linktrainer, a simulator. I also did instructions in Morse code and telegraphy due to my experience at sea before the War.

I think back on those five months in Toronto with great joy. The locals have to take a large part of the credit for it.

Back home in Norway, I had a bicycle, and I had no real prospects of learning to operate another land vehicle. But in Canada, I bought a car. Pure and simple. I only had to pick the used car I wanted at the local dealership, sign up to a contract for repayments and off I went. I named my car 'Sebastian'. We often drove out into the wild and explored. I also drove down to Niagara Falls.

As we acted as instructors, we also trained ourselves on more advanced types of aeroplane, such as the Curtiss Hawk, during the day and at night. I was also temporarily transferred to Stinson seaplanes to instruct trainee naval pilots. 'Little Norway' was situated very close to Lake Ontario, so we had a great chance to get as much practice as possible in take offs and landings.

'I think we're across the border now!'

Finn's pupil is pressing his face against the window to get a view of the USA stretching out beneath them. Finn grins in response to the lad's excitement.

'Oh yes, we're definitely not in Canada any longer.'

Nobody seems to get too upset if a small Stinson seaplane flies over the border for a short period of time. The sea looks calm even if the weather isn't at its best.

'Listen, let's take her down for a short break and a cigarette,' says Finn.

Finn Thorsager enjoying a day in the sun in Canada, summer 1941. (*Wilhelm Mohr*)

Finn pulls back the throttle and prepares for landing. Floats are a good thing. You may land wherever you want, as long as the sea keeps calm enough.

'Flaps, please.'

He gives the order calmly, but loud enough so the lad hears the message with absolute certainty. The pupil puts out the flaps and the Stinson slows down. A good descent is established with the proper nose up. Soon they're flying slowly just above the small waves before they put her down with a light splash on the water. Finn decreases what's left of the throttle and then shuts it off completely. With one last huff from the engine, the propeller stops turning. It's suddenly all quiet. The Stinson rocks a little on the gentle waves and they listen to them lapping against the floats.

They turn off the electrical system before they step onto the floats. They pull out cigarettes from their inner pockets and start talking about the War, those back home in Norway, and about flying. One could almost think it was peacetime. They both know it isn't so, but the feeling is good anyway. The War isn't going all that well for the Allies. They're uncertain about how it will end.

Finn puts out his cigarette and flicks it into the sea.

'Let's get cracking again. Alright?'

The boy agrees. Finn lets him start the engine. Blue smoke covers them for a second before the engine is running smoothly. Then there's nothing left except a cigarette floating around in the water and a low humming from the engine up in the skies.

We had all arrived here to be accepted into the RAF, so after our stay in Canada had served its purpose, the time arrived for us to travel to England. This happened at the end of May 1941. For security reasons, we were sent up to 'Vesle Skaugum' in northern Canada, a property owned by the Royal Norwegian Air Force. We stayed there, both pilots and ground crew, for about nine days. We kept ourselves busy doing all sorts of sports like canoeing and shooting with revolvers. We had, in advance, taken a course in shooting with the Canadian police. We had some great days there. We also packed up all our belongings, ready to be sent to Norway after the War was over. A company in Toronto would take care of it all while the War was on.

Finn getting in some practice shooting in Canada, summer 1941. (*Finn Thorsager*)

Chapter 9

Training with the RAF

Johan Christie[4] would be our supervisor on the journey to England, and each and every one of us had instructions to follow. Personally, I was a 'policeman' in charge of about five men, and we would each make sure, by force if necessary, that people followed the appropriate disciplinary codes. After three days on a train, we arrived in Halifax, from where the convoy would set off.

'I can't stop being amazed by this massive convoy.' Wilhelm Mohr crosses his arms, and breaths cold air in and out from his lungs, clearly impressed at what he's seeing. They both look at the convoy on the horizon. It's an impressive sight of battle cruisers and destroyers.

The allies have suffered heavy losses in the Atlantic Ocean, and they're taking no chances with this convoy. Five big liners packed with military personnel on their way over to Great Britain. Three battle cruisers, eleven destroyers, and submarines in the waters around them, all as protection against German U-boat attacks. The allies are losing a sickening number of ships, but looking around him, Finn feels pretty safe. But maybe he's being naïve; there have been several alarms already, even though this must be one of the biggest convoys ever to cross the Atlantic, at least in the number of men.

It's gradually been getting colder since they left the Canada. Finn puts his arms in his side pockets and draws in a good amount of the cold sea air, looking at Wilhelm.

'Any idea where we are?'

Mohr shakes his head. He doesn't know more than what they've been officially told. The rumours are saying they're somewhere off the coast of Greenland. The cold air may suggest that this is right, but they can't be sure. They've calculated among themselves that the crossing will take around two weeks.

Left: Wilhelm Mohr at Catterick in early 1942, shortly after arriving. (*Finn Thorsager*) *Right:* Reidar From at Catterick in 1942. He later took over 332 Squadron from Finn. (*Wilhelm Mohr*)

'We're about half way, I'd say,' responds Mohr, after thinking it over.

Finn looks out at the dark sea and the huge number of boats around them. They will soon set foot on English soil. In the meantime, they had better make the best of it.

We had a lovely time on board, and arrived in Glasgow after about ten to twelve days. Upon arrival, we were all brought to a transit camp. We had been quite spoiled food-wise, so we were in for a hard time. We practically starved, but luckily, our stay lasted just a few days. From Glasgow, we – the pilots – were sent to an OTU at Sutton Bridge. Here we got to fly Hawker Hurricanes while learning proper RAF tactics. This went on for a month and a half.

The boys have just made their way through the gate at Sutton Bridge in Lincolnshire when they hear the sound of Rolls Royce Merlins in the air. Finn Thorsager, Wilhelm Mohr, Werner Christie, and Reidar From; all of them Norwegians, and all equally excited about getting into the cockpit of a Hurricane.

In perfect formation, two Hurricanes fly past the boys at low altitude. Just above their heads, one of them breaks off to the right and up towards the low cloud cover. The fighter to the left waits a few seconds before it does the same. Not long after, they're both on their final approach with wheels down. A small bump and the first one touches down on the grass field. The other

Reidar From, Wilhelm Mohr, and Finn Thorsager at readiness, Catterick, spring 1942.
(*Wilhelm Mohr*)

one does a more-or-less perfect three-point landing. The Merlins give out a few monster-like crackles, while the Hurricanes, in dark green and brown camouflage colours continue down the field. The noise made by the Merlin engine sounds like a dangerous wild animal. In the right hands, it is a beautiful killing machine. It is soon to be in Finn's hands, and he can hardly wait.

While the boys walk towards the barracks, Finn makes his first acquaintance with Sutton Bridge. The station doesn't seem have any permanent runways. There are three grass strips crossing each other east to west, north-west to south-east, and east to south-west. Concrete has been laid around the field, encircling it, and there are shelters of concrete all around the perimeter for parked aeroplanes. Finn can spot about fourteen different hangars, two of them very large.

'Welcome to Sutton Bridge!' says an RAF officer, pulling Finn out of his thoughts. 'Good to have you here, gentlemen.' He smiles and shakes hands with all of them.

'Before you go to meet the commanding officer, I'll give you a brief introduction to the place.'

The officer turns around and talks while he walks. You simply don't waste time in the RAF. He continues talking while the boys keep up as best they can.

'RAF Sutton Bridge was built in 1932, but it wasn't fully opened until '36, so we're a new and modern base. We have had several squadrons here. Among others, 266 Squadron, flying Fairey Battles, and 254 Squadron, with their Blenheim IVs, have been here. You, gentlemen, are here to learn RAF tactics, and that's what we're going to teach you. For you, this place is an OTU. That is, gentlemen, an Operational Training Unit. Please follow me.'

The Norwegians straighten up and walk after the officer towards one of the buildings further away from the field.

'The commander here at Sutton Bridge, Lieutenant John Bisdee, is a veteran from the Battle of Britain, so show respect and salute him properly. He likes things to be in order and puts discipline high on the list, so don't do anything stupid. Relax, boys. You will, with time, learn proper tactics and the RAF style of things. By the way, we call him "The Bishop", but not to his face and all of that, you know.'

They meet the famous Bishop in his office. John Bisdee is a tall, blond man, exuding confidence. A natural organiser and a very popular chap in the RAF, he's known for his humour and for having the right attitude. Finn can see why the RAF love to have him around. For Bisdee, Sutton Bridge is just another break before he 'straps on' a Spitfire, ready for real combat once again.

The boys stand to attention before Bisdee while he speaks. Finn knows right away that this man will make a lasting impression.

★

'Alright,' says an RAF officer, standing on the wing of Finn's Hurricane. 'Get yourself seated and learn the switches and the instruments by heart. It is of absolute importance that you know everything without hesitating.'

Finn pays close attention.

'Always keep your eyes on your equipment, especially your 'chute. If it's not alright and you have to jump, contrary to popular belief, you can't come back and get another!

'Sit here for a while and sort everything out in your head. When you're ready, give me a quick wave. I don't think it will be too much of a problem, not with your experience.'

The Englishman lets go of the cockpit and jumps off the wing. Finn looks at the control panel. It is more advanced than that of a Gladiator, although the stick is similar with the characteristic doughnut-shaped top. There are several more instruments, but that's to be expected. Finn is sitting pretty high up too; the sides of the cockpit almost reach up to his face. He feels safe where he is, until it dawns on him that there are only a few centimetres between him a deadly 20-mm bullet.

Finn studies the cockpit down to the tiniest detail. It is a bit confusing that the RPM needle is in a completely different place to the throttle and

Finn at Catterick, 1942. (*Finn Thorsager*)

the fuel mixture, but he can't do much about that. Gears and flaps are on the same stick, separated in an H-pattern. It looks a little bit like the gearstick on a car. All in all, he's very pleased with what he sees. He gives the officer a wave.

'Alright then. No problems?'

'No, everything's good.' Finn smiles with confidence.

'A few checks first, and you're ready to go.'

The officer jumps off the wing again and a mechanic comes forward. He pulls out a screwdriver and taps the exhausts gently. They give off the correct sound and he seems pleased. A signal is given to Finn in the cockpit. All ready for ignition; it's time to get this bird into the air. Finn moves his hand to the left of the cockpit and switches the fuel to its ON position. Battery ON at the right side, DC master, start master and then booster coil ON. Fuel pump ON and then back to the left side for the start button and the primer. Finn primes it six times, as instructed by the officer.

The engine starts up almost instantly. Flame bursts out from the exhausts before it turns to blue smoke and disappears behind him. Finn sets the mixture to 'auto rich', and the engine runs at 800 rpm. All OK so far. The mechanic pulls away the chocks in front of the wheels. He gives Finn a thumbs up. All set!

Finn is careful with the throttle. He doesn't want the Hurricane to tip over on its nose. From what he's been told, it's happened many times, caused by careless pilots.

He pushes the throttle and the Merlin engine roars willingly in response. A short taxi to the end of the strip, and he's ready to take off.

Full power to the Merlin, and the Hurricane speeds off down the grassy field. With his right hand, Finn selects undercarriage up once the Hurricane is in the air. The aeroplane is quick; much quicker than a Gladiator or a Harvard. The type-VA engine isn't the quietest, but the power is superb. It vibrates and makes a lot noise, but that doesn't matter one bit. Not at a time like this.

Cruising over Lincolnshire, Finn keeps the engine running at 2,000 rpm, with a speed of 200 mph. The stick feels easy and simple to hold, and the aeroplane is stable. He tries a few turns; the Hurricane responds easily. The thick wings give the fighter the ability to turn very tightly. Finn pulls the plane into a loop and rolls it back around at the top. No problems at all, except maybe a little slow to accelerate.

Time passes quickly and before he knows it he must prepare for landing. The only problem could be to get the Hurricane down to 120 mph so he can select flaps and undercarriage down. No problem, though; he slows down enough in good time. Full flaps out and 96 mph over the perimeter fence of the airfield. A little bump and he's back on Mother Earth. Not bad for a first trip! It may not be as pretty as a Spitfire, and not as fast either, but it certainly gets the job done.

Finn is pleased with a Hurricane right now, but later on he knows he will wish for a Spitfire. The legend of this aircraft has already reached the Norwegians in Canada.

The RAF officer is quickly on the scene after Finn has switched everything off and the propeller has stopped.

'Everything alright then?'

'Absolutely. I liked it very much.' Finn can't help grinning. The Norwegians are in for some happy days at Sutton Bridge.

★

Among our fellow pupils at Sutton Bridge, usually English pilots, were also a few American pilots. Before the USA entered the War, many were more than willing to participate as volunteers in the RAF. They were not very experienced, but after a while, they became good enough to form their own American 'Eagle Squadron'. They were full of spirit.

Summer was at its height in those days. It was warm and the sky was dotted with big white cumulus clouds, around which we flew aerobatics in our Hurricanes. We practised battle formations and did target practice, and we felt in good shape for becoming RAF fighter pilots. This short period at Sutton Bridge was a good time. We got used flying in the RAF and its operations. We got into it all quickly.

'Right then. Now, listen carefully chaps.' The instructor leans forward over his desk, looking up towards the boys in the classroom. He's young, maybe no more than 25, but he probably has a lot of battle experience, maybe from France, Dunkirk or the Battle of Britain. Finn can only speculate. The Englishmen clears his throat and continues.

'I will teach you RAF tactics, and I expect you to learn them down to the tiniest detail. Different squadrons use different tactics. The point is to know them and learn them by heart. Without them, you're sitting ducks. Different tactics may be equally good, but make sure to know them!'

Finn can't help but smile at how the instructor talks. He's obviously done this a few too many times. It's not that he's not good at it – far from it, the man knows his stuff – but he runs through it all like a machine, barely without stopping.

'Forget the stories from the First War about lone fighters hunting for prey. In this war, a squadron is more like a football team. "Solo shows" are only allowed once the formation has split up and the squadron leader has given the order.

'Most squadrons are split up into three different flights, each with four aeroplanes.' The Englishman raises his arm and pulls down a map with black silhouettes of aircraft as a way of illustrating his point. Blue, Red or Yellow for each flight, 1-2-3-4. 'The Squadron leader is usually Red 1 and is in the middle of the three flights. About five hundred yards out to your right there's Blue 1, and on the left side is Yellow 1. Notice that we're not using surnames or anything of the kind. If you're flying as Yellow 4, you're exactly that.' He uses the stick to point to each of the planes on the board while he speaks.

'If you use this method of covering each other, everyone will see what's going on behind you, which is absolutely vital. Yellow and Blue stay behind Red, while keeping a distance of about a hundred yards between each aircraft in their own flights. Each flight is then split up in two pairs or "sections" of fighters that stick together. Red 3 and 4, for example, need to stay together. Keep in mind that two fighters together are a threat against the Hun, whereas single fighter is an easy target.

'Once airborne, your first task is to keep your eyes out for enemy fighters. If you have the element of surprise on your side, you will most likely win the fight. All twelve pilots in the squadron will keep their eyes out at all

Ground crew working on a Spitfire Vb at Catterick, winter 1942.

times. The sharper your vision the better.' The instructor takes two steps forwards towards Finn and the other pupils. He lowers his voice and stares right at them.

'Beware of the Hun in the sun. Words to live by. The sun is our friend and our enemy at the same time. It can hide you well enough to catch a flock of 109s by surprise. Unfortunately, it can also be used by the Hun. A sad number of pilots have been lost because they didn't pay attention to it.'

Finn takes notes as the instructor talks. Much of what he's hearing he already knows from before. Nonetheless, it's a whole different game now. These are rules and lectures based on experience paid for with blood. The first phase of the War didn't go very well for the RAF; their initial tactics were proved to be totally impractical in combat.

'Always remember your squadron call sign. Never use the radio for useless chatter. Always use a pilot's codename if you have something to say to him or about him. Never turn on the radio and yell out, "Turn! You've got a Jerry on your tail!" Others will hear the same message, and everyone will stop what they're doing and take action. Speak clearly, calmly, and in proper English. If you see a friend under attack, think of the sky as a clock face.

Finn and Reidar From investigating a newly purchased camera, Catterick, spring 1942.

Start with the squadron's call sign. For example, "Rabbit Red 2, break, 190, ten o'clock high." Get it?'

The pupils nod slightly and continue to take notes. 'If the bastard comes from underneath you, it's 10 o'clock low. Make sense?'

A Hurricane roars over the building, low and fast. Finn sees the fighter pull up and go into a roll, still at low altitude. The instructor collects the papers on his desk and mumbles angrily before continuing.

'Right then. Sorry about that, chaps. Let's go on. I'll continue with a few words on deflection shooting.' Finn sits up immediately. He's already experienced how hard deflection shooting can be. It will be very interesting to hear what this man has to say about it.

'If you're a fighter pilot and can't shoot, just pack your bags and go home. You're not of any use to anyone.' There is a pause as the Englishman stares at his class. 'Never shoot from too far a distance. Get in as close as possible. Fire short bursts and correct your aim if you see that you're missing. When you're firing, keep the bloody aeroplane steady. After you're done with the Jerry, don't forget that there will most likely be another one on your tail trying to blast you out of the sky. If you're alone, don't panic and think all your friends are dead. One moment the sky is full of planes, and they're gone the next. It's common. If you're alone, dive down to ground level and get home in one piece.'

He takes a look at the clock hanging on the wall. 'That's it for today. See you all tomorrow.' All the chairs are pulled back at once, and the boys are out of the classroom in no time. Lectures can be interesting, but Finn would rather spend the days flying a Hurricane with Mohr, dogfighting each other for fun.

With the sun on its way down, the four Norwegians jog through the terrain around the airfield. They keep a good pace. They kept themselves busy in the same way in Canada. While they jog, they keep each other company with stories, discussions, and jokes. After long days of lectures, flying, and training, it feels nice to stretch the legs and keep fit.

They pass a couple of RAF pilots and say hello. The pilots say hello back, but are clearly puzzled by their behaviour.

'Say, what d'you think they're after?' asks one.

'Well, you know … Norwegians,' replies his friend, and they both laugh.

It dawns on Finn that the British don't get involved in physical activity if it doesn't include some form of sport or gambling. The Royal Air Force is no exception to the rule. Football, cricket, rugby and squash are all popular activities, but just to jog without any particular goal is incomprehensible. Although there are little cultural differences between the Norwegians and they're British allies, Finn feels they all get along very nicely at Sutton Bridge.

After the exercise is over, the boys relax with a refreshing bath. This is definitely one of the better sides of life.

We ate local vegetables every day. We bought them from the farmers, and I especially remember amazing tomatoes. Homesickness, considering the situation at home, was not in my thoughts at all. But these happy days of training had to end sometime. We left Sutton Bridge at the end of August 1941 and were sent to Castletown, up north in Scotland, where the Norwegian 331 Squadron was based.

At 9.15 a.m., three pilots arrive at Castletown – Finn Thorsager, Henning Leifseth, and Reidar From – excited young men straight from OTU. They report to Squadron Leader Odd Bull, ready for duty at 331. The name of their squadron leader, Finn is sure, has already been joked about to death.

331 Squadron pilots outside Golf Links Hotel in Dunnet, Scotland, not far from their base at Castletown, late August 1941. Finn can be seen far right beside Morten Ree. (*Finn Thorsager*)

Outside, the mechanics are working hard on their ageing Hurricanes. Some of these planes date back to the Battle of Britain – long ago in wartime. The squadron came into being just months before at Catterick in Yorkshire. It is slowly on its way to becoming a formidable force in the RAF.

Finn can feel the tension rise in his body. If only they can get a chance, they will show what they can do. Finally, the goal he set out for a year ago is becoming a reality.

Old friends from Norway show up and shake his hand, wishing him a very warm welcome. There is a lot to catch up on and people are interested to hear how Finn escaped from Norway, and what it was like crossing the Atlantic; he gladly tells them everything. New faces unknown to him show up as well. They shake his hand and seem happy to be getting experienced people in the squadron. Some of them have already been in other RAF squadrons gaining experience. Others are still there, somewhere down south.

Those with civilian backgrounds seem to be a bit sceptical of those with a military education, but there isn't any conflict and all are friendly and forthcoming. Most importantly, Finn has finally reached his goal. He's now with a fighter squadron in England, ready to pick up from where he left off on 9 April 1940.

We had lots of practice sessions; formation flying, shooting, and night flying. It was hard in rough weather. There were a lot of mountains around, and we had barely any navigational aids. We had to keep in touch while flying to the best of our ability, and it's not that easy with dark mountains and the cold North Sea wind.

Chapter 10

Skeabrea

'You've got to be joking! Please, tell me you're joking!' cries one of the pilots in astonishment. 331 Squadron have just heard of their imminent transfer to Skeabrea.

'The Orkneys? Bloody hell!' Another pilot throws his newspaper down onto the table and walks out in disgust. No one can hide their disappointment, not even Finn. This was not part of their plan. Won't they fight the Germans after all?

Finn tries to focus on the positive side. He tries to look beyond the disappointing aspects. He has to say something smart to the frustrated boys.

'Listen, maybe we will get to fly Spitfires. We can finally get away from these Hurricanes. They should have been scrapped a long time ago. Maybe one or two Germans will pass over, so we can have a go at them.'

'Oh yes...' says a young pilot at the back of the room, 'I want a German, even if I have to fly all the way over to Norway to get him.'

Pilot Henning Leifseth pulls at his moustache with two fingers. He's not pleased. 'It's not much to write home about,' he says, despondently.

Finn has to agree. Skeabrea is cold and bare, with no vegetation, and the only buildings seem to be the Nissen huts that will be their home for the next few months. It's all far from the lush surroundings of Kent down in southern England, where they had all hoped they would go.

'I'll tell you one thing,' says Pilot Officer Fearnley, carrying on from Henning's comment, 'Air Force Headquarters can go to Hell. It's all their fault we're here in this mess. Where are the Germans? They're not here, that's for sure! We will sit here all winter freezing our arses off. What's the point?'

Pilot Officer Fearnley has been with the squadron for a while, and he's had enough of the situation they're in. Finn wouldn't use the same

Pilot Officer Fredrik A. Sverdrup Fearnley, 1941.

language, but he admits Fearnley has a point. To make matters worse, their 'new' Spitfires were terribly misused by the Polish squadron that had them beforehand. Spare parts never show up, the weather is terrible, there are continual difficulties in keeping the Spits flying, and people are constantly falling ill. Finn is sure that no other squadron is living in worse conditions than this.

The Nissen huts are drafty, people getting out of bed in the morning have to be careful not to slip on the ice. However, some of the boys seem to be alright. Many of them, including Finn, go off hunting in the area.

> On my time off, I used to walk around the area. Sometimes I took a Smith & Wesson and shot rabbits. We also stopped by the farms and chatted to the locals. They were hard to understand, but they were keen to talk to us. Some of their words were clearly of Norwegian origin. They were all very kind people. I remember we bought plenty of eggs from them. Some even had goats as house pets. It was Viking history right in your face!

Others, on the other hand, seem depressed, and at times, there is unnecessary conflict between them. Lots of letters are written in loneliness.

Depressing thoughts written to family, friends and girlfriends. But Finn feels he's doing alright, considering the situation.

Talk of fighting the Germans is always guaranteed to cheer people up. When darkness arrives at Skeabrea, and the Spits are nicely tucked away for the night, the men gather indoors while the weather howls outside. Some of them pull out a map of Norway and dreams unfold of heroics by excited boys hunting down their enemy.

'Listen, I know this area as well as my own pocket. It's doable to fly a Spitfire in at low height here and just blast away at them. The Germans are stationed here, and here. I saw them before I escaped. No problems at all.'

Finn listens while the boys discuss these tempting targets in Norway. One of the pilots points to a long fjord on the map, suggesting a low-altitude attack with Spitfires and light bombers. They all dream of ways to hurt the Germans, to throw them out of their homeland.

Finn leans over the table and looks at the map. He knows it's all wishful thinking for the moment, but it's good for the spirit. The boys are hungry and willing.

I was stationed at Sumburgh on the Shetland isles during the Christmas of 1941. We were here with a flight of six Spitfires and the Dane, Kaj Birksted, as commanding officer. We participated as escorts during the raid on Måløy. We escorted light Canadian bombers back to Shetland. Some of them were pretty shot up. I saw a Blenheim do a belly-up landing here for the first time. On Christmas Eve, we had our own little party in one of the huts with a special greeting to our popular Danish boss, Birksted.

At Skeabrea we also had Nordahl Grieg[5] living with us for a couple of days. We often sat by the fire place and toasted our bread at night. One night, I had a long conversation with him. He had a very distinctive, calm way of speaking. He was very peaceful and relaxing, but could often disappear into a world of his own sometimes. He was definitely not in ours!

Chapter 11

A Taste of Things to Come

In March 1942, 332 Squadron was formed with pilots and ground crew. Because of my experience, I was ordered to join them as a flight commander. I met many familiar faces when I arrived at 332 Squadron: Marius Eriksen[6], Jon Ryg, Jan Eigil Løfsgaard, Torstein Strand, and Svein Nygaard, as well as those I knew from 331 Squadron. Each squadron had two flights, A- and B-flight. 331's old squadron leader, Odd Bull, commanded the squadron initially, before Wilhelm Mohr took over.

We were based at Catterick, an airfield in North Yorkshire. We did a lot of practice and created a good bond between ourselves. At one point, I was with B Flight over the coast, west of Hartlepool. We did a lot of shooting at target drones there and had several interceptions with Germans. I'm sure several of them got hit. They did shoot back, though. One of our pilots got unlucky during one interception and got hit in the eye with a fair bit of damage.

The boys run towards the lonely Spitfire, coming to a halt at Catterick. They see it's Piltingsrud, one of the two pilots who went up earlier. Finn, inside, can hear them chatter wildly.

'Where's Liby, his number two?' There is no sign of the second Spitfire.

Finn puts his equipment aside and looks out the window. The boys are already gathered around Piltingsrud, just out of his Spit. He's pointing, chatting and explaining what happened. Finn goes outside and walks over to the crowd, interested to know what's going on. He grabs the first man approaching him.

'What happened?'

'Not entirely sure, sir, but Liby has landed at some other airfield. They just called from there now. His cockpit is a mess. Some of the shattered remains of it hit his eye. He's been bleeding quite a bit, I hear.'

Wilhelm Mohr at Catterick in 1941. He took over 332 Squadron from Odd Bull around the time this picture was taken. (*Wilhelm Mohr*)

Finn is here seen with Squadron Leader Odd Bull, shortly after arriving at 332 Squadron in the winter of 1942. (*Finn Thorsager*)

332 A-flight pilots at Catterick during the early spring of 1942. Bottom left to right: Søren Liby, Thor Wærner, Reidar From, Odd Bull. Top left to right: Arne Sunde, Torstein Strand, Finn Thorsager. (*Finn Thorsager*)

331 Squadron landed at RAF Catterick in May 1942, en-route to North Weald. 332 Squadron, having not received their orders to follow their sister squadron down south, were beyond envious. (*Finn Thorsager*)

Finn reaches Piltingsrud, who is telling people what happened.

'We got up to 25,000 feet and went straight after him. Couldn't have been more than 3 miles away.' Piltingsrud holds his hands up in the air, showing them where the German was, and where the Spitfires were attacking from.

'I just couldn't get close enough, but Liby got in on his tail.' He closed his right hand on his left to where Liby attacked from.

'Liby fired off a burst and hit him well. I think it could have been a Junkers 88, but I can't be sure. The bastard fired back at him, and hit him right in the cockpit. I tried to get in a burst at him, but he disappeared into the clouds. We had no choice but to turn back. They always seem to have some clouds to hide in.'

His voice is remarkably calm when he speaks, but Piltingsrud is not new in the game. He's been in the thick of things before. Liby, on the other hand, might be less calm, wherever he is. However, with a bit of luck, he will be back after his wounds have healed.

332 is still a fledgling squadron. They've been sent out on several scrambles in the past month, but they have rarely ended up in combat with the Luftwaffe. When things suddenly do happen, it's a brutal reminder about what they are doing every day. The Germans are good shots, as Liby just found out.

Another view of 331 Squadron's stopover at Catterick in May 1942, much to 332 Squadron's jealousy! (*Finn Thorsager*)

Arve Aas (far right) resting in the sun while a group of pilots are playing cards, Catterick, spring 1942. (*Finn Thorsager*)

Finn turns away and walks back. There will be more of this kind of thing. He's sure of that. It might be more difficult to live through this than he first thought, but there's little he can do about it. He'll just have to take each day as it comes.

In the meantime, they gather valuable experience by doing their jobs well at Catterick. 332 Squadron might not get into a fight with the Germans every day, but the practicing they do is vital for things to come.

One lovely spring day, 331 Squadron drop by at RAF Catterick to refuel on their way to RAF North Weald in Essex, their new permanent home. Finn can't hide his jealousy when he sees them, and he's not the only one. 331 are going down to where things are really happening, within flying distance of enemy territory. That's where they all want to go. He can only wish that 332 will soon follow suit.

It wouldn't be long before he got his wish.

Reidar From is desperately trying to put a feather in Finn's hair, while Finn tries to stop him. Catterick, spring of 1942. (*Wilhelm Mohr*)

Finn Thorsager at readiness at Catterick, spring 1942. (*Wilhelm Mohr*)

Chapter 12

'Open Up and Start Weaving'

We were to be transferred to North Weald, belonging to 11 Group, the most important and active fighter group in the UK. 331 had already lost a few pilots before we arrived, among them Jens Müller, who survived being a prisoner of war and later wrote a book about his escape from the prison camp.

Life at North Weald was very special. We ate well in the mess hall, and the living room area was nice with good chairs, sofas, and a fireplace. For breakfast, we got eggs and bacon. It was definitely an advantage in belonging to 11 Group. The dinners were also quite good. Pretty often, we had official evenings with nice outfits. During dinner, it happened that people started knocking on the table, and would call for a particular name. This meant that the person had to give a speech in English. A lot of British officers usually attended. The British learned Norwegians songs from us, and we learned some British ones from them. For example, we learned 'Tipperary', 'Roll Out The Barrel' and 'Over The Ocean'. We also had an open bar every night. Usually we drank beer, but also scotch and soda. Most of us had enough brains to drink responsibly, but sometimes a few men stood out from the rest of us. Not that that was odd for young men in their early twenties. We basically spent all our time together, so we felt like a family.

Our spirits were high, and we had Wing Commander David Scott-Malden as our Wing Leader. He was a young chap of 22, a veteran from the Battle of Britain, and we had a tremendous amount of respect for him. He was very British. He was always calm and level headed, and we felt we could trust him.

We had our Spitfires parked around the perimeter of the airfield, and each of them was protected from bombing attacks by walls of concrete around them. The pilots usually stayed around the duty barracks, a Nissen

Hut, where we kept our parachutes, training equipment and all sorts of games to pass the time. We had really good chairs as well, and in better weather, we put them outside in the sun. It was necessary to stay together as a unit and become well acquainted with each other, so we could react to each other well when we flew together.

The ground personnel were a very important part of an operational squadron. In our case, they consisted of former seamen, whalers, and all kinds of other people with different backgrounds who had escaped from home. Many of them had applied to be pilots, but were not accepted due to a lack of qualifications or medical flaws like colour blindness. But each of them was given an in-depth education in a specific field. A superb relationship existed between the pilots and the ground crews.

We also had our own telephone watch, whose primary task was to receive messages from the main control. If the control had something mysterious on their radar, they contacted the station that was in the best position to deal with the problem.

Each airfield had at least four aircraft on readiness, and they could be in the air in about one minute's time. If a message of enemy activity came in from the main control, the telephone watch would shout 'Scramble!' with all his might. The pilots would run out to their aeroplanes, where the mechanics were busy getting the Spitfires ready. Parachute ready, helmet with goggles, and radio on. Then, the pilot got into his seat, strapped on his parachute, put his helmet on, and was ready to start up the engine. North Weald was a huge area of grass, so we could simply go straight out from our boxes. Once he was airborne, the pilot received his next instructions.

Finally, the day came when Scott-Malden said we were ready to fly into enemy territory, across the Channel. For us, this was very serious – a big deal.

'This is the moment you've been waiting for, chaps.' Wing Commander David Scott-Malden's words are directed at 332 Squadron in particular. They are in the briefing room, standing in front of a big map of southern England, the Channel, and the north-western part of the Continent. Over the map, there is a transparent plate, where the routes and heights for the forthcoming mission are drawn up. The men of 332 Squadron listen intently to their leader's voice.

Scott-Malden is younger than many of the Norwegian lads, but when he speaks, Finn listens with the utmost respect. He has chosen the Norwegians as 'his' wing, and Finn has wondered many times why he chose them. Does he know something about them that they don't know? For him, it's hard to tell, but they have shown a considerable amount of initiative already, escaping from occupied Norway. It would count for something. They're 'keen', as the British would say.

'Today I will introduce you to what it's like over enemy territory.' Their mission – their first from North Weald – is to go out on a 'ramrod', with the aim of getting the Luftwaffe into the air, and engaging them, while a squadron of Boston bombers will attack Dunkirk and Neiuport. 331 and 222 Squadrons will join 332 in the air, all from North Weald.

Mehre and Mohr, squadron leaders of 331 and 332, close the briefing; with wishes of good luck to all, the lads gets up from their seats.

Finn's AH-J is ready and the ground crew are finished with their preparations when he arrives. A couple of words are exchanged between him and his crew before he pulls on his 'chute, which has been prepared for him and placed on the wing. They wish Finn good luck, and he climbs up into the cockpit and begins his start-up procedure.

> We could not stay on the ground for too long, because the undercarriage hindered the engine from cooling properly.
>
> Scott-Malden started up, and we followed him. After take-off, we were told to fly at tree-top height until the wing commander started the ascent. We would follow him up. During the climb, radio-silence was still strictly kept. Sometimes, we had extra fuel tanks under our wings, and we would drop them when Scott-Malden did. With these extra tanks, we could fly for longer.
>
> We flew across the Channel at 10-20 metres height to avoid being spotted by the German radar. Suddenly, we saw Scott-Malden start to climb, and we stuck to him like glue. It was a very special atmosphere, sitting alone in the cockpit. It was pleasant to look over to the closest Spitfires, seeing the faces of comrades. It was an unspoken, warm feeling of camaraderie.

Scott-Malden's voice crackles on the radio. No point in keeping the Wing's mission hidden from the Germans any longer. They've seen them already. At Scott-Malden's command, Finn ejects the extra tank under the Spitfire, disappearing somewhere beneath. The others do the same, and a large group of empty fuel tanks fall towards the sea. If they got tangled up in a dogfight before doing this, a hit in the extra tank would most likely cause a huge explosion.

332 Squadron pilots, summer 1942. Finn was on leave when this picture was taken. From left to right: Bjørn Ræder, John Bernhard Gilhuus, Olaf Tandberg, Thor Wærner, Svein Nygaard, J.A.K. Goldthorpe, Jan Eigil Løfsgaard, Marius Eriksen, Erik Hagen, John Ryg, Gabriel Joachim Urbye, Hans Kjell Hansen, Olav Djønne, Esten Lindseth, Egil Ulstein, Søren Liby, Odd Kristiansen, Roald B. Sørensen, and Per Bergsland. (*Wilhelm Mohr*)

Spitfire Vs of 332 Squadron at North Weald, winter 1942. (*Wilhelm Mohr*)

In good weather, we would see the enemy coast very well. First as a belt of light on the horizon, and then we saw the landscape appear behind it. The question was, what could happen during the next minutes?

'Open up and start weaving,' says Scott-Malden, his voice safe, calm, and clear.

The Wing spreads out, and starts banking side to side to keep a look-out for what's going on around them. Big black puffs of smoke make Finn tighten his grip on the stick. Dark thoughts sneak into his mind. Where will the next one explode? What can they do? He will just keep hoping the next one doesn't happen anywhere near his Spitfire. Never before has he seen a thicker carpet of anti-aircraft fire.

Back from the Continent, 332 Squadron flies in formation over the English countryside. (*Finn Thorsager*)

A section of 332 Squadron is in charge of escorting half of the Bostons to Neiuport; they break out of the formation and follow the bomber boys to their target with a dense carpet of flak all around them.

'Look at all the black smoke!' One of the 332 pilots comes on the radio. He seems scared and excited at the same time.

'Yes, I see them too.' The Wing Commander's voice is there and gives comfort. It calms Finn as well. It feels comforting to him to have a veteran up front, even if he is a mere 22 years old. He knows what he's doing, he's seen it all before. To Finn, it feels like nothing can bring Scott-Malden down.

'Do you see the red fires in the explosions?!' The Norwegian pilot is there again, not yet feeling safe with the flak around them.

'Yes, I see it too, but don't touch it.' Scott-Malden answers sharply this time, and the Norwegian goes quiet. It will take time to get used to the flak, but as with all things, it will be alright with time.

In the meantime, the other group of Bostons have reached their target, and dropped their cargo over Dunkirk as planned. Finn can see several hits around the harbour area.

'Keep your eyes out for fighters,' says Scott-Malden, reminding Finn and the rest of the Wing about the threat lurking somewhere around them. He turns his head around, focusing on several spots in the sky, but there is not a single Luftwaffe fighter around.

Safely back at North Weald, the intelligence officer quickly arrives to get all the details from their mission. The ground crew approaches Finn when he jumps off his Spitfire's wing. They want to know what it was like over on the other side of the Channel. The red tape over his gun ports is still intact, but they want to know what happened. Without their amazing efforts, he wouldn't even have a Spitfire to fly in the first place. Wilhelm Mohr has told them specifically to talk to the ground crew, and keep their spirits up. They've been instructed to have a little chat with them before they go to give their official report of their mission. It's good for morale.

Finn gladly tells them what went on. Their faces light up when he speaks. They smile, satisfied with Finn's tale, and start to work on his Spitfire, while Finn walks over to Intelligence to give his report.

He searches his pockets for his tobacco, and lights up a cigarette while he speaks to the 'spy'. Several explosions on the ground, many ships in port; he gives his details to the man with the note book before he strolls off to get a cup of tea.

'Plenty of flak over Dunkirk, right? Didn't think it would be that thick.' Finn talks to Mohr, sitting in a chair outside a Nissen hut with a smoke and a cup of coffee. Mohr saw a lot of the same last year in a British Hurricane squadron. They had specialized in attacking German ships in the Channel.

Finn grabs a chair, and sits down with him.

Mohr nods, 'No Germans, but they'll come sooner or later.'

When he gets up, Finn can feel his legs are a bit shaken, almost numb. He looks at his friend, but Mohr is too busy looking at the ground crew working on his AH-W. The excitement of today is still in Finn's body. He wonders if he will be able to sleep. Tomorrow they will be flying again.

We – Norwegians in the RAF – were told that we might encounter certain problems if we were shot down over enemy territory and taken prisoner. We did come from occupied territory, and might possibly be treated differently than the British. That's what our government thought, anyway. So, we were advised to fly with fake names – English ones. I changed my identity to Frederick Thorpe, as it was easy to remember in dangerous situations, after all, my brother's name was Carl Fredrik Thorsager, so it had a connection.

We also thought about who would inherit our possessions if we got killed. Some of us wrote a little paper which stated who should inherit what. These documents were found to be invalid later on.

Chapter 13

The Cost of War

'It doesn't look good. He's still just officially missing, but really, it doesn't look good.'

332 Squadron pilots are gathered around their squadron leader, who is trying his best to be professional. One of their pilots is missing.

'As we all know, pilots can survive in the Channel for several days if they're in their dinghy. However, as time drags out, the odds get worse. We all know the drill, chaps.'

Mohr looks down to his feet, as if he's gathering enough courage to keep talking about the subject to his pilots. He's not the only one. They all feel the pain. No matter how adaptable they are to their surroundings and situation, the bad feelings are always there, somewhere. It makes a great and lasting impression. Now, Finn and the rest of the boys would have to come to terms with the fact that Lieutenant Arve Aas is unlikely ever to come back.

'Do you think I should have paid better attention today? Kept a better look-out?' Finn asks.

Mohr thinks before he answers. A hard question to answer, but if they can, they have to take some wisdom from what has happened.

'Well, maybe. It's bloody hard to know. It all happened so quickly.'

The pilots walk off, leaving each to his own thoughts about the mission. They had been escorting bombers on their way to Hazebrouck. 332 Squadron had been placed at the back as support, and the rest of the Wing had spread out to their places in relation to the bombers heading over the Channel.

Their problems had started with engine trouble. Per Bergsland's engine had started to act up even before they crossed the English coast at 25,000 feet. Bergsland had to turn back, which meant his wingman, Thor Aarbo Wærner also had to go home. They were minus two Spitfires before they even reached the middle of the Channel. Later, Marius Eriksen started to

332 Squadron A-flight leader Arve Aas. He was killed during combat off Calais on 29 June 1942. (*Finn Thorsager*)

lag behind; he also reported engine problems. They had all heard how scared the 18 year old was.

Eriksen was number two to Arve Aas, and Aas turned back home with Eriksen, to give him cover on his way back to North Weald. Just when they turned back towards England, five Focke Wulf 190s dived on them. Eriksen saw Aas dive down towards the Channel with thick smoke coming out of his Merlin engine. It was the last he saw of him before Eriksen himself had four 190s on his tail, and had to throw his Spitfire hard around the sky to avoid being shot down. Luckily, he got away, and landed at Manston for refuelling before flying back to North Weald. Another pilot, Ringdal, reported later on that he had seen a Spitfire go down in the Channel in the same area as Eriksen saw Aas for the last time. Ringdal said he saw a parachute. Could it be the same Spitfire?

The Focke Wulfs had clearly been lying somewhere over them, sneaking around unnoticed. When they saw Eriksen and Aas break formation, they attacked with force. Everything had been in the Germans' favour. Height, speed, and surprise. Thankfully, Eriksen got away. It could well have been two missing pilots instead of one. The thing most troubling Finn was that they had not seen the 190s above. If they had spotted them, Aas might still have been alive. Even if they didn't spot them overhead, they should have seen them when they dived down on Eriksen and Aas. Now Aas is most likely killed. They are in need of a new leader of A-Flight, a position Aas had filled since the squadron was formed.

A-flight at Catterick, spring 1942. From left to right: Egil Ulstein, Johan Bernhard Gilhuus, Peder Mollestad, Torstein Strand, Finn Thorsager, and Thor Wærner with squadron mascots Dante and Ole. (*Finn Thorsager*)

Finn is tired from the day's sad events. Tomorrow, there are rumours of the squadron heading down to Manston, most likely for convoy support. Finn's first summer at North Weald is rapidly moving forward. It's soon July already.

★

It is still early when Finn sees Henning Leifseth land his Spitfire at North Weald. Minutes later, a second Spitfire comes in for landing. It's Morten Ree, Henning's wingman. Finn usually keeps track of his old friends from 331 Squadron. Henning has been a friend for a long time now, dating all the way back to their days together at Kjeller. One can't help but notice Henning on the ground and in the air. He's a very skilled pilot, and a man who can always make people laugh and feel good in his company. Finn can just spot Henning getting out of his Spitfire and strolling off to dispersal, most likely on the hunt for a cup of tea.

Hours later, 331 and 332 Squadrons are in the briefing room, ready for Henning's second mission of the day.

Finn is going on his first 'show'. The briefing is detailed and to the point. A massive 'rhubarb' is in the making from North Weald. They are

Henning Leifseth.

to fly low, destroying anything they can on the ground, while exposing themselves terribly to anti-aircraft fire. Together with 222 and 121 Squadrons, the Norwegians will cross the Channel, heading towards Belgium, close to the French border. 331 will be low, while 332 will be at about 1000 feet above them as top cover, in case the Luftwaffe is tempted to show up.

Henning has a serious look on his face when he hears the briefing. Low attacks against French targets are dangerous. In fact, they all know rhubarbs are extremely dangerous. Usually, it's not experience or knowledge that count for survival, but pure luck. Dogfights against 190s are one thing; if, at least, you have some experience like Finn does, you might survive. To fly low over the French countryside with cannons hammering away is something else entirely.

Henning gives a nod when he's told he will lead 331's Yellow section, while Finn is given orders to lead 332's Yellow section. They both get the picture. The Germans might take the bait and come up to greet them. If not, it will be hard work with the massive flak from the ground. It's a show with high stakes.

After the briefing is over and wishes for a successful mission have been given, Finn and Henning are standing outside. The last checks are done on their Spitfires.

Henning is worried, and shakes his head in seriousness.

'This is dangerous stuff, Finn. You have to alert me if we find ourselves over Dunkirk. The place is packed with flak batteries. You'll see better from your height than I will.'

'I'll do my best, Henning.'

Henning gives off a quick smile. What more can Finn promise? They both know how dangerous these rhubarbs can be.

Finn also knows that Henning always talks about the mission being dangerous. It has become a sort of character trait of his. Maybe he does it out of habit, maybe for superstitious reasons. Finn doesn't know. Henning is, after all, a very good pilot, they all agree on that. Maybe he's even a bit better than average. Maybe, in a few months, he will take over 331 Squadron as squadron leader.

The two of them split up in front of the barracks at North Weald, heading their separate ways to 331 and 332's areas, ready to lead their respective Yellow sections.

Henning's Spitfire is filled up with fuel, and ready for its second mission of the day. Finn's AH-J is ready too, standing proudly with the other Spitfires of 332. Newly washed, it's shining in the sun.

Soon, the propeller is slowly starting to turn. Then the flames shoot out of the engine's exhaust pipes. Finn's Spitfire shakes violently when the Merlin engine awakens. The ground crew run forward and pull the chocks away from forty-eight Spitfires all around North Weald. A tremendous volume roars through the entire base. Then they are all just small dots on the horizon. The ground crews stroll back to the hangars and the barracks, hoping they all will come home in one piece. They have to endure a long and nervous wait.

We, the Norwegians, were to meet the two other squadrons just north of Vlissingen in Holland.

332 has got Wing Commander David Scott-Malden as leader. Over Frinton, he sets course for the Channel, with just a few feet separating them from the sea.

They cross the Belgian coast not far from Dunkirk and climb upwards, with 331 in the lead further below. As he promised, Finn is keeping a close eye on Henning's Spitfire below.

Suddenly, there is a tangled mass of Spitfire squadrons in the area, and Finn loses track of Henning in the chaos that follows. It's impossible to find one specific Spitfire with so many about. Finn keeps looking, but to no avail. Henning has merged with all the others.

331 pick out their ground targets and shoot at anything that might pose a threat. Finn is still higher above with 332's Yellow section; he keeps looking for Henning, but with no luck. In the meantime, the Germans are firing everything they've got at the North Weald Wing, who are racing over the flat landscape of Belgium, heading south-east towards France. Dangerous black dots of smoke keep appearing everywhere around their Spitfire Vbs.

One explosion is extremely close to one Spitfire; the shrapnel hits it hard, but it keeps going.

Henning pushes 331's Yellow section low and fast. Fields, trees and roads are passing them at great speed. If they can stay away from Dunkirk, as they intend to, things should be ok for the time being.

The range of a Spitfire over the Continent is short. It's time to turn back before Finn even thinks about it. Scott-Malden is on the radio, giving orders to pull out and head for home. Finn banks his Spitfire in a long turn back towards the coast, and his Yellow section follows him, still intact. The coast is not far away, swept in a thin layer of haze.

Meanwhile, Henning and his wingman have picked out a cement factory and a water tower as their last targets before heading back. Henning keeps his Spitfire low and level, and aims for the tower. The Germans on the ground open up at the two Spitfires with everything they've got. Henning and his number two are flying straight into an inferno.

Through dark explosions and heavy flak, Finn sees Dunkirk show up not far away. They will pass on the city's right side, their left. Seconds later, he spots a major flash of light that draws his attention away from Dunkirk; it is a Spitfire burning below him, close to the outskirts of the town. The stricken plane is engulfed in flames. Finn can barely see the roundels on its wings through all the fire. It's been hit by ground fire.

'Spitfire going down. Looks like Yellow One!' One of the Norwegians from 331 is on the radio. Finn quickly realizes what's going on. Henning has been hit, and he's going down.

Henning's wingman pulls up and goes in for another attack, avenging his fallen leader. He gives the machine gun position that just shot down Henning a long burst of fire, and leaves it burning.

Henning has no hope of ejecting. He goes down into the ground, a burning wreckage.

> I was very sad at Henning's death, and I remembered his last words before we left North Weald. But I had done my best. That's just the way it was.

332 Squadron escapes out of France at only a few metres' altitude above the sea. The Germans are still giving them everything they've got, while they are trying desperately to get out in one piece.

Finn looks left and right. The weather has been nice the entire day with little wind. The sea, on the other hand, is bombarded with projectiles meant for the Norwegians. The intense firing from the Germans makes the water look like it's boiling. Finn throws his Spitfire around. Up, down, right and left to avoid the flak the best he can. It's simply a miracle they all escape. All except one, left burning on the beach at Dunkirk.

On his final turn into North Weald, Finn pulls the cockpit hood back. He wants to see as wide a view as possible, in order to land safely. The big Merlin engine obscures just about everything straight ahead. He selects wheels out, a bit of trim, and his Spitfire is ready to touch the ground. A little bump and he's back home.

With his engine off, everything falls into silence. Apart from a few Norwegian Spitfires still taxing back to their respective spots, everything is oddly quiet. Finn feels warm, and pulls off his goggles and headwear. He pulls his blond hair back and sighs heavily. For a moment he thinks of Henning and the days they had at Kjeller before the War; Henning's face, full of smiles and laughter. Finn feels he is about to cry, but tightens up and pushes his emotions as far back into his mind as he possibly can. When his ground crew arrives he's his old self again, giving them his unofficial report as it happened. Then he walks off silently.

As darkness arrives at North Weald, and the last Merlin engine has been shut off, Finn sits quietly inside one of the barracks as the squadron adjutant writes down the report of the day. Not far away, he can hear the humming of the first bombers heading for Germany. Wellingtons, Stirlings and Halifax bombers are taking off from airfields in the North, heading south-east. Soon, they will release their deadly load over German towns. Maybe one of the bombers will end up over Dunkirk on its way back, where Henning's Spitfire lies.

Finn stops for a second, listening to the distant sound. He takes a deep breath as the adjutant finishes off his report: 'It is thought to be a million-to-one chance that Henning Leifseth could survive his crash, so we shall miss very much his lively good humour. He had been A-flight's commander since last April. Henning was a very fine pilot with a great deal of flying experience. He was always ready for a party.'

Later on, in the officers' quarters, Finn is still awake, thinking about the events of the day. Henning's last words are still there in his mind, bothering him. He had done his best. What else could he have done? 'His time was up,' as the British say. It had been Henning's time to die. But, no matter what excuse Finn manages to find, his friend will not disappear from his mind. It's not his fault. He had done his best. To keep an eye on a single Spitfire, with almost fifty others around in a hectic situation, with flak and explosions, is almost impossible. He knows that, but it doesn't help. Finn twists and turns in bed. Nothing can be done, but he knows that he will never forget this day. A feeling of guilt will follow him forever. Finally, he falls asleep.

From now on, we participated in a great many missions to the Continent. We escorted daylight bombers to the western part of Europe. We flew 'sweeps', usually two squadrons working together, flying over France and Belgium, trying to get the Germans into the air and shooting them down. It was all about destroying as many German aircraft as possible, with a future invasion of Europe in the back of everyone's minds.

We also had these 'rhubarbs' to fly. Low flying with the purpose of destroying as many things as possible, such as shipping, trains, artillery and barges. There were German boats lying in the rivers, thought to be intended for an invasion of England.

★

To help us deal with the stress of flying mission after mission, and the strain of losing friends in battle, we were given time off to relax, and bring some form of normality back into our lives.

Quite often, we went to the little town of Epping, about five kilometres from North Weald. In town, there were several different stores, restaurants, and pubs. The most popular one for us pilots was the Thatched House.

Most of 332 Squadron pilots in front of a Spitfire IX at North Weald, possibly autumn 1943. Finn can be seen to the right of Wilhelm Mohr, underneath one of the Spitfires blades.

We spent a lot of free time here with friends and colleagues. It was a pleasure. All this made us feel right at home. We didn't feel we were in a foreign country because the people were so kind to us.

We also went to London often. A train took us there, taking about half an hour into Liverpool Street Station. In London, there were several enjoyable clubs, especially the Royal Automobile Club, where we were made honorary members. We had a great time there, relaxing the British way. They had Roman baths, steam baths and swimming pools. Tea and biscuits were served while we relaxed. Great stuff.

The underground was always interesting. People laid down here, packed like sardines, sleeping. It was safe from German bombs. Travellers had to step carefully between people sleeping to get to their destinations.

Sometimes we went further for our holidays. In late July 1942, I went with Reidar From to St Ives for a well-deserved rest. It was really warm in Cornwall, and some tropical fruits were grown there. Plenty of good beaches as well, and we stayed at a superb hotel. We almost forgot the War, but when we returned, there was a terrible reminder.

The squadron, with Mohr leading, had been out on a 'rodeo' on 31 July. Having received a report of enemy fighters below, 332 Squadron was called down to help out and promptly got caught in a heavy dogfight. In the chaos that followed, they lost each other and became vulnerable. At this moment, several 109s dived on them, targeting four Spitfires; Hansen, Nygaard, Tandberg and Hagen all 'bought it'. Mohr had several splinters in his leg, and some damage to his face. He managed to get his Spitfire back to base, and did a wheels-up landing. Neither undercarriage nor flaps functioned.

It's a tough pill to swallow when four pilots go down on the same mission. Later, they might be able to take revenge and shoot down a few 109s, but it won't bring the lost men back. Maybe some of them will send word from captivity in Germany, or maybe they all died. It was some comfort that Søren Liby had claimed a 190 destroyed. Mohr had claimed one damaged. But, overall, the Germans had not got away with it.

Chapter 14

Dieppe

A significant event during these times was the raid on Dieppe on 19 August 1942. We were sent to Manston with the ground crew. We didn't know what was going to happen, but we did understand that something special was taking place, and we were right. In the evening, there was a secret briefing where we were told how many warships were already on their way across the Channel to participate in a big raid on the French coast. This was also meant to be a test invasion to gain experience. 331 and 332, as well as many other squadrons from other airfields, would support the ships and the landing of the troops. It was the biggest and most complicated operation yet, and many thousands of troops would be put ashore, mostly Canadians.

It's four in the morning when Finn finds his seat with the rest of 332 Squadron, together with the Wing from North Weald. They're being briefed on Operation Jubilee. Outside, the ground personnel are working their hardest to get all the Spitfires in tip-top shape. They make adjustments and last-minute repairs, and double check everything so that nothing is left to fate. All the Spitfires have to be ready for the day's task over Dieppe. Take off has already been set for 6.20 a.m. from Manston.

Just after six o'clock, Finn is strapped into the cockpit, going through the normal procedures before take-off, managing to sneak in a cigarette too, before the word is given.

At the exact time given by Scott-Malden, the Rolls Royce Merlin engines roar to life, and the squadrons leave Manston behind, heading towards Dieppe. Finn pulls the hood into place just after take-off. With Scott-Malden leading, they fly at sea level towards the coastal town. Finn thunders over boats, soldiers, tanks, and weapons in the Channel, all heading for the same place. The soldiers stretch their arms into the air and wave at the Wing from North Weald as they pass over.

Ground crew hard at work cleaning a Spitfire before the ill-fated Dieppe raid in August 1942. The Norwegians, however, got nothing but praise for their efforts. (*Wilhelm Mohr*)

Finn lets his eyes wander around, keeping a good lookout. He is Yellow Three for this show. It's a wonderful morning in August, with just a little haze in the Channel. It's common for this time of the year, and the summer is slowly fading into Autumn.

Finn hears the reassuring voice of Scott-Malden, and pulls upwards while opening a little more throttle. His Spitfire is more than willing. The first ships have already arrived and are below the Wing, the fighting has begun. Finn sees them from his Spitfire, small dots on the beach, running toward the German positions. Many of them stop moving, falling to the ground. The sand around quickly turns red.

Just under the cloud cover, 332 is flying in perfect formation. Suddenly, a swarm of 190s go in for an attack on 332 Squadron in sections of three or four aircraft. Within a moment, the air is filled with Focke Wulfs and Spitfires, whirling around in the sky. A Spitfire gets a 190 on his tale, and a Norwegian pilot yells out a warning, 'Watch out Spit, you're being attacked from behind!'

Too late. The Spitfire is doomed, spinning towards land. Another Norwegian throws his Spitfire into a hard turn, seeking revenge for his lost comrade.

Finn keeps turning sharply around while being pressed into his seat. The Germans are diving down on them from everywhere. He pushes his Spitfire to the limit to avoid the attackers, trying to get on the tail of one of them.

His body is heavy one second, the next he's in a negative dive, and he's being pressed against his straps.

A 190 appears dead ahead and Finn opens fire almost before he has time to think. His Spitfire shakes from the force of his guns. To his great shock, the two of them are heading straight for each other; Finn just keeps firing, hoping he can obliterate his enemy.

Seconds later, the German is gone. He saw several hits, but he didn't see what happened. The 190 just seemed to disappear.

Suddenly, Scott-Malden's calm voice comes on the radio, 'Back to base!'

Finn takes a quick look at his fuel gauge. The needle is dangerously low. The order came just in time. He turns around and dives towards Manston. Forty minutes later, he's on his final approach.

The Spitfire bumps across the grass at Manston. Finn pulls himself out of the cockpit and jumps down from the wing; he knows there will be more flying today.

The ground crew arrives, refuelling and doing a quick check. They grin when they see that the red tape over the cannons and machine guns has gone.

Wilhelm Mohr lands his Spitfire shortly after Finn, and taxies it up to the Nissen huts. Beside him, a third Spitfire shuts off its engine. The pilot gets out and gives Wilhelm Mohr a few words of support when he sees that one of his boots is filled with blood. But Wilhelm is stubborn. He just wants to refuel and take off again. He has to give in when the others arrive and insist that he gets his wound treated. A bullet has gone straight through his leg, making a neat hole in the map he had in his pocket. The hole is not far from Dieppe, which sparks a few jokes from the nearby pilots, much

Finn on a short break, Dieppe raid, 1942. (*Finn Thorsager*)

to Mohr's annoyance; 332's squadron leader is not the easiest person to be around when he can't fly his Spitfire.

Finn is given orders to take over 332 in Wilhelm's absence. For the rest of the day, he will be leading them over Dieppe. A chilling thought, but he's up for it.

It is 11.10 a.m. when the squadrons leave Manston again. They know exactly what they are heading into now, and they set a direct course.

For the second time that day, Finn throws his Spitfire around in the sky, trying to get on the tail of a Focke Wulf. They are out in numbers.

332 spots a formation of Dornier 217 bombers below. The Norwegians are hungry for more targets, and dive down on the Germans, machine guns and cannons blasting away. One Dornier is already doomed. Black smoke pours from one of its engines. The Norwegians see the easy prey and go after it like a flock of vultures, lining up to have a go. They are so keen on firing that they get in each other's way.

Finn dives down on another Dornier, with his number two, Nils Jørgen Fuglesang, on his tail. This one, too, is already burning from an attack made by two pilots from 331, having mixed themselves in with 332. Finn keeps going down anyway, closing in. With his thumb already on the firing button, he hesitates when he observes something strange from the cockpit; a mysterious white light is obscuring everything in the cockpit area. He holds his thumb ready, but he's confused. Is it directed at him? Some sort of signal? There is no returning fire from the Germans either, and Finn doesn't understand why.

He makes a decision, and decides to go in closer, firing a long burst from his machine gun. He sees no clear result, no pieces falling off. Still no return fire. The bomber just keeps going in a shallow dive towards the sea.

Just north of Dieppe, the Dornier hits the water with a gigantic splash. Finn banks his wing to the left to observe it disappear into the sea. That was it. The bomber was finished. With Fuglesang still on his tail, he pulls up again, gaining altitude. His conscience is troubling him though. He tries to get higher, keeping a look-out for German fighters.

On the ground, the fight continues. Finn sees several explosions with thick black smoke rising into the sky. Some of the explosions seem to be happening right where soldiers are running. It's not a pretty sight.

In the battle in the sky, a lonely Spitfire is jumped by several 190s coming in from the sun. The unknown pilot rolls his smoking Spitfire over, and jumps out. The parachute opens, and the pilot is picked up by a friendly ship. He hardly even gets wet.

Scott-Malden breaks in on the radio and pulls his men out of the show. Back to Manston. A little breather before they go out again. Maybe something to drink, and a few pieces of bread for those who can eat.

At 2.45 p.m., Finn leads 332 towards the Channel and Dieppe for the third time. Ten minutes later, 331 takes off as well. Again, they fly low over the Channel, and they start their climb before reaching Dieppe. Finn, now as Red 1, navigates his squadron with ease over Dieppe and the convoy outside Dieppe harbour. He twists and turns in his cockpit, looking for the Luftwaffe. He knows they're around, and remembers to keep a particular eye on the sun; the Germans always like to come out of it, diving down with machine guns firing, going straight through a squadron of Spitfires without turning at all. Finn knows about the danger, and he knows very well where they are at their most vulnerable.

Suddenly it happens. A section of 190s dives on 332 from above.

'Tally Ho!'

Finn banks his Spitfire into a sharp turn, climbing up and into the attacking Germans. 332 follows straight behind. Finn fires a long burst of cannon fire against one of the attackers. He sees the German aeroplane being hit by his cannon shells, but loses it a second later in the chaos of Spitfires, Focke Wulfs, and parachutes opening around him. Suddenly, it's all quiet. Everyone has disappeared.

Deciding to go for the deck, Finn dives westwards towards England. A single Spitfire is an easy target for the Luftwaffe; they wait for chances like this. Thankfully, another RAF squadron of Spitfires shows up in his area, and he follows them back to Manston.

> During our missions over the Continent, we sometimes got separated from each other, and had to find the way home by ourselves. From time to time in bad weather, we had no idea where we were. But, usually, it was just a matter of flying a direct course, and an airfield would pop up sooner or later. We could then refuel, and ask for directions back home. The south of England was packed with airfields. It was almost like a big carrier ship.

It's 3.55 p.m. when Finn meets his ground crew. The red tapes over his machine gun ports are burned off by bullets, not long ago hitting an Fw190 over Dieppe. The men on the ground are pleased. They want to hear all the details. Finn gives them the story with pleasure.

Dusk is starting to arrive when the Wing from North Weald takes off for their fourth and last mission over Dieppe. The convoy is on its way home. The attack has turned into a defence of tired and wounded soldiers.

A captured Fw190 gathers plenty of interest at North Weald, summer 1943. (*Finn Thorsager*)

Just over the convoy, 331 spot something in the distance, straight ahead.

'Aircraft 12 o'clock, on collision course. Looks like 190s!' The Norwegian pilot's voice is excited and tense.

The two squadrons meet head-on, and one of the Norwegians opens fire. Too late, they notice the markings and the actual shape of the 'enemy'. They are Hawker Typhoons.

Their leader flies straight ahead for a few seconds after the engagement before his Typhoon goes into an uncontrolled spin downwards. It hits the ocean at extreme velocity. It's not possible to survive such an impact, if he wasn't dead already. Finn can do nothing more than watch the disaster happening. A terrible start to their last mission of the day. It won't be the last time it happens, for both Allied and German pilots. It's all part of the game. It's just the way it is.

Like big swarms of bees, the Spitfires are positioning themselves over the convoy, with the Luftwaffe circling close by. One 190 loses position and is quickly attacked by angry Spitfires. The Focke Wulf explodes in a big ball of fire. The smaller pieces fall down like leaves.

Then the two air forces engage. A 190 dives down on a Norwegian pilot who pulls his Spitfire up towards the German. The Norwegian is desperately trying to gain height, while making himself as small as he possibly can in the cockpit. The 190 shoots, but misses when they pass each other with a marginal clearance. Another Norwegian has to bail out after his Spitfire is attacked by several 190s. The pilot is quickly pulled out of the cold water by an Allied vessel.

Finn sets a course for home with 332 behind him. He dips his wings at the ships with the surviving soldiers heading for England. They've suffered terrible losses on the ground. On several of the ships, there are Norwegian pilots who have been shot down.

While dusk settles over Manston, Finn comes in to land his Spitfire for the last time that day. It's starting to get really dark when his engine is finally turned off. He gets out of his Spitfire, and walks towards the barracks. It's been a very hectic day at work.

At dinner, there are two chairs empty in the mess hall.

The 'big day' was over with big losses on both sides. However, the Allies did collect necessary experience for the full invasion of the Continent, which had to come sooner or later. Our ground crew and mechanics coped exceptionally, and were given special thanks for their quick and reliable efforts.

After Dieppe, Scott-Malden left us for a very well deserved break from operations. Wilfrid Duncan Smith took his place as our Wing Commander.

Six Bostons to St Omer

'This is good stuff for a joke, but are we really supposed to do this?' The briefing room falls quiet at the words from the Norwegian pilot, Olav Ullestad. They're all feeling rather poorly from last night's party. Normally, when 'Zulu' Morris arranges a party in the officer's mess, they have the next day off from flying. Not this time. Finn and 332 have been sent down to Manston in the early morning, still feeling a little drunk from last night. None of them knows what to say. It is the most dangerous mission the squadron has ever been given.

Mohr clears his throat after Ullestad's comment, choosing not to reply to it, and continues with his briefing. The conditions are bad, with low cloud and rain. They will be flying low, exposing themselves to massive amounts of ground fire. The Norwegians are shaking their heads in disbelief.

At a specific time, in a specific position, we would rendezvous with a squadron of Boston bombers. These bombers would bomb the airfield at St Omer and then St Ingelvert. We were to fly just ahead of them and shoot up flak batteries. It is pretty hard to meet up with other squadrons at low altitude, because we can quickly disappear from each other's view, due to our high speed. St Omer was also one of the most heavily defended airfields in our area of operations.

'We've done some dangerous flying before, but this is just crazy, you know...' says Marius Eriksen, 332's youngest pilot, to Finn after the briefing. The tension is building. Both of them remember Mohr's chilling choice of words, 'The survivors from St Omer will proceed to St Ingelvert to do a second low level attack.'

Eriksen and Finn head for their Spitfires lined up on the field; Finn with his regular AH-J, and Eriksen in AH-P. With Eriksen strapped in his cockpit, waving a short and gloomy goodbye, Finn walks the last metres down to his own Spit.

'Finn, wait a minute.' It's Mohr, catching up with him on his way to AH-W. 'Listen, I got hold of Wing-Co Duncan Smith on the telephone. He tried to cancel the entire affair, but it was simply impossible. He couldn't talk them into dropping this doomsday show.'

'At least he gave it a try,' says Finn, 'we can't ask for much more.'

Mohr seems tense and nervous when he walks down to his Spitfire and grabs the parachute from the wing. It's a rare sight for Finn to see their boss like this.

Waiting to take off, Finn lights a cigarette and smokes it quickly. Finishing it, he starts on another one. The nerves are running high, and he wants to calm them down with a few puffs.

To his left, Thor Wærner and the Dane, Kjeld Rønhof, get ready in their cockpits. Finn can hear Wærner's nervous voice before he jumps up on the wing of his Spitfire. 'Well, goodbye then Kjeld,' he says. 'We won't be seeing each other again.'

It sends shivers down Finn's spine. The chaps are giving themselves little chance of survival, and with every right. It's verging on a suicide mission.

Finn strapping on his Spitfire MkIX at North Weald, spring 1943. (*Finn Thorsager*)

At 9.30 a.m., they're all ready. Twelve Spitfires ready for take-off from Manston with Wilhelm Mohr leading. It's a solo escort, without the rest of the Wing. Only 332 this time around, and just six Boston bombers to look after. The task will be difficult. Trying to keep track of the bombers in poor weather and low cloud is terribly hard work. In addition, they are expected to do low-level strafing on machine gun posts and flak positions around the airfields before the Bostons come in. Even if the Luftwaffe doesn't show up, there will be plenty to do.

Small particles of water hit Finn in the face as he straps into his Spitfire. Light drizzle is not the best Spitfire weather. He simply has to hope for the best, and that the weather keeps itself steady enough for the mission. They have to get those bombers over to France, and back home again. It feels like an impossible mission for those bombers, beating up extremely well defended airfields.

'Friendlies in sight!' Just five minutes after take-off from Manston, Mohr spots the slow bombers in formation over North Foreland, just about touching the extremely low cloud base. Mohr gives his messages over the radio, and Finn spots the bombers just where their boss said they would be. They've made contact.

Just under the dark grey clouds, 332 is flying ahead of the bombers towards the French coast. Over Calais, the Germans fire their first rounds towards them. The bombers keep on flying courageously towards St Omer as if nothing has happened, never wandering off their course.

Finn looks over to his left. He has one of the Bostons relatively close, just a little behind. He can vaguely see the pilot and the men behind their machine guns. The pilot stares ahead, busy keeping in formation, while the flak explodes around him.

Suddenly, the Germans hit their target. The explosion rips through the doomed bomber. It rises steeply up in the air with its rear half engulfed in a massive fire, before it flips over and crashes into a farm in a gigantic ball of flame.

No one saw any parachutes. The bomber was too low for any of them have a chance of getting out. Now there are five left and they still have a good way to go before reaching their target.

We continued flying in a zone with plenty of flak, with tracers flying all around us. To avoid German flak, we had to fly as 'wild men', up and down, and turn as much as possible. It was also important to stay as low as possible. Sometimes, we came back with leafs and branches on our Spitfires.

332 Squadron's Peder Mollestad with mascot Mads on the engine of a Spitfire V, summer 1942. (*Wilhelm Mohr*)

332 crosses the coast just 6 miles east of Calais. A hailstorm of ground fire meets the Norwegians from the sand dunes. Finn spots one of the Norwegians open fire on one of the several Germans positions on the beach; the German soldiers around it fall dead to the ground.

Suddenly it goes quiet again. No hostile Germans, just friendly French civilians waving a warm welcome to their squadron of Spitfires. Finn keeps his Spitfire as low as he possibly can, supporting the Bostons. They have no choice, over them there is just a massive layer of cloud.

Then the fire opens up again. They have no choice but to fly through it, and Finn desperately tries to make himself smaller where he sits. Then it happens; one of the Bostons gets it bad. The big bomber suddenly pulls sharply upwards before it stalls and goes straight down. Finn can clearly see a Spitfire swerve to avoid a collision with the stricken bomber; it misses by a hair's breadth. With it's bomb load still intact, the explosion is enormous. It crashes into a French farm, totally destroying the entire group of farming houses. No one had a chance, neither those in the bombers, nor those on the ground.

Finn has no time to think more about the incident; the squadron race into a heavy rain shower with the Germans still firing everything they have got at them. Taking his eyes off the horizon in front for a mere second, Finn can spot a church to his right. He is shocked when he realizes he has to look up to see its spire.

Closing in on St Omer, the Bostons are already split up. 332 leaves them to do their job, and Mohr leads the squadron up. Finn breathes out in relief when they finally have a little height and go into 'line abreast' formation.

Mascot Mads, left alone on the massive engine of a Spitfire V.
(*Wilhelm Mohr*)

'This is Red 2. My glycol system is hit!' Finn sees Red 2, Thor Wærner's Spitfire, in the formation. White smoke pours out of the doomed engine. 'I will try to climb for altitude and bail out!'

Wærner pulls his Spitfire upwards. With not enough speed, and a bad engine, it will never hold. He will never manage to get enough height to take to his 'chute. Wærner realizes the same just seconds after Finn and aborts the climbing, tipping the nose of his Spit down again.

'This is Red 2. Good luck, boys.' Wærner's voice is cracking up, full of horror.

'I think you need it more than us,' responds a Norwegian pilot.

Finn can see the glycol is gushing over the Spitfire's windscreen. He can see Wærner aim for a small field just ahead. The last thing he sees is the wheels appearing underneath the ill-fated Spitfire. The field is big enough. With a little luck, he will make it there safely. However, there is a poor chance of seeing Wærner again anytime soon.[7]

'Bandits, ten o' clock!'

The warning is given. Finn sights the formation of 190s ahead, just where they were reported to be. They are a good distance away from the flak that 332 have to endure. They won't attack as long as 332 is being fired at from the ground. Too risky. If none of the 332 Spits drop out of the formation, they will be relatively safe for the time being. It's more than enough to handle the stuff they get from the ground.

The Bostons finally give up their mission with the call of 190s in the area. They drop their bombs wherever they may be around the St Omer area and head up into the cloud to fly home.

332 climbs to 6,000 feet, into the deep grey clouds, and heads for home. The Germans fire off their last rounds just when the clouds give them cover. They're out of the worst part now, with one man less than they came with. Flying into the fog, Finn's Spitfire is met by a wall of rain, hail, and wind. He doesn't care as long as they get themselves out of France. A few minutes longer and he's convinced more of them would have gone down.

Halfway over the channel, Mohr gives a call for them to drop out of the clouds again. Finn can breathe more easily now, but his body is still shaking from the low flying and extensive ground fire they had to endure for so long. Mohr reports a sighting of oil on the water in the channel, and they circle the spot until another squadron of Spitfires takes over.

Finally approaching Manston, Mohr calls up on the radio, asking specifically to be given room to land first. Mohr says he can smell fuel in his cockpit and needs to land at once. Finn can see him go straight in for landing, and looks to be alright.

The fog slowly covers Manston like a grey carpet, engulfing 332's Spitfires in wet drizzle. They will probably have to stay at Manston for the night. Shaken, Mohr got down in one piece, his engine stopping when he touched the ground. A couple of bullets had hit his fuel system. Jolly good luck he made it home. Johan Gilhuus had been the Spitfire that just avoided the stricken Boston. With a gloomy face, he tells them he was so close he had seen the face of the tailgunner of the Boston before it hit the ground.

Finn can't deny the fact that even with a bad result, 332 did pretty well in a very difficult situation. A near to perfect rendezvous with the Boston bombers in horrid weather conditions. They never lost their place in the formation either, even with plenty of flak and lots of poor luck. Even if the result was not the best, they had showed they could work superbly as a team. It was something to be pleased about, but even so, many of the pilots thought that a mission this dangerous should not have been attempted.

Sometime later, in 1943, we got a message about a briefing for 332 Squadron involving an attack on Boulogne harbour. We were to hold a minimum of height over the Channel, as usual, in order to give them a big surprise. We were not told if there were any special targets in the harbour for us to attack, but we did understand that there was something there. We were to shoot at what we felt was right, and concluded that the harbour must have some important ships. We were also told to shoot up any flak positions. I think we all understood that this was a very dangerous mission, and had our quiet thoughts. We were given a time to start, and I was to lead the squadron.

We cycled back to our dispersal after the briefing, and got ready. However, I was then given message that the start was postponed. The message said we were to wait until further orders.

This kind of waiting could be nerve-wracking, and I noticed that many of our pilots were very nervous. After a long time, at least a couple of hours, we finally got the message that the entire thing was cancelled.

I was later informed that there had been discussions in the RAF about the risk factor involved. It did not stand up to the hopeful result of the mission. This was a very interesting episode, and truly showed that things did go on 'behind the curtains' at a high level.

Chapter 16

More Friends Gone

With parts of 332 assigned to convoy duty for the day, the rest of the squadron were to do some practice flying. Finn decides to send two of the new pilots, Tandberg and Hansen, out to practise dogfighting over the Thames Estuary. The cloudbase is high, but the haze is thick. With Mohr off somewhere for a much needed rest, Finn is acting squadron leader, and he decides it's the right day to get in some much-needed practice.

Having given them some pointers and wished them good luck, Finn watches Tandberg and Hansen speed off down the runway in their Spitfires. He keeps his eyes especially on Tandberg; the boy had taken the same route as he had from Norway, all the way through the Soviet Union to Canada. Just as Finn, he had acted as an instructor at 'Little Norway' before coming to England and joining 332 Squadron.

With the Spitfires disappearing into the haze, Finn walks back to dispersal and grabs a cup of tea before he's off with Gilhuus for convoy patrol.

At 2 p.m. sharp he's lined up at North Weald in Spitfire BS508 as Yellow 1 with Gilhuus as Yellow 2. After a quick look in his mirror to see that Gilhuus is where he should be, he pushes the throttle gently forward. Up in the air, the haze is as thick as expected. With Gilhuus on his tail, they soon reach the convoys and cover the slow moving ships for forty minutes before they are given orders to return to base. Not a single German in sight.

Back at North Weald, things are normal and quiet. Most of 331 are still somewhere practicing over Southend, and the rest of 332's pilots are inside dispersal playing cards.

Finn asks if Tandberg and Hansen are back yet; the chaps give a short 'no'. Finn finds it odd, as they should have been back by now, but he decides to give them another thirty minutes before checking further. In the meantime, Finn sends Gilhuus and Bjørn Ræder off for some mock dogfighting. Better make most of the day.

With almost forty-five minutes gone, the phone suddenly rings. Finn answers it with a short 'hello'. His face drops instantly. He hangs up the phone and looks to the boys playing cards. They can see something is up. His face must have gone very pale.

'Something has happened to Tandberg and Hansen,' he says, 'I don't know what exactly, but I was told they have crashed mid-air.'

'Are they alive?' asks Eriksen urgently.

'One of them is.'

'Which one?'

'They didn't tell me, they don't know.'

'Jesus Christ,' says Eriksen, still with a deck of cards on his hand.

In the evening, Finn recieves more news. Hansen is the one who survived. Tandberg has been found dead near Gravesend, all mashed up.

The next morning, Finn drives off with pilots Hassel and Fuglesang to visit Hansen in the hospital. The weather is too bad for flying.

Poor Hansen is in a bad state. He tells Finn how he almost froze to death coming down in his parachute, and Finn instantly thinks how Tandberg must have died of the cold on his way down. The British have put Hansen in a soft bed with plenty of good food and drinks; they thought he was an officer. Poor Hansen couldn't even mutter his own name when he arrived. Finn notices the mistake, but doesn't say anything. For all he knows, the English will move him to a less fancy spot in the hospital if they find out the poor boy is only a sergeant.

Later that evening, Finn's thoughts of Tandberg freezing to death turn out to be wrong. By the state of the body, poor Tandberg wouldn't have been able to open his parachute at all.

★

The men from 331 Squadron are unusually quiet.

After Finn lands at 2.30 p.m. with 332, it's not long before the depressing news comes in. Stein Sem, an especially skilful pilot with 331 Squadron, has gone missing.

Sem and another pilot, Ottar Malm, had to turn back because of a problem with Sem's supercharger, and oxygen issues on Malm's Spitfire. Just before crossing the French coast, they were attacked from behind by two 190s. Malm had warned Sem about the danger, but too late. He had seen Sem climb violently upwards with white smoke coming from his engine. He then came on the radio saying something Malm had not been able to understand; probably a warning about the attack from the 190s, because

Malm was hit by one of them just when he got the message. Sem then reported a 'Mayday', and probably bailed out.

Both squadrons roar out from North Weald in search of Sem. They think he might be 'in the drink' somewhere off the French coast. Finn flies with 332, but neither of the squadrons see anyone in the Channel, and they have to go back to North Weald empty handed. Finn had known Sem for a long time, way before coming to England. Sem had even flown Gladiators with Finn before the War.

Finn doesn't feel well when he lands at North Weald after their unsuccessful search for his friend. However, their preparations for Christmas carry on as if nothing has happened. The squadrons have big plans for a party on Christmas Eve. Wing Commander Duncan Smith also leaves the Norwegians, and is replaced by Wing Commander Jameson. Finn instantly likes Jameson and they form a friendship.

For most of the Christmas period up to New Year, Finn and the rest of the North Weald Wing stay on the ground. The weather has been horrible with fog, rain, cold, and even snow. Finn had heard some of the chaps getting up as early as 5 a.m. to shovel off the snow from the runways.

In February 1943, things starts to pick up, and on the 4th, 331 and 332 gather together at 10.30 a.m. for a briefing on 'Rodeo 159'. Wing Commander Jameson briefs the Norwegians, and Finn listens carefully; he's on the list of pilots to fly this mission. The mission will include three Wings; Northolt, North Weald and Biggin Hill. Each Wing going in after one each other, with the Norwegians being withdrawal cover for the Northolt Wing. As for the area they're going to, Finn has been there numerous times before – north-east France and Belgium. Jameson informs them he will be flying with 332 Squadron.

At 11.45 a.m., Finn is ready in his Spitfire. His BS508 AH-J never lets him down, and they take off in the sunny weather. After nine minutes on the deck, Jameson pulls the Wing up into the sky east of Dunkirk. Reaching Ypres, Finn takes a look at his altimeter. It shows 21,000 feet. Minutes later, they're at 30,000 feet with the sun behind them. Heading slightly down again, two Focke Wulfs are spotted dead head, going straight towards Jameson and his number two, Westly. Finn can clearly see the two 190s break off before reaching their formation, and Jameson sets off in hot pursuit with Westly on his tail. Jameson is not one to back out of a fight.

Suddenly, the sky is full of 190s. Finn spots one on his right and pulls hard to get onto its tail. Instantly, the 190 half rolls the other way and disappears below. Thinking twice before going after him, Finn lets him go, and focuses on not losing 332 Squadron. Another pair of 190s speed past him on his left, but he has no time to react. Turning towards home again, another pack of twenty-four 190s dive down on 332 Squadron, but Finn can't see anyone being

331 Squadron mascot Varg with 332 Squadron mascot Mads at North Weald, 1942. They did not always see eye to eye. (*Wilhelm Mohr*)

Finn's Spitfire Vb AH-J R7335 at Catterick, early 1942. (*Finn Thorsager*)

hit. The Germans don't look to be going in for another attack either, and the Norwegians dive out of Walcheren, all in one piece. All through the tangle, Finn has heard plenty of shouts on the radio, so someone must have been lucky.

Back home, they are all laughs and smiles. Westly claims a 190 damaged, Rolf Arne Berg from 331 claims one shot down and Jørstad, also from 331, claims another damaged. They decide to head over to the Kings Head in the village for a few pints and one or two glasses of whisky. Things have been going smoothly the past couple of days.

★

In early February, we had been over Holland, and we were flying home in formation just off the Dutch coast.

It had been a messy trip over to Holland. Nothing had gone as planned. When they took off, they could hardly see further than 500 yards ahead. Foggy, rainy, and grey; typical British winter weather. 331 and 332 had lost each other in the poor weather. They tried to find each other again over England, but had to give up. Soon afterwards, Birksted, leading the Wing, had trouble with his radio. Ground control also gave up and called them home. High over Flushing, at 25,000 feet, Reidar Kluge Watne, one of the less experienced pilots in the squadron, gets on the radio.

'This is Yellow 2. I have engine problems.'

Finn can see him losing height. The engine is still running, but he is having serious problems maintaining altitude. It's still a long way to go until they reach the English coast. Finn knows clearly what the conclusion will be. Watne will never make it. The only thing that can save him is if the engine suddenly comes to life again.

To land in the sea with a Spitfire was hopeless. This was a grey, cold and windy winter's day. The sea was dark and unfriendly, but Watne had lost a lot of height, so we agreed that he had to prepare to bail out.

A decision is made. Finn presses his radio button, and gives his message to Watne in the doomed Spitfire. 'Yellow 2, prepare to bail out.'

They are several kilometres from Manston, and Watne is already down to 6,000 feet. It is a correct decision. Better jump out than ditch it. The sea is way too rough for anything like that anyway.

Finn watches Watne while he pulls back his hood. The young man climbs out of his Spitfire in the biting cold winter air. He kicks the stick of his Spit down, and is thrown clear. Watne's Spitfire continues onwards for a moment, before it turns right and dives sharply towards the sea.

Having got out OK, Watne is under his parachute, preparing to land in the ice-cold sea.

> He landed OK, but wasn't able to release his dingy in the high waves. I didn't lose sight of him, even though it would have been easy to do so. I lead the Squadron on this day, and most likely had a bit more fuel left than the others, so I stayed behind, circling over him.
>
> The RAF air/sea rescue had heard everything over the radio, so they were prepared. I was in radio contact with a speedboat on its way. When it came closer to Watne's position, I made sure to dive towards Watne several times, so they would get a fix on his position.

Finn keeps circling, waiting for the speedboat to arrive, keeping one eye on the man in the water, and one on his surroundings.

Suddenly, the wind grabs Watne's parachute and drags him under water. He hasn't managed to release himself from it. After a horrific long moment in the dark water, he pops up again to the surface. He finally looks to be able to release himself from his 'chute; he is trying to swim forward for a few metres, but then he suddenly stops still.

Watne is lying motionless with his head down in the water.

Finn dives down on him for one last time. The speedboat is close, and he's running out of fuel. On his last pass, Finn sees no motion in the sea, only Watne's lifeless body. Another quick look at his fuel gauge, and Finn heads for home. He takes one last check for the speedboat. It's now arrived where Watne is lying.

> They found him, but by then, he was already dead.
>
> This was not very far from the Dutch coast, so the Germans knew what was going on, but they did not cause any trouble. I hope this was a gentlemanly gesture. Not much of that happening during the War.

The weather isn't any better when Finn lands at North Weald. He is the last one coming in, right after Ulstein. He was also circling Watne for almost as long as Finn was, until his fuel, too, was critically low. The others arrived several minutes ago, and are already giving their reports with stiff faces.

Finn looks over at Ulstein, parking his Spitfire close by. Ulstein's face is white with stress and troubling thoughts. Finn shakes his head, tightens his lips and gets out of his Spit. A horrible mission.

Squadron Leader

On 22 February 1943, I was promoted to Major, and Squadron Leader of 332. Wilhelm Mohr's mandatory rest period was coming up, and the Squadron was given to me.

The fog is as dense as the day before. Finn can't even see across the airfield. Their Spitfires are parked in their respective places, all with their noses pointing towards the sky, wrapped with necessary covers for the wet weather. Even on the ground, their Spitfires seem ready and eager to fly.

Inside the barracks, Nils Jørgen Fuglesang of 332 has found himself a chair and a newspaper. He looks up and nods when Finn enters.

'Bloody foggy, isn't it?'

Fuglesang is annoyed about the poor weather, but still pleased about a quiet morning. Plenty of time to relax with a cup of tea and yesterday's newspaper.

'You know British weather. Rain, fog and plenty of mud,' answers Finn.

Fuglesang, a 24-year-old Norwegian from Florø, escaped Norway by boat. Very different to what Finn did. It was especially risky to bet one's life on a small fishing boat in the Nordic Sea. Fuglesang came to fight the Germans, and he does it well. It's only a couple of days ago that he was out flying a recce with Mohr just off Dunkirk. He eagerly wants to fly again.

'So, I'm sure there will be a good speech and a nice parade today, since Major Mohr is saying his goodbyes,' says Fuglesang, looking up from his newspaper.

'Oh, I believe so,' replies Finn, smiling, as he tries to find something interesting to read, going through a stack of magazines on a table. Fuglesang grins and nods back before returning to the article he's reading.

Left: Nils Jørgen Fuglesang of 332 Squadron at Manston during the Dieppe raid in 1942. Fuglesang participated in 'The Great Escape' and was murdered by the Nazis after being captured. He was nicknamed 'Birdpip' by his friends, as his Norwegian last name translates to 'Birdsong'. (*Finn Thorsager*)
Right: Spitfire MkIIa P7929 (with the number three) was just one of several Spitfires Finn flew while with 331 Squadron at Skeabrea. Here it is later in the war, now with 53 OTU. The Spit was scrapped in 1944. (*Peter Arnold Collection*)

Wilhelm Mohr's time with 332 is now up. He's led the squadron for a long period, and he's been around since 331 came to Castletown, just one day after Finn back in '41. Now, the two friends will separate for the time being.

With the dark fog still lying heavily over North Weald, they're all outside to listen to Mohr's little goodbye speech. With the time getting close to 3 o'clock, Mohr begins. He clears his throat, and offers his greetings to all of those who have been with him. Some, like Finn, all the way since Canada.

'I would like to thank you all for the support you have given me while leading the squadron.' Mohr's voice fills the airfield. He gets right to the point. 'The squadron has had both good and bad days since it came into being. We have truly become a great team, and that's why we must never forget to back each other up, both in the air and on the ground.'

Finn knows filling Mohr's shoes will be a hard task. He's been a truly popular leader, and he's a great pilot. Maybe one of the best they have.

A couple more words and it's done. Mohr is no longer Squadron Leader, Finn is now the boss, and he has his work cut out. There's no doubt that the coming months will bring trouble for the RAF. The Luftwaffe can still show up in good numbers, and when will the invasion of Europe come?

Before the end of the gathering, Jon Ryg is given command of Finn's old A-flight, while Torstein Strand takes over B-flight for the time being. Captain Jameson, their Wing Commander, is awarded a DFC.

At 4 o'clock, the men are relieved from duty. Some make for the King's Head, others find a good book, or write a letter to a girlfriend in Canada. The next day will bring new challenges for the newly promoted Major Finn Thorsager, Squadron Leader of 332.

A couple of days after Mohr's goodbyes, just before 11 a.m., all twelve Spitfires of 332 are airborne, together with the rest of the North Weald Wing. Wing Commander Jameson flies with 332 for the day.

Course to Lympne is given and 332 banks into a turn. Just in front of Finn's Spitfire, Jameson is wagging his wings before breaking away. Radio trouble. He disappears in the haze back to North Weald. Without a functioning radio, he's of little use in leading the Wing.

As second to Jameson and squadron leader, Finn is now commanding the entire Wing. He can feel the heavy responsibility on his shoulders, but he will do his best. He trims his Spitfire to the finest detail, and lets his eyes run over the sky the way he always does.

The English coast is soon behind them. They continue to climb, and reach 21,000 feet with 331 Squadron as top cover. No sight of the Germans in the air – so far.

Over St Omer, the Wing turns back and heads for the Channel. No show today. But then a new message is given to Finn from ground control.

'Bandits to the west at 25,000 feet.'

He turns his Spitfire left while climbing to meet their enemies. However, he still can't see even one German. Again, they turn for home before ground control, Appledore, contacts the Norwegians for a second time.

'Reports of several Germans over Cap Griz Nez.'

Finn changes course yet again, while they all keep their eyes peeled for the Luftwaffe. Just a couple of kilometres off the coast of France, Appledore is on the radio again.

'This is Appledore. You are in a bad position. Suggest return to base.'

Finn pushes the transmitting button on his radio and confirms the message.

'Returning to base.'

Just after noon, they're all back safely. Finn makes a quick note in his log book. Uneventful. He leaves his Spitfire to the ground crew and gets something to eat. All of that effort, and it's put down as a simple 'Uneventful'. But, in the end, that's what it was. But he was actually leading the entire North Weald Wing. It doesn't sink in before he's safely back down again. Today was a very special day. He has never that much responsibility before. It all went alright. Maybe he'll get another chance some time.

Late in the afternoon, they all gather at the Thatched House in Epping, ready to celebrate Finn's new position as squadron leader of 332.

The weeks keep passing quickly with escorts, patrols, and offensive sweeps over Europe. They keep the intensity up. Sometimes, Finn feels tired. It takes its toll on him, flying all these missions. But he can't lose concentration. He

Finn and Wilhelm Mohr in England, *c.* 1943. (*Finn Thorsager*)

Finn Thorsager at North Weald, 1943.
(*Finn Thorsager*)

has responsibility to lead the squadron as best he can. He knows he's almost an idol for many of the younger lads, full of respect and admiration for his skills and leadership. They come to him if they are unsure of something or need advice. He just has to keep going.

Sooner or later, he will be posted for a rest period. If he stays alive, that is. He has to admit, he does feel tired.

Chapter 18

Tally Ho!

'Tally Ho. Tally Ho. Going down!'

The call is given by 331 Squadron. Finn can see sections of Spitfire IXs turn almost over on their backs, diving towards the ground, hunting down the bandits underneath. The British red and blue roundels on their wings shine in the sun as they dive. The Norwegians level out somewhere below Finn, now covered by their camouflage colours over Dutch fields.

Finn is Red 1, flying with 332 who are cover. They maintain their height at 24,000 feet, keeping a look out for more trouble.

Finn dips his wings left and right. He needs to know what's happening. 331 have disappeared from his view, but they have to be down there somewhere. His eyes shift from the events below to a movement over him.

Black dots are above them. Finn keeps looking at them, growing in size by the second. He can count fifteen now, looking like they're coming down towards 332 like an angry swarm of bees on a hot summer's day. There's no doubt in his mind now, they are Focke Wulf 190s.

'Tally Ho, fifteen bandits coming down from above, one o' clock high.'

He pulls the stick towards him, climbing up to meet the 190s. Two of them pass him and his number two, John Bernhard Gilhuus, at great speed before they start to climb again, most likely going in for another dive in a few seconds' time.

It's a bad move on their part; Finn has enough power and speed to spare to give them a short burst when they start their climb. He manoeuvres his Spitfire into position, making sure he's ready for a deflection shot. The cannons of his Spitfire come to life with a thundering sound. Several times the closest 190 is hit by his cannons, all over its silvery body. He can see some of them hit the cockpit area, but he has no time to reflect on it.

The 190 flicks over and starts burning. It continues to spin downwards until Finn loses sight of it at 6,000 feet.

A feeling of relief comes over him. He is still alive, and he has most likely shot down a 190. This 190 seemed sure enough as a confirmed kill, even if he couldn't see where it went. Finn was always reluctant to claim things he couldn't prove, but this time around, he was sure. He had done his job.

He takes a deep breath of the oxygen from his mask and releases a sigh of relief. Gilhuus comes up on his wing. Finn can seem him clearly in his cockpit, putting on a huge grin while raising his arms and applauding him. Bloody cheeky. Finn laughs and waves back. He can't wait to get back to North Weald and give them the report for the day. Today, he got one of them, and on a pretty tricky deflection shot. It doesn't really matter if he gets it officially or not. The job was done anyway.

Flying back with Gilhuus following, they keep good pace low over the English countryside, hoping the rest of the Squadron did well with no losses to their own chaps.

Finally, Finn spots the familiar radio masts in the distance, a well-known landmark for the North Weald Wing. Keeping their distance from the tall masts, they come in to North Weald.

★

I remember one incident when we were out on a rhubarb to shoot up German flak positions. I was on my way home when I found myself over the harbour of Vlissingen. I spotted a German cargo boat of about 10-15,000 tons.

It's tempting. The cargo boat is a big, fat target.

Finn pulls his stick forward. The Spitfire obeys willingly, and the speed increases rapidly, diving on the boat. The Germans open fire from their positions. He can see the tracers coming towards him. At first sight, they seem to be missing him by miles, but then they make a sharp turn straight towards him. The Germans really know how to shoot with deflection. Luckily, they miss, and Finn aims for the boat. He fires both cannons and machine guns.

Nothing happens, not one burst of fire can be heard or seen from his Spit.

He lifts his finger from the firing button, and then tries another burst, expecting a loud cracking sound from his guns. Instead, he can only hear the Merlin engine. Bad luck, the boat is already behind him. He went through that low attack under fire and wasn't able even to fire one shot.

Spitfire IX BS251 getting some attention, spring 1943. (*Finn Thorsager*)

Finn pushes left rudder with his foot, at the same time banking the Spitfire left with his stick, making up his mind at the same time.

He'll go around for another try.

Bit of elevator in the turn, and the Spit IX doesn't lose too much speed going around. Again towards the boat at full speed and ready to give a good burst. When the ship pops up in his sights, he fires. He expects his load to hit the boat, but again, nothing happens.

The Germans have summoned themselves now and the tracers are coming closer, just passing him on his right side and a bit over him.

Finn changes course yet again and roars over for a third time with no result. Clearly something must be wrong with his guns.

Safely back on the deck, I found out why my guns had not worked. The man who was supposed to arm my Spitfire had forgotten about it. On a matter of principle, he was sent to a military court for this incident. The result was that he got a very hard punishment. He was usually, though, a very skilled man. During this episode, I remembered what happened on 9 April 1940. During my second flight that morning, my machine guns stopped working. This, too, was due to them not being rearmed after my first combat that morning.

Chapter 19

'Forts in Sight!'

Finn feels like he's barely closed his eyes when he's awakened early in the morning by his batman.

'Good morning sir. Lovely morning. Raining cats and dogs by the bucket. It will clear up, though. Briefing at 8 o'clock, sir.' He makes sure Finn is awake before he closes the door.

Finn twists around in bed a couple of times before he decides to toughen up and just get on with it. He gets out of the bed, stumbles over to the window and glances outside. It's still a little dark, but some of the men are already cycling away towards the briefing room. They all look to be half asleep when they pedal past his window.

Finn throws some water in his face and pulls on his uniform. Briefing at 8 a.m. He can only guess what they're up to today. Escorting Flying Fortresses would be his best bet.

The English grass is fresh, green and moist. Finn's bicycle leaves a trail behind as he makes his way over to the briefing. At 8 o'clock sharp, they are all there; 331 and 332 together in the briefing room. Low rumblings can be heard. Some have managed to swallow down some early breakfast after a few too many pints the night before. Just as well to get some energy before they head out. Today's show doesn't seem to be cancelled.

'Good morning, gentlemen. Today, we will escort 200 American Forts to Lille where transport centres will be bombed...'

When the Americans joined the War they specialized in daylight bombings. They went out in large formations, sometimes in the hundreds. When just one of them had thirteen big machine guns, and plenty of ammunition, you realize the awesome firepower they had. The Germans had respect for these bombers.

332 Squadron area, North Weald, winter 1943. (*Wilhelm Mohr*)

'...They will come in from the south, and turn left after their cargo has been dropped. You will stay above the Americans, keeping the Germans away if they see fit to attack from above. Several squadrons will escort the bombers – Biggin Hill, Hornchurch and Debden Wings. They're all there. Wing Commander Mehre will lead 331 and 332. Engines start at 11.32 a.m. The French coast will be crossed over Calais at 16,000 feet. Good luck.'

There were more rumblings among the pilots when we left for our Spits. 16,000 feet over the coast was uncomfortable. Spitfire IX, which we now used instead of the V, had about 1,500 bhp, and its best performance against German aircraft was at altitudes of over 20,000 feet. At 20,000 feet the supercharger went to work. We felt it like a kick in the buttocks. It sometimes happened that the supercharger didn't work or disconnected itself in formation at over 20,000 feet. If that happened, you couldn't follow the formation and lagged behind the others. This was very dangerous, as a lone aircraft was easy prey for the Luftwaffe; you were usually told to head on home with a section of Spits escorting you.

We biked back to our own dispersal and got ready; parachute, overalls, helmet with goggles, microphone and oxygen mask. In our boots, we usually had a Smith & Wesson revolver. We also had some emergency equipment with us, such as French money, some French words and expressions on a piece of paper, different sorts of pills, knife, compass and a map.

We usually walked out to our aircraft in good time before take-off. Many of us had our own Spitfires to take care of. I had AH-J.

A last check on AH-J is done as Finn approaches his mechanics. Nothing serious with the Spit. Some minor adjustments and then everything is 100 per cent ready. The mechanic wipes off some oil from his fingers with a dirty cloth, and helps Finn with his equipment. Then Finn slides into the cockpit.

The mechanics were specialists with good training. One was a specialist on the Rolls Royce engine, one on radios, one on the aircraft itself with ailerons and rudders, and one focused only on the weapons. We all had two cannons and four machine guns in the wings.

Finn is in no rush. No stress. Everything has to be perfect. One little look out to his left, and he sees Helge Mehre's Spitfre. Three, four puffs of blue smoke from the newly appointed Norwegian Wing Commander's engine, and the show is about to get under way.

The mechanics removed the blocks, and we taxied out to formation start. After getting airborne, we followed the boss at tree-top height, usually

Hard at work cleaning Spitfires, North Weald, summer 1942. (*Wilhelm Mohr*)

south towards Kent. Down there, the farmers were standing in their fields, waving at us when we roared past them; I found it very inspiring.

Once over the Channel, we started our climb to our given height. At 12,000 feet, I connected my oxygen, and a bit later, Wing Commander Mehre dropped his extra tank. Then we all did it; twenty-four tanks whirling down towards a French farmer's field.

'Forts in sight!'

The radio comes to life. 200 B-17s split up into boxes fill the sky like a phalanx of Roman soldiers on an ancient battlefield. Each box, with an enormous number of machine guns, lines up in a perfect defensive structure over France. There are thick, white lines of condensation coming out of all four engines from every bomber in the sky. Around the bombers, the squadrons of Spitfire fighters are finding their positions. They're everywhere, as far as Finn can see. Over the North Weald Wing, Finn can spot another big wing of IXs. Maybe the chaps coming from Biggin Hill. They are at a perfect height, but their position, compared to the North Weald Wing's place in the formation, worries Finn. No time to dwell on it though.

Underneath, France unfolds as a big green carpet, with little rivers crawling through the scenery. The sun burns through Finn's hood; the hard winter is behind them and they are done with numb fingers and ice crystals forming outside the cockpit for the time being. Still, flying at 12,000 feet is very cold, whatever the time of year.

The control breaks through on the radio: 'The St Omer boys are getting up. They're at Angels 20, and they are 20 plus.'

This meant that the Germans from St Omer now had started. There were more than 20 and they were reaching 20,000 feet. We usually managed to prevent the Germans getting through to the bombers, but sometimes some of them dived down on them, only to be met with a very warm surprise. We, in the RAF, were a bit reluctant to get close to the American bombers as they tended to be a little 'trigger happy', and not all of them were familiar with all types of aircraft.

The bombers closed in on their target. Here, the Germans had prepared a lot of defensive positions, so the entire target area was filled with exploding shells. It looked like no aircraft could ever penetrate their defence. But they flew straight into it anyway, and there were always bombers being hit. There was no point in us going into this mess, so thankfully we could stay outside, and watch the show while we kept the German fighters away.

The bombers drop their deadly cargo, and the air is filled with small black dots falling towards the buildings below. Black smoke then pours from the target area as the bombers turn left. No German aircraft have been reported so far, even if control has said that several are in the area.

Out of the thick smoke, the Americans appear with their big bombers. Several of the big boxes of Fortresses have wide holes where bombers are missing. Many have been hit by the intense flak, and are now lying somewhere in France with no chance to come back to England. The Wing comes closer to the B-17s, and Finn can clearly observe that many of them have serious damage. Some have one or even two engines dead, big holes in the fuselage, and oil spattered on their wings. Several machine gun positions no longer seem to be manned. Most likely the men have been hit by flak, now lying dead or injured somewhere inside the slow bombers. Some of them have taken a very harsh beating. Just making it back over the Channel will be a challenge. These are the ones that need special attention from Finn and 332. Still no reports of German bandits, but they might be around, waiting for an opportunity like this. With some luck, the stragglers will make it safely across and home to their base in England. If some Me 109s will show up, the Spitfires will deal with them as best they can.

Dogfight over Vlissingen

Finn sits in his cockpit and lets his thoughts wander before they take off for the day. To him, it seems that the Germans aren't as eager to meet their Spits as they used to be. There had been a little increase of activity in the spring, and he clearly remembers the German he unofficially shot down a few months ago.

After those missions, it had become quiet again. Just as much flying, but more of the routine type – escorting the Americans into France, and then meeting up with them again on their way home, or basic patrols along the coastline.

The bombers keep pounding the German industries; maybe the decrease in German activity means that the bombing is working. Finn is not sure, but he hopes he's right. He gets the feeling that the War has now finally turned around for the Allies. Thoughts of survival start to sneak up on him. Back at Catterick, being introduced to the first glimpses of warfare, the idea of surviving seemed almost unreal. Now, there seems to be a fair chance he can get out of if alive. With each mission he puts down in his logbook, the more days go by. It's still important to keep the chaps on their toes. It's dangerous if they get complacent and don't concentrate fully when they're out flying. A pair of Focke Wulf 190s might suddenly attack out of the sun and send two or three Spitfires into the ground before they know what's going on. It has happened before, and it can happen again.

Finn pulls the shiny Spitfire hood over his head. He feels tired when he does it. Yet again, another check on the instruments, looking for the wing commander's turning propeller, and keeping formation heading out of North Weald.

The sound of his Rolls Royce Merlin engine reminds him that, yet again, he's going out with the Wing on a mission. He doesn't even remember 'pressing tits'.

Spitfire BS 248 AH-O at North Weald, winter 1943. (*Finn Thorsager*)

Finn's eyes scan the field of fast-moving Spitfires as he searches for Red 2. Finn finds him straight ahead; he pulls the stick back and pushes the throttle forward. The Spitfire happily responds to his orders. Finn gets himself in position behind Red 2; he's Red 3 today. Wing Commander Helge Mehre is leading 332 on this mission. They will act as support for bombers and fighters now coming back from Belgium. They've taken the route several times before.

The formation looks to be tidy and the altimeter shows 14,000 feet. They continue to go upwards to 26,000. Finn double-checks his oxygen, fearing he might lose consciousness through the simple mistake of not putting it on.

'Tally ho. Tally ho!'

A sharp-eyed pilot reports twenty-five bandits about 10,000 feet below them. Mehre knows his stuff, and leads the Wing higher up before he pulls them into a turn, which positions them directly against the Germans from above. The enemy is there under them, still in formation. If they don't see the Spitfires soon, they will be in for a big surprise when the battle-hungry Norwegians from North Weald fall upon them.

'Going down, now!' calls Mehre and Finn pushes his Spitfire downwards with the wing commander leading. He tightens his grip on the stick and tries to keep up with the leading Spitfires. The ailerons get heavier the faster the Spitfire dives – Finn is fully aware of it, it's one of the few problems the Spitfire has. The faster it dives, the heavier all the controls get.

Finn checks his reflector sight. It's on. Cannons ready to fire as well. Everything is in order. Where's Sandvik, the pilot who is supposed to be covering him? Finn has a short glance behind. The wingman is right where he should be. Good. This bounce looks to be going very well. Finn stares at the formation of Germans straight ahead. He lets his eyes scan the dots of aeroplanes. The one to the left seems to be the perfect target, and he picks it out as his prey. He holds his fire, waiting to be close enough.

Finn opens his cannons; the Spitfire shakes brutally but keeps flying straight. His target, a shiny silver Focke Wulf 190, is taken completely by surprise. The German takes several hits from Finn's guns. Two black puffs of smoke emerge from the engine before it stops dead. Seconds later, black smoke gushes out from it. Violently, the Fw190 flicks over to the left. Finn pulls hard on his stick to avoid crashing into it. His arms feels like lead, the oxygen mask slips off of his nose and is pressed down from his face by the heavy gravitational force. The turn is so hard that he can't pull his head up enough to see ahead. The only thing he can see is his legs and the stick he's holding with both hands.

Far down to the left, the Fw190 explodes in a giant ball of flame after Sandvik gives him a final salute from the Vikings of Norway.

Finn pulls his Spitfire on to its back and pulls down and to the right. Dirt from the floor hits him in the face while he's upside down. He desperately tries to find Sandvik behind him, but to no avail. He quickly concludes that his number two must have missed him when he pulled away from his first attack. Finn knows there's no time to back out now, and keeps going.

Something grey passes Finn on his left side. It's another 190, alone. Finn rolls the Spitfire over and begins the chase. It's one on one; there will be no help from either of their wingmen.

The 190 keeps jumping around in his gunsight. Finn fires, but the deflection shot misses its target. Suddenly, he is too far away to fire any more. The 190 keeps diving towards earth. Finn thinks for a fraction of a second before he decides to follow, and then, keeping track of his enemy, he presses the Spitfire into a hell-bound dive. He knows it well; this is absolutely not the place to be for long. He has told inexperienced pilots so many times about how dangerous it is to be alone in the sky. Way too many times.

He is catching up, but in a flash, he loses the German. Finn can feel the panic rising as he frantically looks around the skies; he imagines the 190 on his tail, ready to fire at any second.

Suddenly, Finn sees something in front, coming straight at him. He just manages to fire his guns before the German passes him at terrific speed. He sees hits around the cockpit area just before the enemy plane disappears.

Viking Spitfire

King Haakon's previous visit to North Weald, autumn 1942. (*Finn Thorsager*)

King Haakon talking to Finn Thorsager with Crown Prince Olav to their right, autumn 1942. (*Finn Thorsager*)

Now he's gone and Finn is alone. A real close shave. His altimeter shows 8,000 feet. He's not staying here a second longer. The area is probably swarming with enemy planes, and being alone, he's no match for them.

Finn presses the throttle forward as far as it goes, contemplating going through 'the gate', but he doesn't want to risk the engine. He heads for the coast. It doesn't seem to be too far. He can't have flown as far east as he thought.

Sandvik appears over the Channel and waves his wings at Finn. He can see him sitting there, in his cockpit, showing him thumbs up. Finn lifts his hand and waves back at him. It feels numb, and more than a little shaky.

Safely back at North Weald, they round up the numbers. It has been a very good day. Thirteen shot down with no losses. In a couple of days, the King and Crown Prince of Norway will arrive at North Weald; a great honour for the Norwegian pilots. Finn feels he can meet them proudly after this little show of his.

With a cigarette hanging from his slightly shaking lips, Finn reports one 190 destroyed and one 190 damaged. He could easily have been sitting in a Belgian field right now, his backside covered with dirt, and a parachute he's desperately trying to hide before the Germans arrive. He's been lucky, and he knows it.

Chapter 21

Radar Control

One day I was going to lead the entire Wing – four squadrons, a total of forty-eight Spitfires. That morning, we had all been over to France with Mehre leading, and when we were back at North Weald, we were called into briefing again. I was to be the leader. The different routes concerning the show were drawn in on the large map. These orders were always sent on secret D-forms from Uxbridge. We were given information about our courses, who was participating, the goal of the mission and so on. When the 'spy' had cleared all the specifics, it was up to the leader, in this case me, to express his specific wishes about how he wanted things to be done. I have to admit, I was a little tense when I gave my orders in English. I said I would lead 332 low, and 331 would be over, covering us. We were going up to 25,000 feet. The mission would take us over St Omer, and then towards Abbeville. The purpose was to find and shoot down Germans, if they came up to meet us. We would be under Appledore control, the latest in radar control technology.

The communication between the aeroplanes and RAF's control centres was of great importance. The RAF controlled the airspace over England, and the important parts of the Continent with the help of their radar stations, always under development. For communication, we used the most advanced VHF of the time.

We got underway, and when we reached 25,000 feet over St Omer, I spotted a bunch of 190s. These were not reported on our radio. I gave an order to bounce them, and we dived down. When we were a few thousand feet above them, the Germans turned into a clever defensive manoeuvre, so I turned my squadron accordingly. Then, several more Germans attacked from above, ones we had not seen before. The English controller asked about our position after the fight was underway, but I was so busy I only managed to say, 'We are engaged!'

It was chaotic, with plenty of dogfights; those were some very hectic minutes. The fight eventually died out, and the Germans left for home, so I decided to do the same with our Spits. I called on the squadrons to form up behind me to the best of their ability. We managed to get home with several 190s shot down, and luckily with no losses to our own. The controller later told me the Germans had managed to stop their radar by sending out some kind of disturbance.

★

One day, I was up for a test flight with a Spitfire after an overhaul, and I was going up to 4,000 feet. The test was reported to the controller, and I was heading towards London.

'What is your position?'

The controller is on the radio, and Finn reports back his position and waits for a reply. He's right over London, and can easily see the River Thames. The visibility isn't the best, but good enough to spot landmarks. Suddenly, he remembers a joke he was told a few days ago; if he didn't know where he was, the best thing to do was to head for the thick, grey foggy area – London would be right underneath it. The joke did have some truth to it. The factories in London pump out plenty of smoke, thick as soup. The balloons are also in place, and are put strategically around the city for protection. The Londoners are still scared of German bombing, even if it's decreased quite a lot over the last year. They hardly get any intruders over these islands any longer.

'Look out! There's a bandit very close to you. Same altitude!'

The controller is back on the radio and Finn twists his head around to spot the German. He pulls the Spit into hard turns, fearing the intruder might have sneaked up on his tail without him knowing. But there is no one to be seen. Could it be a lone and brave Fw190 hunting for easy prey over London? It sounds very odd. However, lone 190s have come over British airfields from time to time, dropping a bomb, and then turning back for home before anyone can take off and have a go at him. But Finn isn't low either, he's quite high up. Could it be a stray bomber? Maybe a Heinkel 111 off course, mistaking landmarks and ending up over London.

He continues to look sharply around. Still no German. Finn half rolls the Spit so he can see straight down. No Germans there either, and he finishes his roll with ease. Suddenly, another call comes in on the radio:

'Sorry about that, you are the bandit.'

Finn sets course back to North Weald, feeling a little dazed. It had been a lot of manoeuvring for nothing.

When I landed, I spoke to the controller on the telephone, and he told me it had been a misunderstanding from his side. The air sirens had gone off over the entire London area, and in the next day's newspapers, there were pictures of my contrail, and an explanation of the entire affair.

Chapter 22

Wingman

The squadron has been getting a lot of new chaps lately, all 'green'. Finn took them for a dinghy drill just recently. They were all keen, but very inexperienced. It was an absolute priority to get them up to speed for all their missions. It wasn't an easy task.

As squadron leader, Finn tries to think of everything he can to give his pupils as much information and knowledge as possible before they're sent out for the first time. Time is crucial. He hoped to give them more time, but they're on the roster now, ready to participate in 332's actions over the Continent.

One day, one of them is on for a show. Finn can see his eyes widen when he sees his name on the list, as number two to Finn himself. Perhaps the chap is a little quieter than normal too, finally getting his chance. Finn has observed the lad's flying, and he's shown a great deal of skill. Finn is an experienced pilot now, and he knows how to train others to fly from his Little Norway days.

Flying as number two to Finn is a good way to start. The safest place to be is behind an experienced pilot who knows what he's doing. Experience is the key. Too many times, green RAF pilots have been killed or ended up in POW camps after just one mission.

Finn is early today, and it's still pretty dark outside. Soon, the first beams of sun will break through. Layer after layer of clothes are pulled on. After a routine check of his equipment, he strolls down to his faithful AH-J, quietly waiting his return to the cockpit. When he flew with 331 at Skeabrea, the Norwegians got a lot of praise for being quick into the air during scrambles. He intends to keep that good trend going, and hopes the debutant is up for it. Finn makes a mental note to tell him again before take-off, just to make sure.

Inside dispersal, some of the chaps have already started to gather. The new lad sits in a chair and reads a magazine of some sort. Others play a game

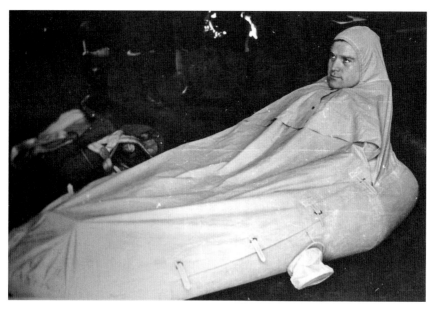

331 Squadron Spitfire pilot John Ryg demonstrates the proper use of a dinghy, 1942. (*Wilhelm Mohr*)

of cards. Some keep a conversation going, trying to settle their nerves. Finn can tell the lad is excited.

'Now then,' he says, 'ready for today?' Finn ruffles the boy's blond hair and grins. The boy is tense and jumps a bit in his chair, but pulls himself together quickly. No one noticed anything.

'As ready as I can be,' he says.

Finn can see he is tense, but he's not the only one. Several of the chaps get up every now and then and walk over to the toilets. More than usual – just the way it is before a show.

'You'll be fine. Just remember the most important bits. Alright?'

The lad puts his magazine down, thinking for a few seconds before he answers. 'Yes, stick to your tail and keep an eye for enemy fighters. No mindless efforts if we see fighters around. Keep the speed up and never lose any height if you don't need to. No straight flying, but keep weaving and always turn your head around to look for bandits.'

Finn nods, pleased with the quick reply. 'Remember, though, if you lose me, try to form up with the closest Spit you see.'

'I'll keep that in mind, sir. I just hope it will go well. I've heard the first times are the most dangerous.'

'You'll be alright. Just don't lose me up there.'

The phone rings and the room falls quiet.

'Scramble!'

Cards, books, and chairs go flying as the pilots run to the door and out to their Spitfires. Finn hooks on his parachute rapidly. In the corner of his eye, he sees the new lad having some trouble with his, but he manages to get it in order within a few seconds.

Finn attaches the oxygen mask to his face, and presses the start buttons. His number two is also ready in his Spitfire, and everything looks set. No problems so far.

The throttle is where he left it. Full forward. Seconds later, the wheels lose their firm contact with North Weald, just as quick as at Skeabrea. Radio on, the hood closed and wheels in. Things are running automatically. He just hopes his number two does things right. He should be behind him, on his right. A short glimpse in his mirror, and the Spitfire is where it's supposed to be.

The radio comes to life, bringing them the latest; American 'Forts' coming out of Abbeville are in trouble. They're being attacked by plenty of fighters from the Luftwaffe. Finn repeats the correct height and course given by the controller before he sets course directly towards the Americans. The lad behind is still there, keeping up with him.

332 surges upwards, pushing their Spitfires hard. Finn is pulled back in his chair while the Merlin engine roars towards the clouds without missing a single beat.

Time to open up the formation. Finn gives the order. For a moment he remembers it was only a year ago that Scott-Malden gave the same order to green Norwegians. To Finn, it feels like an eternity since they flew down from Catterick to North Weald. The excitement of that trip was immense. He can still feel it.

The squadron opens up in formation and Finn's number two stays where he should be, and at the right distance. Reflector sight is on. The firing button is released from it's safe position. 332 goes into a long turn, while keeping their eyes open.

One of the chaps calls out for unknown aircraft below at ten o'clock. Finn sets his eyes on them. Plenty of dots in the sky – big ones – looks to be the bombers from Abbeville. Black puffs of smoke appear all around them; if his number two wasn't excited before, he must be now!

Another glance towards the sun and several small dots appear. They can't be anyone other than the Luftwaffe.

'Bandits two o' clock high, coming down now. Break right!'

It is absolutely crucial that the boy is awake. Finn pulls his Spitfire sharply to the right. If his number two loses him now, they're both in

Finn Thorsager, *c.* 1943. (*Finn Thorsager*)

trouble. One Fw190 arrows past them, and Finn fires a short burst, but to no avail; the German disappears somewhere below. No point in diving after him.

Finn pulls hard left, half rolling his Spit, going down after the 190. He doesn't even get the chance to fire before the silver enemy has disappeared from his sights. Where's the lad? Gone? Finn's mirror is filled with a Spitfire's spinner and large propeller. A bit too close for safety, but he's there, and he didn't lose Finn when the 190s came down. He's doing alright, as long as he doesn't cut off the tail of Finn's dear AH-J.

The Forts are slowly pulling themselves out of harm's way. The Germans correct their line of fire and hit one of them. The massive bomber catches fire and is quickly engulfed in huge flames. The B-17 dives straight down, leaving a long trail of fire and black smoke. Finn sees several white spots in the sky. Parachutes. He counts them. One, two, three, four. Half of the crew. The rest probably never had the chance to bail out. Their bomber is just a massive ball of fire now. He's seen that sight too many times.

Finn pulls his eyes away from the stricken bomber, and starts focusing on the other B-17s.

More 190s appear, now below. Yellow section pulls away and dives on them. Another 'break' is called from the left of the squadron, and Finn pulls another hard right. This time, the 190s stay to fight. Finn fires short bursts whenever he has one in his sights, but can't see any hits. Another 190 flashes by his port side, tracers flying past moments before. He didn't even have time to get away from it.

And suddenly, they're gone. The skies are empty. A lonely Spitfire is somewhere down to the left. There's no chance of seeing who it is, but Finn's number two is no longer on his tail. Most likely he couldn't follow him through the last fight with the 190s. Finn hopes he's alright.

Back at North Weald, several of the chaps have already landed, and are having a chat with the 'spy'. As he comes to a complete stop beside Reidar From's Spitfire, Finn looks around for the lad, but can't spot him anywhere. More Spits coming in, though.

He lets out a sigh of relief as he can see his number two follow another Spit in for landing. So, he made it back in one piece. The boy makes a bad landing, jumping all over the place down the runway, but that's a minor detail on such a day. It had been exciting; a good start to his hopefully long career with the Royal Norwegian Air Force.

'You flew well,' says Finn, grabbing his young friend on his way to talk to the spy. 'For a moment there, you were a bit closer to my tail than necessary.

I was a bit frightened you might chop it off! But, all things considered on such an eventful day, you did well.'

Finn smokes a cigarette, giving his number two one from his pocket at the same time. The boy smiles and wipes a few drops of sweat from his forehead.

'Keep it up, and you might become an Ace!'

Chapter 23
Back to Canada

In July 1943, I was given my orders for my mandatory rest period. The squadron was taken over by my friend, Reidar From. I had flown 124 offensive missions.

Suddenly, it was all over. Having taken over the squadron from Wilhelm Mohr last winter, Finn had had his six months in charge, and he'd survived.

He feels tired. It had been quite a year at North Weald. He doesn't want a big fuss. Just a short speech and a little party in London with his friends. It's hard to say goodbye to them, but it's also a relief. Finn has been flying since the autumn of 1941. His body feels the strain. Now, it's Reidar's turn to lead the squadron. He's an excellent pilot, and a good friend.

Now, a new life had started. After a goodbye party at the Odd Spot in London, I took the night train to Glasgow. Here, I boarded RMS *Queen Elizabeth*. It would take me and a couple of thousand Americans to Halifax.

The deck is full of Americans on their way across the Atlantic, all going back to the USA. They all have a life vest, given to them when they came aboard. Everyone is holding theirs tightly while they await further instructions. Finn listens to the conversations going on around him; they all have their stories to tell about their time in England. The captain's voice breaks through on the speakers and the chatter lowers itself automatically.

'May I have your attention, please. We will shortly cross the Atlantic and run the risk of meeting U-Boats. The life vest you have received must be carried at all times, and you must regard it as your best friend.'

He has hardly finished the sentence before a life vest is clumsily dropped on the floor by an American standing next to Finn.

'Oh, my best friend!' yells the American as he scoops it up in a flash and pulls it hard to his chest. Everyone around bursts into laughter.

The long journey got underway. This boat was quick. About 30 knots. We were to be going out alone with no escort, so a zig-zag course was necessary in order to confuse the U-Boats. For a long time, I had been having tooth ache, and the pain was now really hard to bear.

Finn lets his finger run across the aching tooth. Just a gentle push on the area gives him a shot of intense pain. Going up to the deck, a couple of soldiers bump into him. It just makes it even worse. They were just a few centimetres from hitting his tooth directly. The soldiers say their polite excuses and hurry on. There's no way out of it. He'll have to see a dentist. Luckily, there is one onboard. Tooth ache is not something new within the military.

A short look at the plan of the boat and Finn finds his way to the dentists' office. He's obviously not the only one with problems. The entire hallway is filled with people. He gets in line, and hopes things will move quickly along, but eventually he decides to give up – the line is going nowhere. He manages to find some aspirin which make the pain bearable for the rest of the journey.

After four days, we arrived in Halifax. It was a beautiful summer's night. The Canadians had made bonfires along the coast, and they had these little boats, very like those we had in Norway before the War. From Halifax, I took the train to Toronto.

On the train to Toronto, Finn touches the aching bump in his mouth. It has grown further, and feels even more painful than before. He hopes he will be able to get to a dentist soon.

At the station, Finn is met by a Norwegian airman and taken to the Norwegian headquarters.

'Dear lord! What is the matter with you?' exclaims Ole Reistag, Commander of Little Norway, when Finn presents himself in his office. Reistad points to his mouth. The tooth. Of course. Finn hasn't seen a mirror in a while. If he looks anything like he did on the boat, possibly much worse, no wonder Reistad is shocked.

Reistad called Island Airport, and ordered a Cub to be at my disposal for the trip up to Muskoka, our training base. This flight went well, and our

Ole Reistad, commander of 'Little Norway' in Canada. Reistad has become a legend in Norwegian aviation history. This photograph was taken in the early 1940s. (*Wilhelm Mohr*)

Norwegian dentist there, Sognæs, just pulled the tooth out; the relief was immeasurable. Sognæs became a very famous professor in the USA after the War.

From Muskoka, I went to Montreal to report for duty in Transport Command. However, there was no room for me there yet, so instead I got a surprise holiday with superb trips in the big forests and beautiful lakes. I met my friend Holger Hannestad here, also on holiday. Crown Princess Martha was also there with her children Ragnhild, Astrid, and Harald. We used to swim together, especially Astrid, who was pretty wild in the water.

One day, I was walking in shorts by Lake Interlaken, and walked by a very lovely family living in a tent just by Vesle Skaugum.

The children are running around the tent, screaming and laughing for joy, while their father sits quietly in a chair outside, reading from a big pile of documents and papers on his lap. He looks up from his papers and greets Finn as he walks by.

'So, is it a long time since you left Norway?' he asks.

The man shows immediate interest in how Finn left Norway and made his way to Canada. Finn can hardly believe that it's been a few years since he escaped. How time flies. The man tells him that he's in the Norwegian Air Force in Canada, although not as a pilot.

'Have you thought of applying for pilot training?' he asks Finn.

The question takes Finn a little by surprise, but he's not in uniform, and the man can't know that he's been flying Spitfires for almost two years.

'Oh, I'm already a pilot,' Finn replies, modestly.

The man nods. 'Where are my manners?' he says suddenly. 'I'd better introduce myself properly. My name is Thor Heyerdahl.[8]'

'Finn Thorsager. Nice to meet you.' Finn smiles and shakes his hand. It doesn't seem right to introduce himself as a major. He's on holiday, after all.

That night, in the mess, we met again, and now I was in uniform. To his great surprise I was a major. I remember it all well, but I'm sure Heyerdahl has forgotten this 'intermezzo'.

Time went by quickly, and Transport Command in Montreal still didn't want my services, so I wanted to go back to England and start flying again. But Reistad did not agree; he thought it inappropriate to come all the way to Canada to do nothing except have a holiday. I was therefore sent to a training base called Bagotville in northern Quebec. They had a huge airfield there, and it was far into the wilderness. To top it all off, they had too many instructors already, so it quickly became the worst experience I

Finn in Canada, 1943. (*Finn Thorsager*)

had through these years of war. There was nothing to do apart from read and walk around, so I felt pretty useless.

One day I was called in to represent Norway at a big Rotary meeting in Kingston. I had the chairman on the other side of the table. It was a nice, civilized party until all of a sudden, the Canadians started to bang the table with their fists, shouting, 'We want Norway, we want Norway!'

The chairman leans over the table, and explains the Canadians' wild banging to Finn.

'You see, Major,' says the chairman, 'they want a Norwegian song. You know a few tunes, right?'

Finn feels caught off guard. A song? He hasn't prepared for any singing. What on earth can he sing to these wild, noisy Canadians? Song titles rush by in his head. It'll have to be something simple. 'Kjerringa med staven'[9] will do.

'Major, this man will accompany you,' says the chairman, pointing to a man in the audience who gets up from his chair and jumps up on the small stage. There's no way out of it now. Finn clears his throat, and the Canadians go quiet in suspense, ready to see what this Norwegian has to offer them. Finn hums a few bars introduction for the pianist to work with, and then begins.

It is going alright and the Canadians seem to be enjoying it, but two verses in, Finn completely forgets the rest of the lyrics. But it doesn't matter; they won't notice the difference. Finn just makes it up as he goes along, a whole big mess of words. A few more verses, and with a nod to the pianist, he brings the song to an end.

Afterwards, the crowd applauded me greatly. They're very polite, these Canadians.

Chapter 24

Transport Command

I regularly sent Reistad letters asking to be sent back to England. I kept writing these letters for two months, and finally the order came to return to Montreal and Transport Command.

I was to fly B-25 Mitchell bombers over the Atlantic to Scotland. I got myself a small apartment and a blue Dodge, and started school at Dorval Airport. First up was a technical course on the B-25, and then pilot training. I had never flown twin-engined aircraft before, and in addition, this was an advanced bomber with a nose wheel. For me, it was a big change from a Spitfire.

Soon I was ready to fly my first aircraft to Prestwick. Initially, we flew to Goose Bay in Labrador, then to Narsarsurak in Greenland. Then onwards to Reykjavik and to Prestwick.

The flying from Goose Bay to Greenland was special. It was my first time, and the winter in Goose Bay was very cold. We were to start early in the morning when the sun got up, so we were woken at night for the briefing. It was a very special atmosphere, with car exhausts wafting up in the light of the electric street lamps. We got into the briefing room and drank coffee while some experienced American pilots told us about flying to Greenland. The airport in Greenland was situated far into a long fjord with high mountains all around. A radio tower was placed out by the coast; from this tower to the airport we could not afford to make any mistakes. If we flew into the wrong fjord, we would be lost – they would be too small to turn around in. It had happened before with tragic results, so this briefing was crucial. We saw a film of one flying into the airport, and this was repeated many times so that we would get a good picture of it in our minds. It was pretty easy to find the right fjord in good weather, but in bad, it could be tricky.

On this first trip of mine, all went well. We filled up our tanks, and flew to Iceland and then to Prestwick. From Prestwick, we got a ride with an RAF transport back to Montreal.

I was also put on a course to fly a DC-3 to an airfield just outside Casablanca in Morocco. This was due to the invasion of Italy. We made the flight during the night. Gander in Newfoundland was our first stop to refuel our tanks. Then the second stop was the Azores for another refuelling, but after a few hours flying, the weather got much worse, and we decided to change course.

The DC-3 is wrapped in thick clouds and the strong winds throw it around in the air. Finn has to correct their course constantly. He feels his arms getting more and more tired from holding the big machine on its right course. They can't afford to lose any height or speed. He'll have to try and take the DC-3 higher up, over this horrible weather.

The altimeter slowly crawls up to 15,000 feet. It won't go any further. It seems to be impossible to make the machine climb higher. Finn can feel the tension in the cockpit. He's the only pilot onboard. The rest of the crew consists of a navigator and a wireless operator. It is he who sits by the controls, and he's the one who has to make a decision.

He jumps in his chair when he hears loud bangs on the fuselage. Ice has been packing itself on the hard-working propellers. The sound is terrifying when it flies off the propellers and hits the aircraft. Another look at the gauge and Finn has to admit that they're losing height. He simply can't keep the bird flying at 15,000 feet. If he pulls more on the stick, they will stall out, and if that happens there will be little chance of survival. Instead, he gives maximum power to the engines and flips on the de-icing system with one hand kept on the heavy controls.

Another look at the altitude. His actions did not help; they're still losing height. The ice keeps flying off the propellers, cracking into the DC-3 further back. What's more, he's having increasing trouble with the windscreen. Large chunks of ice build up, making it impossible to see anything ahead. It's starting to get serious, and he'll have to make a decision.

'We will never be able to get to the Azores in these conditions!' yells Finn to his navigator. The navigator nods back with a serious look on his face, but keeps calm and continues on with his tasks.

They set a new course back to Gander. A long turn around, and they're set for 'home'. But it doesn't seem to help their situation. They've lost too much height, it's becoming critical.

The discussions in the cockpit quickly turn to emergency signals. Should they send them out? They decide to wait it out for a little while longer. Using strong torches, they see the ice still building up on the fuselage, while they keep losing height. If the ice doesn't fall of soon, they won't even make it back to Gander. They will end up in the 'drink'.

Finn keeps fighting the winds outside. The DC-3 is responding better now, though the altimeter shows that they are very low. It can't be long now until they touch down in the rough waters. He keeps looking at the altimeter, hoping the ice has started to fall off so that they stop losing precious height. Suddenly, their height seems to have stabilized. Low, but steady.

'I think the ice is starting to melt off!' shouts the navigator with enormous relief written across his face.

For Finn, it is only a matter of keeping the DC-3 flying with a little more height, hoping the weather will not get worse on their way back.

We finally made it back to Gander, and there was an incredible amount of ice on the DC-3 when we landed. After we had refuelled, we started up again, but this time in daylight. We had much better information about the weather this time around, so we avoided trouble and made it to the Azores without further difficulties.

After all this, we were quite tired, so we slept on the base for the night. We took a short walk into the 'town', although it was more like a little village in Norwegian terms. We ate a good dinner with splendid wine, before we started our walk back to base. We strolled across a piazza on our way back, and heard guitar playing and singing coming out of a house. It turned out to be the local police station! We stopped outside from curiosity, and a couple of police officers invited us in. I think they saw we had RAF uniforms. We stayed for a few hours, drinking wine and singing some songs, having a great time. Finally deciding to go home, we were given a ride on a cart, pulled by a donkey. The donkey was so small and skinny, the three of us got off the cart several times and helped it up the steepest hills.

The next day, we flew to Morocco, and the day after we were given a ride back home to Montreal by a British BOAC aircraft.

Meanwhile, several of my friends from North Weald had arrived in Montreal. Reidar From, Svein Heglund[10], Jon Gilhuus, and Olav Ullestad had all arrived for their rest period in Transport Command.

I kept on flying B-25 bombers to Prestwick after the Morocco journey. On one of these flights during the winter, we got a weather forecast predicting very bad weather between Goose Bay and Greenland. I started,

Arvid Piltingsrud and Finn Thorsager in civilian clothes, possibly during his BOAC period, 1944-45. (*Finn Thorsager*)

and so did two others. The weather got really bad with snow and heavy winds, and low visibility between the icebergs. I had to go all the way down to sea-level to get my bearings. What the two other pilots did, I don't know, but the weather kept growing worse. In the end, I had no choice but to turn 180 degrees and fly into the clouds back to Goose Bay, where we performed an instrument landing.

It turned out the second in our group had also turned around, but the third one was never heard from. The next day, we had to go up to look for the missing B-25, and I was given an area north of Goose Bay. Fortunately, the weather was alright.

After a couple of hours searching for the missing crew, Finn spots a group of people on a frozen lake in the wilderness. He flies over them as low as he can, and can easily spot their blue overalls. It fits with what the missing crew wore when they took off from Goose Bay. They all normally wear blue overalls in Transport Command. When passing overhead, the people on the ground wave back at him. He's sure they must be the missing crew; who else would be so far out into the wilderness at this time of year?

Finn pulls the aircraft up from the frozen lake and contacts Goose Bay so they can pinpoint his location by radio. Happy with his discovery, he heads back to Goose Bay, sure that the missing crew will be rescued.

An aircraft was sent out to pick them up, and landed on the frozen lake. The group of people told the rescuers that they were hunters. It was a terrible disappointment to all involved.

We later continued on with our journey to Prestwick, and returned to Montreal in a DC-4. We were about twenty RAF pilots on this return trip. We all had to hand our equipment over as cargo, with no chance of getting to it after the flight was underway. The cabin and the cockpit each had one heater. Sadly, the one in the cabin broke, and we could all now look forward to fourteen hours of extreme cold. Because of the weather, we had to fly at over 20,000 feet, so we had to constantly move around to keep warm, but moving around, we couldn't use the oxygen system. We all got really worn out by the cold. When we finally reached Montreal, I checked myself into a hotel at the airport, and defrosted here for several days.

Later on, I got orders to deliver another B-25 to Prestwick. We stayed the night in Narsarsurak. When I tried to get up in the morning to fly to Iceland, I simply couldn't. I had bad pains in my back. The pain was a result of how cold I got on that freezing trip back to Montreal. My crew saw what was happening to me, so they called for an ambulance. To my surprise, the Americans had built a big modern hospital in this backwater to treat injured war veterans. The hospital was fully staffed with doctors and Latin American nurses.

I was treated like a king, and examined in every way possible. I started to feel better almost instantly! However, they wouldn't let me go and diagnosed me with the early stages of pleurisy. I was marched off to bed with blankets and plenty of refreshing fruit juices. But my crew were waiting for me, so after a couple of days, I got out of bed and said my goodbyes. The people at the hospital were all kind and helpful, and they gave me an unforgettable experience.

In the spring 1944, I was sent back to England. My rest period was over, and I was rejoining active service. I flew the last trip from Montreal in a Lodestar to Prestwick. From there, I was to report to Kingston House, the headquarters of the Norwegian Air Force in London.

Chapter 25

Stockholmsroute

While I was stationed at North Weald, I became friends with famous Wing Commander John 'Cat's Eyes' Cunningham. So did many others of us Norwegians. He had promised me a place in his Mosquito squadron when I came back to England after my rest period. Unfortunately, I was not given permission from the bosses.

I was instead ordered to something called 'Stockholmsroute', which was also very interesting. I moved up to St Andrews in Scotland where they were stationed and became an English citizen for the remainder of the War; I flew in a civilian English aircraft with a British passport, and used British Overseas Airways uniforms. It was assumed that, if we were shot down, the Germans would treat civilian Norwegian pilots badly. Therefore, it was decided that we had to become British.

We were to fly between Leuchars in Scotland and Stockholm in Sweden with priority passengers and cargo such as ball bearings, medicines, and the like. We could obviously only fly when it was dark, and by the least risky route across the North Sea, which took us over the south of Norway and into Sweden. Kattegat and Skagerrak had to be avoided because of the German night fighters. In these areas, one of our aircraft was shot down with passengers onboard.

I met my old friend Holger Hannestad again. He was a telegraphist in Scotland, and he joined my crew.

The route to Stockholm gives Finn some extra inspiration. They will fly over Norway. He's wanted to fly in Norwegian skies ever since he left home, but it's not been possible until now. He knows Norway very well. The same goes for all of them. But it will not be easy to fly a civilian aircraft over enemy territory with no chance of defending themselves against German fighters. It is a highly dangerous business and he will have to be careful not to fly over any 'hot spots'. The Stavanger area is one of those places. So is his home city of Oslo. The Germans don't distinguish between civilian and military aircraft. An unknown aircraft is a suspicious aircraft and it will be fired upon. They will be flying on the same terms as B-24 Liberators, or Norwegian Mosquitos from 330 Squadron.

Gradually, the disappointment Finn felt when he was forbidden to join Cunningham's squadron began to wear off. He can't deny that the route to Stockholm also sounds very interesting. So, no Mosquitos right now, but maybe later.

In the winter moonlight, it was fantastic to see all those familiar places again. It was good weather for flying very low, and it was more difficult for the Germans to spot us and shoot us down that way.

We also had an instrument on board with different kinds of lights. If the red light came on, we knew that the anti-aircraft radar had seen us. If the white light came on, we knew that a radar installed in a German night fighter had spotted us. These lights came on very often.

Before each trip, we had a briefing with the meteorologist. We were also informed about things that were important for the task ahead. After that, we calculated a flight plan. I usually flew a flight plan that crossed the Norwegian coast between Stavanger and Bergen. The critical part of the flight was usually when we had plenty of altitude, reaching the coast. If it was a moonlit night, we kept our eyes open more than usual. If one of the lights came on, we were 'on pins'.

The German espionage department knew about the Norwegian route between Leuchars and Bromma, and we were informed about this by the British Embassy. The Germans had their people out at Bromma, reporting back on everything of interest to them. They knew the names of the crews, what kind of aircraft we flew, even our flight plan! We even ran into them from time to time at Bromma airport.

One time, just outside Stavanger, the white light appeared, and, seconds later, a German jet fighter passed us. His speed was so high he hadn't had time to fire. Jets were still at an experimental stage then, and especially at night. Another pilot, Fridtjof Giørtz, also flying on this particular night, and very close to me, had the same thing happen to him. The event was of great interest to the British when we landed back at Leuchars.

Another incident happened when we were on our way back to Scotland. We were over the Norwegian coast, flying into rough weather, so we were quite low, and the white light came on.

The Lodestar is shaking violently in the terrible weather. The radio operator struggles to stay in his seat. The white light is still on but, no matter how hard they try, they can't see any enemies outside. It's simply too dark. Finn puts the Lodestar into a left turn, pulling hard on the controls to maintain their altitude. The white light disappears from the instrument. It takes just a second of level flying before it comes back on. Finn pulls an opposite turn this time, banking hard right. The feeling of not being able to defend themselves is nerve-wracking. At any given time, the German can get close enough for an attack. They will most likely not even be able to think before their aircraft is on fire.

Finn levels out again, and the same thing happens. White light back on. To the crew, it feels like a never ending danger lurking just outside their cockpit. Finn decides to dive. Pushing the control forwards, he feels his body becoming weightless, pushing itself against his straps. There's no point in looking out. It's all black. He keeps staring at his artificial horizon, making sure he's not diving too steeply, losing too much altitude.

The altimeter was set according to the air pressure the meteorologist had given us at the English embassy, so we went as low as possible, putting our trust in it.

Finn pulls out of the hell-raising dive when the altimeter has crawled so far down he doesn't dare to go any lower. He can't be entirely sure it is 100 per cent accurate. By his calculations, they should be over the sea, so he leaves the thoughts of crashing into a Norwegian mountain behind him. The white light is still there, almost mocking their fight for survival. No matter what he does, it comes back on after he's done his manoeuvres.

With his altitude lost, Finn pulls the Lodestar left and right as violently as he dares. To the despair of everyone aboard, the white light simply comes back on again. They just have to keep going.

Another hard pull right, followed by a quick contra manoeuvre to the left. Finn starts to feel exhausted. It takes its toll, pulling all these turns. He's been waiting for that devastating bang for a while now, but nothing comes. It's almost as if he just wants it to be over it. Anything is better than their current state. Finn sets a steady course for Scotland. The white light is not shining at the moment, but he's sure it will pop up again. He's ready for it, sitting with his leg on the rudder pedal, ready to kick it in the moment it appears.

Seconds pass, and still no light. Only the roar of the two engines can be heard, fighting against the weather outside. Holger smiles, and gives Finn a thumbs up. No white light. They finally got away. Finn takes a deep breath; it had been some very tough minutes. It suddenly dawns on him that his passengers must have had an absolutely horrifying time.

> We managed to get home to Scotland in one piece. There had been plenty of hard manoeuvring on instruments only, so most of our passengers lying on a big mattress in the back had vomited.

Finn enjoys coming back to Scotland. He feels at home there. After each trip, when their Lodestar is parked, they are served tea and biscuits from the ground crew at the base, who really care about the men flying to Sweden. He usually manages a quick smoke before bed, too. Finn feels Stockholm is very different to Scotland. Everything there is lit up. There are no restrictions, and the life of the average Swede is mostly going on as normal. For Finn, Scotland represents what he's involved in; no street lights; blackened houses. There's a war on. To go to Stockholm doesn't feel real. It's almost morbid; a world he's not participating in.

> We lived in private homes, renting apartments, and we had our meals at restaurants in St Andrews. Since St Andrews is the birthplace of golf, we were well introduced to the sport during our time there.

★

Finn turns the Lodestar quickly around when he gets the depressing news from Bromma. If this one is to end well, they will need all the fuel they have. Bromma is completely fogged in, and the order has been given to return to Scotland. It truly is a last-minute order. They're already well into Norway. Finn can't waste time with discussions. If they're going to make it home, they have to turn around now. In the meantime, the navigator calculates a new course home. Finn can see him shaking his head. They won't be able to reach St Andrews. Too little fuel, too much head wind.

They decide to try and make it to Sumburgh. Finn knows the place well from his time with 331 Squadron there. He didn't expect to return to Sumburgh ever again. Their chances are marginal, but within the limits. With the current fuel state, they will just make it. But if the wind increases further, they won't.

The Lodestar keeps going towards the Shetland isles. Finn takes a quick look at the fuel gauge every other minute. It's lower than he expected.

'We can't rule out that we have to ditch in the sea.'

The navigator understands the seriousness of the situation as well as Finn does. He ponders the chances of survival if they were to ditch. If they don't go down with the plane, the chances of surviving in the North Sea for very long are not great. It's a cold place to end up.

Suddenly, we heard the Swedish beacon transmitting again.

Bromma is open again, they can turn back. They set a course for the Swedish capital. No problems with fuel this way. They will be in Sweden in a relatively short time. With luck, they will get down with no further trouble.

The fog worries Finn, but he can only assume that the worst of it has disappeared. Perhaps it happened very quickly. He can't really get his head around it, but concludes that the people on the ground know their jobs.

This new message was Urbye's work, our administrative boss. He was, by chance, in Stockholm at that time, and was told of our situation. He got in touch with the controllers at Bromma, and told them to let us land, as he thought this was our best option, and he knew we could do it.

Another case involving poor weather happened on our way to Bromma. It was raining. The visibility was bad, and we had a low cloudbase all the way to Sweden which made it very tricky to take visual reference from the ground. We saw trees beneath us, flashing by in the dark, and sometimes we saw lights from Swedish homes. Our radio operator tried to get a fix on Bromma, so we could find our way, but the radio conditions that night were extremely poor. Even our own radio compass didn't work. The man worked under great pressure, but kept changing calmly and systematically from one frequency to another. As time passed, we had to think of the possibility of landing over the Baltic Sea. Finally, he managed to get a positive fix from Bromma. It saved us from another potentially fatal landing.

The other aircraft that night flew into the same conditions and had to ditch in the sea, all the way up at Umeå. The Lodestar was lost, but the crew survived.

★

Ever since they departed from Stockholm, the wind has done its best to blow them off course. Finn is flying on his instruments through thick, dark clouds on their way back to Scotland.

He takes the Lodestar lower. No one is quite sure where they are. They need to know for certain, hoping to spot known landmarks. Finn's gut is telling him they must be somewhere over the eastern part of Norway, maybe near Oslo, but he doesn't know for sure.

The Lodestar appears out of the dark clouds, and Finn levels it out. His eyes widen with shock when he sees where they are. The moonlight makes long and twisted shadows on the buildings below them. His gut was right, it's Oslo. They are right over the Ekeberg area.

Finn automatically starts thinking of his departure from home, and how long it's been. He can see all the known landmarks – the harbour, the city hall, the castle – they're all there, just like they were when he left in 1940.

The joy is soon forgotten as Finn remembers the massive anti-aircraft positions all around the Norwegian capital. He suddenly feels desperately vulnerable. It's that horrible feeling of being exposed. At any moment the Germans will blast away with all they've got at the low-flying Lodestar. The red light is on, flickering in the pitch-dark cockpit. They need to get down to tree level as soon as possible. Finn pushes the Lodestar down as low as he dares. A quick turn over Alnabru, and he puts it on a course just north of Oslo. Still turning, he can suddenly see his parents' home at Bestum, shining dimly in the moonlight.

The sensation is unforgettable. Here he is, flying a Lodestar almost right on top of his parents' house. If only they had known. Finn gets a strange feeling from it. It is almost unreal. He desperately wants to open the small window and scream out to them. He's right here, flying over them, alive and well. He's not been home for almost five years, and now he's there, but still so far away.

Bestum disappears in the darkness and Finn lets his emotions go with it. He continues flying south-west to Scotland. Luckily for everyone on board, the flak stayed away. Most likely, they never managed to react quickly enough.

Safely down at Leuchars, Finn sees another Lodestar that was flying that night come in for a landing. He grabs a cigarette from his pocket, waiting for the aircraft to stop. Giørtz has been flying behind him down to Leuchars, although he never saw him during the trip. He climbs down from the plane and makes his way over to where Finn is standing.

'How did it all go?' asks Finn, taking a long drag from his cigarette.

'Well, we came out of the clouds over Oslo just like you. Maybe five, ten minutes later? They were prepared for us, I tell you. We got all of it on us. Reminded me of the time when I flew bombers over Berlin.'

Once again, Finn had been lucky. He could have been shot down over his home town. It would have been a strange ending to it all.

Chapter 26

Home At Last

Finally, the War was over, and it was strange, to put it mildly! On 15 May, I was finally given orders to fly to Gardermoen with a bunch of high-ranking officers.

We flew up to Oslo, having the coast of the south of Norway beside us the entire time. It was fantastic. No Germans shooting at us, and we all felt the joy of being safe in the sky. When we passed my home at Bestum, I dived down and threw out English newspapers with my personal greetings. Sadly, they were never found by my family.

We landed at Gardermoen, and taxied up to our designated parking area. There were plenty of people there to greet us.

It's a big moment. Finn has landed in Norway! He can't even begin to imagine how many times he has dreamed of this moment. He pulls off his headphones and turns off the aircraft's electrical systems. There is an eerie period of silence in the back of the plane. Instead of exiting the aircraft, all the officers stay sitting down. Finn turns around, about to ask what's going on, but one of the officers beats him to it.

'Captain and crew first, please.'

They all smile at him, understanding his desire to set foot on Norwegian soil once again. Finn smiles back at them, nods in gratitude, and jumps out. As his feet touch Norway, Finn's emotions run high. Instinctively, he bends down and grabs a few blades of grass from the ground. He smells them with pride, making him almost dizzy with happiness and joy. After five long years, he's finally back home.

At Gardermoen, we were given a ride in an open truck to the Bristol Hotel in Oslo, where some kind of command centre had been established. I was asked where I wanted to go, and two chaps from the Home Front drove me to Bestum in a jeep. We heard gunfire around Frognerparken, and I was told it was from a few die-hard Nazis, still going at it. The jeep stopped outside my home, and I thanked the men for their help before they drove on.

Finn gently walks up to his home, hoping his parents still live there after five long years. He hesitates, wondering whether he should go right up and knock, or be more cautious.

He tip-toes up to the door. 'Thorsager' is written on it in bold letters; he's at the right place. Everything looks the same around him. Then he suddenly remembers the time; it's the middle of the night. He backtracks and rethinks his approach. He doesn't want to scare his parents by knocking on their door in the middle of the night. They might think he is a German.

Finn turns around. He'd better do this carefully. He walks over to a neighbouring house, where his brother used to have a good friend. He rings their doorbell and holds his breath, waiting for someone inside to make a noise and open the door. A quiet padding of feet can be heard inside before a dark shape opens the door.

'Hello,' says Finn nervously, 'um, I've just come back and—'

'Gosh! Is it you Finn?'

The man in the doorway smiles in the shadows of the darkened house. Finn can see it's Carl Fredrik's old friend, just a little older than he remembered him.

'You recognize me?'

'Do I? Of course I do! What a fantastic surprise!'

'I didn't dare to knock on the door back home. I wasn't sure how everything was, with the Germans and all. I thought I'd check with you first...'

'Of course, of course! Listen, I have a secret phone line connected to Carl Fredrik from this house. I can simply give him a call.'

Finn feels more relaxed, his decision to come here first seems to have been the right one.

The phone call is made, and Finn walks alone back to his parents' house after thanking his brother's friend for his help. The dark figure of Carl Fredrik stands waiting for him in the doorway. He walks out towards Finn, halfway up the driveway, and stretches out his arms in welcome.

It was amazing to see Carl Fredrik again. We sat down on a little rock in the garden, and discussed how to give mother and father the message of my arrival. It gave me the time to have a cigarette as well.

'Listen, just stay put until I come back out. I'll give you a signal when you can come in.'

Carl Fredrik gets up from the rock he's sitting on and walks up to the veranda and in the back door. Finn nods in return to his smiling brother, happy with their plan. He smokes the rest of his cigarette while Carl Fredrik is inside waking up their parents. In a few moments, Carl Fredrik reappears and beckons Finn to come inside the house.

> Now I finally met my mother and father again. It wasn't with a lot of noise. Just a quiet and honest expression of great joy. I don't remember what was said at that moment, but it didn't take long until we were all sitting around the kitchen table, just like old times.

'Finn, do you remember that morning you left?' says his father. 'I told you I would save a bottle of champagne for you – I'll go and get it now.'

Conrad disappears down the basement stairs. For Finn, it's full circle. The champagne has been there waiting for him ever since he left. And now he's finally home.

> We kept talking while we drank the champagne. It had been such a long time since I had any contact with my family, so it was very hard to find the right words. I couldn't stay for long. I had to get over to the Hotel Bristol again before getting transport back to Gardermoen. I didn't really know how to get into the city either. It may sound strange, but long before I really had to go, I felt like I needed some time by myself to think. I told my family that I had to leave so I would make it into the hotel in time.

It's still early in the morning when Finn closes the door at Bestum to walk to the Hotel Bristol. He's got plenty of time. He just wants to walk and listen to the silence of a city still sleeping. On the road passing Vækerø, Finn makes a little detour and walks towards Maritim.

> I sat down on a wharf to enjoy the silence. The sea was calm, clear, and it was all very quiet. I thought about old times at Maritim. We used to have a little sail boat, a small rowing boat, and a home-made kayak here. I remember it as very sentimental to sit there in that silence.

After a good time with his thoughts, Finn gets up to walk towards the city centre. It is still early to show up at the Bristol, so Finn walks over to a bench in the student area of Oslo and sits down. People are starting to wake up and go to work as normal. It seems people are managing the transition back to normality well enough.

Finn's thoughts still wander back to those five years just passed. Everything he's been through, living under military conditions for so long. He feels he's done his duty. He had followed his orders to the best of his ability, and he had mostly made the right choices. In addition, he had got a first-class education as a pilot. Finn had survived the fights with Focke Wulf 190s, and all the trips to Stockholm and back. It was all so different from what the folks back home had lived through. He knew he was lucky.

Finn takes a look at his watch; time to go to the hotel. He gets up from the bench. The sun has risen higher while he's been out walking. It is a beautiful May morning in Norway.

Finn and Reidar From discussing fighter tactics in front of a Gloster Gladiator, during the opening of National Norwegian Aviation Museum at Bodø, 1994. (*Finn Thorsager*)

Epilogue

Those of us who had been flying the Stockholm route during the War spent a lot of time at Fornebu after the War ended. We lived in a big house by the seaside, not far from the airport. The house belonged to a big farm, and we were given twin rooms in the main building. We lived and ate our meals here, and this was where Norwegian civil aviation took shape.

We sat during the evenings and discussed all kinds of things, even how to start a trade union. We had no real experience in these matters, so we looked to British and, most importantly, American civil aviation. Salary was, of course, a very interesting subject. After a good while, our friendly discussions made it clear for us what problems lay ahead, and what we would have to do to solve them.

During the very early days, when we flew on various routes, our organisation was called '20th Transport Squadron', a predecessor to DNL (Det Norske Luftfartselskap). We mainly used Lodestars and DC-3s on flights within Scandinavia and to England. One group flew Junkers 52s on domestic flights.

Our uniforms were those of the Air Force, and, for quite some time after the War ended, there were German military personnel in the aviation administration. They were very military in their manner and were very well behaved.

During those first years after the War, our flying was pretty primitive and simple. We were three men in the cockpit – two pilots and one telegraphist. We flew how we wanted to fly, if possible with contact with the ground. Navigation aids were few and far between. The main rule was to fly at certain altitudes, depending on our course.

One day, an old colleague of mine told me he'd found a great radio station down in Germany which helped him a lot.

'What frequency and position does this station have?' I asked.

'Oh no!' he replied. 'I won't tell you. You'd better find that out for yourself!'

It was said jokingly, but it gives a flavour of what life was like at that time.

Take off, landing clearance and all other information came from the telegraphist, with no chance for us pilots to check anything. He was, therefore, a very, very important man in those days.

Even in bad weather, our landings were done visually. Every pilot had to rely on his own initiative. Personally, I remember the landings at Croydon as pretty tricky, especially with poor visibility, which there so often was. There was usually plenty of traffic in the air, and the airport itself was just a patch of grass, often hard to find.

It did not take long before we could see changes for the better in the flattened German cities. It wasn't just the cities getting to their feet, but also civil aviation went through plenty of positive changes. The airports were improved, with nice runways and buildings, and the weather services were also improved greatly.

During those first days of peace, my family home at Bestum became quite the information service centre. It wasn't far from Fornebu, and many pilots and crew members had their families spread out all over Norway. Many of them used my parents as a way of getting in touch with their families. It was an arrangement which gave both parties a great deal of pleasure. I remember a Polish friend of mine, Rusietsky, arriving at Fornebu. He knew about my family, and went over to say hello one day. Sadly, I was not home at the time. This chap was a very handsome man and looked like Charles Boyer [a prolific French actor]. My mother opened the door, and he entered, bowed like a gentleman and kissed my mother's hand. I think she almost fainted! She was not used to these gestures. The Polish were envious of us Norwegians during those days. They couldn't go home due to the political state of their nation and the Soviet Union. Their future looked very bleak.

In those days, we pilots lived for the future of aviation. A group of us met regularly and discussed anything to do with flying. I guess we were considered fanatics in the eyes of friends and family! There were so many unknown factors and plenty of challenges for the future of civilian flying, so naturally, these discussions arose every time we got together. We understood early on that aviation would play a major part in the future. When we weren't flying, we used to meet before noon in a restaurant at

A SAS DC-4 in flight. (*SAS Museum*)

Fornebu. I think we all thought we had a positive life. We didn't have TVs back then, and very few of us had cars, so it was important to be sociable. In order to actually purchase a car, we needed a license to get hold of the necessary money, and this was not an easy task.

The technical side concerning our aeroplanes was good, and most of the engineers that were hired were known to us previously. We had worked with them in most of the Norwegian squadrons during the War. We had plenty to do, and we fostered good connections with Great Britain.

In June 1945, I had a very exciting trip when I flew Crown Prince Olav with his escort to Trondheim [central Norway]. It was his first trip there after the War. German Luftwaffe meteorologists briefed us beforehand about the weather conditions. We flew a Lodestar on this trip, and even before we started, we were told that the entire population of Trondheim and the surrounding area was lined up at Værnes airport and all the way into town. Over the mountains, we got heavy thunder, as was forecast. We tried to fly through it. Due to all the lightning and electrical charges, Prince Olav had sparks flying over him. He was sitting just behind the radio equipment, but he was very calm through it all. The turbulence was so heavy that we decided we had to avoid the bad weather, which led to us losing radio contact. We had to fly all the way out to the coast and then alongside it to Trondheim. It was a relief when we managed to establish radio contact again, and could tell the controllers what had happened. We landed at Værnes forty-five minutes after our scheduled arrival.

People were indeed lined up by the road all the way into Trondheim. The crew of the Lodestar was given a ride in the car following Prince Olav's. Flowers thrown at him sometimes landed in our car. Two days later, we returned to Fornebu, this time all according to plan.

The first winter in peacetime arrived, and I could finally be out on skis again. It led to many nostalgic trips in Nordmarka. I felt I was slowly getting back to a normal life.

In March of 1946, DNL was formed. In those days, thankfully – I must say – there were none of today's exams to become a pilot. Today, there are many hurdles a pilot has to go through to get his wings, but back then it was different. You needed to be able to pass a medical test and have a valid pilot's certificate. You also had to be qualified in navigation and meteorology, with some technical knowledge as well. The flying school was established by the government. Flying back then was so new that the names of each student were published in the newspapers.

Our first chief pilot was John Strandrud; he had his office in the old hanger at Fornebu. Other sections also had their offices here. My first yearly salary was, to my recollection, about 15,000 NOK as captain. Co-pilots earned a little less.

The administration had their offices in a modern building by the town hall and the pilots' lodgings were spread out around the Oslo area, while several of us lived in an old villa close by. The Germans had built five or six other huts on the same property, and they were all occupied by families. I too lived in one of them. Everyone was very satisfied with the distance to Fornebu, and also the social connection between us all. I paid 250 NOK a month in rent.

The Lodestars we had were sold quickly after DNL started up. We kept the DC-3s and the Ju-52s. DNL also bought three Sandringham flying boats, used for domestic routes. Two DC-4 four-engined aircraft were also bought for transatlantic flying, but these were also used on European routes. None of them had pressurized cabins.

At the same time, something else happened in Norwegian aviation that had never happened before. Adverts were published looking for stewardesses. The applications came in at a tremendous rate.

Hundreds applied, and only twelve to fifteen were hired the first time around.

I remember well the first DNL flight to London on 8 April 1946.

At 8.45 a.m., the silver DC-3 takes off in a strong head wind from Fornebu. After only 200 metres it takes to the air. Finn is piloting the DC-3, Morten Ree, former 331 Squadron Spitfire-pilot, is co-pilot, and Sigurd Stokken takes up his position as the telegraphist. The stewardesses include Gerd Thoren and Gurli Bøge. For Gurli, it's her first trip to England. The passengers are mostly journalists, while others are only on board for the ride to Sola, Stavanger, where they will refuel before crossing the North Sea. Finn hopes to keep to the planned schedule, with a landing at Northolt in London at 1.55 p.m., Norwegian time.

Finn levels out at their planned altitude level. He lets out a smile when he thinks about how things have moved forward since last year. Now, they have stewardesses on board as well.

A calm knock on their door, and a stewardess appears in her brand new uniform with a wonderful smile on her face. Finn is taken aback by her presence.

'Would you like any coffee?'

She has a spell-binding voice. Of course Finn wants coffee. He wouldn't miss it for the world. No matter what coffee she might be serving, it will be the best one he's ever had. He's sure of it.

'Yes, please,' he says, desperately trying to hide his admiration, but clearly making a mess of it.

'I will be right back then!'

She gives another broad smile, and closes the door. Minutes later, she's back with coffee for the entire crew. Finn puts the hot cup to his lips and takes a careful sip. Just like he expected, the coffee is glorious. Flying will never be the same.

This stewardess was Gurli Bøge, and we got married later on. Gurli had been involved with the illegal press during the War, and she had translated many illegal news articles received from England. For her, England was something of a dream.

A few years later, like many others at the time, we had two East-German boys, aged eight and nine years old, living with us during the summer of 1949. They were refugees from all the chaos in the east. They got new clothes, which they needed, and ate as much as they could. We had a happy time with them. We never heard from

Gurli, Finn, their firstborn son Helge, and dog Lasse up in the Norwegian mountains, 1960s. (*Finn Thorsager*)

them since. I hope they managed well after they went back to East Germany.[11]

DNL had too few captains, so a couple of DNL employees went to England to get hold of a few RAF pilots. Without any of us being informed, they showed up in Oslo with their contracts signed. It was up to us, the captains, to get them up to the standard we wanted. Some of them had to be sent home, unfortunately. Others stayed with us for a few years and did a good job.

It was hard for us to get enough practice in, especially for the new pilots and in regard to instrument flying. We only had those aircraft that we flew to destinations around Europe. I was given a task to go to England and buy two Oxford twin-engined trainers. These were planned to be used for instrument flying practice. It was a very interesting trip indeed. The Oxfords were bought from the British at the factory, and they helped me out a great deal. Obviously, there were so many things to remember and some of it was way beyond my capacity, to put it mildly.

It was indeed a very busy time for aviation back then. I was lucky enough to get two chartered trips to Nairobi in Kenya. We had stops in Copenhagen, Frankfurt, Rome, Athens, Tel Aviv, Khartoum, Juba, Kisumu, and then, finally, Nairobi. I remember we had two Norwegian missionaries with us, a married couple, who disembarked in Kisumu. They were heading way into the unknown without knowing any native

Finn with his parents in front of an SAS DC-4 at Fornebu, sometime in the 1950s.
(*Finn Thorsager*)

language, not even English. I had to help them out with the paperwork because they didn't even know what 'born in' meant. God knows where they ended up, but it was truly a brave thing to do.

After we departed Kisumu, the trip went over vast wilderness. It was very interesting. We flew as low as possible since there were no rules of any kind in those areas then. We wanted to see as much as possible. I saw plenty of crocodiles in the Nile, Rhinos, Elephants and Zebras.

We landed at an airport by Juba, in those days a small village. Today it's a relatively big town. Lined up by the runway, there were naked natives looking at us when we landed. They were all grey-skinned from dust and mud, and seemed completely unfamiliar with such a thing as flying.

I also did a charter trip in a DC-4 to Bombay. The passengers included forty Sikhs with beards and turbans. We flew to Rome, Tel Aviv and Bahrain. The trip was organized in Oslo, especially in regards to landing permits and food for the Sikhs. We arrived in Bombay with no trouble, but ran into problems on our way back. On board, we had Swedish man from SAS to make sure we didn't run into any issues. However, he was completely ignorant about everything that went on. His contribution was entirely negative. There were specific Indian rules he should have known about. He had no clue, but pretended to know everything.

When we started our trip back to Oslo from Bombay, we had some Jews as passengers. At the time we did the trip, there were some problems

SAS DC-8 'Dan Viking' taxiing at Fornebu. (*SAS Museum*)

with Israel and their neighbouring states, and we had reports of other crews getting into problems. We told the Swede of these reports, but he guaranteed no problems would occur. Fuel would also be given to us at different locations.

At Nicosia in Cyprus, the government refused to let the passengers disembark. We were told we had to fly back to Bombay with them. Secondly, they refused us fuel. After a lot of negotiation we were finally allowed to buy fuel, but we had to pay for it in cash using British Sterling. Luckily for us, we still had some money left. To top it all off, no one had sent a departing telegram from Bombay, so we arrived at the various places much to the locals' surprise. In return, we got plenty of experience in handling situations on our own. I wrote a report on the trip, still in the possession of SAS.

For five or six years, I was chief pilot for SAS in Oslo. During this time, there were very turbulent developments in SAS.

In the 1950s, air crew personnel from Oslo were allowed to join DC-4 flights over the Atlantic. We used specially equipped cargo planes, and the cargo often consisted of animals. For example, dogs, birds, and even rhinos. The smell on board could be a little on the heavy side at times. The dogs were allowed to walk freely, so those of us sitting in the cockpit could

A wonderful shot of a SAS DC-9 (note the Caravelle in the background). (*SAS Museum*)

often feel a dog's warm breath on our necks. We made the food ourselves on these cargo trips, and interestingly enough, beer was often the chosen drink to go with the dinners.

I remember one episode particularly. The captains used to have a little badge with their name on, which they put up on the door to the cockpit as information to the passengers. I had been without mine for a long time, and couldn't find it. I mentioned it at the office one morning before a flight and Veierstad, a friend of mine and also a captain, spoke up.

'You know your badge? I've got it.'

'You've got it? Really?'

'Yes, I usually put it up every time I make a bad landing!'

I flew a lot during the '50s, and in addition, I had to go to meetings at the offices in Stockholm regularly. Back home in Oslo, there was always more paperwork that needed to be done. There became so much of it that I felt I was letting my family down. So, after about six years as chief pilot, I quit the position to fully concentrate on the flying. I never regretted it. My situation changed for the better, and I felt much more at ease.

I flew mostly DC-8s on long-distance flights, usually to the USA. Everything was very well organized, and in the end, I felt a little spoilt! I remember back when we started out, when we had to grab the initiative ourselves in most areas. Now, we had superb training, and great dispatchers helping us out in the air and on the ground. On arrival at our destination, a car was waiting to take us to our hotel. No problems!

In SAS, we have a scheme that allows us, after a certain amount of time and experience, to make a request to fly new types of aircraft along different routes. After many years flying transatlantic routes, I wanted a change, and it had to include as little night flying as possible. I wanted to fly shorter flights, with no time differences involved, but with the best equipment.

My wish was fulfilled. I was transferred to flying DC-9s. I flew my last years with SAS on European routes, and also quite a lot in the northern parts of Norway. Northern Norway was a favourite of mine. It was flying with a good number of challenges, especially during the winter, with plenty of bad weather, gusty winds and marginal braking conditions due to ice on the runways. The northerners had little experience of flying, so they were always a pleasure to have as passengers.

In 1974, my brother, Carl Fredrik, died after a year of illness. He had meant so much to me. Soon after that, the day I feared started to sneak up on me – my 60th birthday. When a pilot reaches 60 years of age, their 'D certificate' is no longer valid, and without the certificate, they could no longer work for SAS, nor for any other companies inside IATA [International Air Transport Association].

I believe I took part in a time of fantastic development in aviation. When I think back on my first trip from Bestumkilen in that Spartan, to that day I was 60 years old with 20,000 hours logged, I have to admit that I was very happy in the air. Luckily, I was never involved in any accidents as my time as a captain with SAS for over thirty years. I am very grateful for it.

As an end to these writings, I would like to jump back to 9 April 1940. I wrote earlier that Norway was attacked on that day by the Luftwaffe with their Messerschmitt Bf110s, among other aircraft. One of the pilots in one of those 110s was Hans Ulrich Kettling, and he had been contacted by journalist and writer Cato Guhnfeldt, concerning the anniversary. On that 50-year anniversary, a dinner was arranged by Per Waaler, one of the remaining Gladiator pilots from that morning so long ago. Per Waaler flew bombers later during the War, and was shot down over Dortmund. Kristian Fredrik Schye was also one of the Norwegian Gladiator pilots joining us that day. He was shot down over Bærum in his Gladiator. Waaler,

Finn returning from another day's work with SAS on 17 May, Norway's national day. Gurli is there to meet him with a drink in her hand, *c.*1975. (*Finn Thorsager*)

Gurli and Finn with two of their grandchildren, early 1990s.

Helge Mehre of 331 Squadron (left of the memorial) with Finn Thorsager (right of the memorial) in 1992. (*Finn Thorsager*)

Official gathering of Norwegian personnel at North Weald in 1992, fifty years after their first arrival at North Weald. (*Finn Thorsager*)

Schye and I were the three surviving Norwegians from the 9 April attack, and we went with our wives to meet Kettling and his wife at the arranged dinner. Kettling was shot down during the Battle of Britain, and spent the rest of the War in captivity. The meeting was friendly and respectful. We talked about the old days, and Kettling apologized for what Germany had led the world into. We were together the following day as well. Kettling did what he could to promote peace and friendship, and we did too. Now we exchange Christmas greeting cards and write to each other on special occasions.

Finn Thorsager passed away on 29 August 2000, after a long and happy life with his wife Gurli, children Helge and Ellen, and plenty of grandchildren, Christian, Eric, Silje, and Olav. He is sorely missed.

Finn Thorsager and his Spitfires

Finn Thorsager flew four different makes of Spitfire during his time in Britain; IIa, Va, Vb, IXc. Among others, Finn took these Spitfires to the air:

P7929 IIa
P7359 IIa
R7335 Va
AB184 Vb
EP283 Vb
EN910 Vb
BL579 Vb
BL634 Vb
BS540 IX
BS508 IX
BS507 IX
BS250 IX

BS540 was the Spitfire flown by Nils Jørgan Fuglesang of 332 Squadron when he was shot down over Walcheren and captured by German forces. He later participated in 'The Great Escape'. He was captured and executed on a direct order from Adolf Hitler.

BL634 went to 485 Squadron. It crashed in the sea not far from Dunbar 11 November 1943.

EN910 was converted to a Seafire and was given registration number PA122 in 1943.

R7553 came into Norwegian hands on 17 January 1942, and stayed with 332 Squadron until 18 April 1942 when it was taken by 164 Squadron. It later went to 718 Squadron in September 1944.

The only known Spitfire that has been in Norwegian service and is still flying is ML407. It stayed with 332 Squadron at the end of the War when Finn was stationed at Leuchars.

Endnotes

1. **Rolf Torbjørn Tradin**
   Lieutenant and formation leader of the Gladiators on 9 April 1940. He was later with 611 Squadron, based at Biggin Hill. He was killed in battle with Focke Wulfs in 1943.

2. **Arve Braathen**
   Gladiator pilot at Fornebu, 1940. He was killed later in the War, flying Mosquitos in the RAF.

3. *Blücher*
   German battleship, sunk by Norwegian torpedoes.

4. **Johan Christie**
   Brother of Werner Christie who later flew with Finn in 332 Squadron. Johan Christie flew with the Pathfinder force in the RAF. He survived the war.

5. **Nordahl Grieg**
   Norwegian poet, novelist, dramatist, and journalist. He visited 331 Squadron at Skeabrea seeking inspiration for his work. On the night of 2-3 December 1943, Grieg joined a Lancaster piloted by A.R. Mitchell, 460 Squadron, for a raid on Berlin. 460 Squadron lost five aircraft that night, including the one with Grieg on board. He has no known grave. He became a hero in Norway after the war due to his resistance to the occupation and his anti-fascist poetry.

6. **Marius Eriksen**
   Marius Eriksen escaped Norway on 5 November 1940 when he was

only 17 years old. After arriving in Scotland by boat, he made his way to Little Norway in Canada where he was taught to fly by Finn Thorsager. Eriksen described Thorsager as 'the best teacher I could have had'. After finishing his training, he joined 332 Squadron at Catterick in 1942. Eriksen quickly became one of 332 Squadron's most talented pilots. According to Wilhelm Mohr, he was 'almost too good'. Before being shot down in a head-on battle with a Focke Wulf 190 from Jagdeschwader 1, he had nine enemy kills to his name. Eriksen spent the rest of the War in captivity. After the war he continued with his love for alpine skiing, and he also did some acting. Eriksen passed way in 2009.

7. **Thor Wærner**

Wærner managed to land his stricken Spitfire, avoid being captured and get himself all the way back to England. On his return, he went on a rest period to help him recover from the strain of evading capture and his emergency landing in France. He resumed flying later though, and stayed on active service until 15 April 1945.

8. **Thor Heyerdahl**

A famous Norwegian explorer.

9. **Kjerringa med staven**

An old Norwegian folk song.

10. **Svein Heglund**

Norway's top scoring ace of the Second World War with 16.5 confirmed kills. He joined 331 Squadron during the autumn of 1941, leaving behind his studies in Zurich. He stayed with the squadron for two spells, then left for Transport Command in November 1943. He later joined 85 Squadron flying Mosquitos until the War was over. He then went back to his studies in Zurich. In Norway, Heglund had several positions in the Air Force until he retired in 1982. Svein Heglund passed away in 1998.

11. **The tale of the German boys**

In the spring of 2011, I was contacted by Tobias Neumann from Germany. He is the son of one of the boys who stayed with Finn and his wife Gurli. Tobias is happy to report that his father remembered his time in Norway with joy until the day he passed away. Both of the boys survived the hard times in Germany after the War.

Blessings

an autobiographical fragment

Books by Mary Craig

LONGFORD

WOODRUFF AT RANDOM
(ed.) (Associated Catholic Publications)

MAN FROM A FAR COUNTRY

BLESSINGS

Blessings

an autobiographical fragment

by

Mary Craig

WILLIAM MORROW AND COMPANY, INC.

NEW YORK   1979

For Anthony and Mark,
who will read and understand.
And for Nicholas who will not.

Acknowledgments

James Walsh S.J., editor of *The Way*, for permission to draw on an article I wrote for the January 1973 issue; and the Rev. Canon Michael Mayne of the BBC Religious Broadcasting Department, who made me re-think the material for a Lent Talk on radio (Bare Essentials, March 1977, BBC Radio 4)

Elizabeth Longford, Morris West and David Winter, who read and approved the MS with an enthusiasm which surpassed my wildest hopes.

John Harriott, without whose encouragement I should never have begun to write, on this or any other subject; and Edward England of Hodders who, having read the article in *The Way*, insisted on my writing this particular book.

Pat and Jessica, my much-loved friends, who checked my reminiscences of Cavendish and found them authentic; Sue Ryder (now Baroness Ryder) for the special inspiration she has always provided; and 'the Bods' themselves, in whose debt I shall always remain.

Betty, for what she has given all of us, but especially for her devotion to Paul and Nicholas.

And Frank, whose story this is as much as it is mine, and who has had much to endure.

Cold Ash, Newbury, June 1978.

Contents

The life that I have is all that I have,
　　The life that I have is yours.

The love that I have of the life that I have,
　　Is yours and yours and yours.

A sleep I shall have, a rest I shall have,
　　Yet death will be but a pause.

For the peace of my years in the long green grass
　　Will be yours and yours and yours.

Code poem used by Violette Szabo, the British resistance heroine who worked in France and was shot at Ravensbrück Concentration Camp.

Blessings

an autobiographical fragment

'You Know He Isn't Normal . . .'

IN 1956 THERE were three of us: Frank, my husband, an industrial chemist whom I had met when we were both undergraduates at Oxford, Anthony, our year-old son and myself. We had just had a house built in a village a few miles outside of Derby, but we did not really belong to that part of the country, and the Midlands never felt like home. Home for Frank was Hampshire, whereas I had sprung from the smoke and soot of St Helens, a grey town in what was then called Lancashire. Nowadays it has been re-named Merseyside, much to the disgust of its inhabitants.

We spent quite a lot of time in St Helens, since my widowed mother lived there, and it was not such a very long haul from Derby in our tinny second-hand Morris Eight. Whenever we went there, a little spastic girl who lived lower down the road used to come in and play with Anthony. She was a nice child, very gentle and affectionate, and really very intelligent. But she filled me with horror simply because she was not normal, and I hated abnormality of any kind. I despised myself for it, but every time that Margaret came to my mother's house, a wave of revulsion swept over me. I could not bear to see this malformed and inarticulate child play with my son; and I wished with all my heart that she would stay away.

Where we lived in Derbyshire we had no Catholic church, but attended Mass every Sunday in a hired room above a local pub. Among the fairly small congregation was a woman who came along each week with her three tall sons. I no longer remember the names of the other two, but the middle one, I know, was called John, and he was mentally handicapped. After Mass, the mother always made a fuss of this boy, taking his arm lovingly on the way home. Could she not see how repulsive he was? Did she, I wondered, see him as he really was, or were mothers of such children blinded by mother-love?

Like most people, I suppose, I was frightened by my rare encounters with the unthinkable. I cherished the belief that abnormality was something that happened to others. It couldn't possibly happen to me. But it did.

My second pregnancy was unremarkable, except that I was sick rather a lot, and was unusually nervy and irrational. (On the day when two gipsy-women had called at the house selling clothes-pegs and heather, Frank found me sitting under the stairs, terrified to death, when he came home from work.) For the birth itself I went over to St Helens, where I had booked an amenity bed in a small teaching-hospital near my mother's home. The night that I went into labour, I remember speaking to a friend on the telephone, and telling her that I was scared stiff, much more frightened than I had been the first time. And it wasn't really the pain that I was afraid of; there was a deeper, free-floating anxiety which I was at a loss to explain.

It was, in fact, a very difficult labour, followed by a high forceps delivery and a breech birth. I lost an inordinate amount of blood, and afterwards felt exhausted and ill, with none of the elation which I had felt when Anthony was born. The baby, another boy, was large, about 8lbs 12ozs, and when they showed him to me, declaring that he was beautiful, I shivered. Flesh seemed to droop off him, like an overcoat several sizes too large. To my own dismay, I felt no urge to take him in my arms or cuddle him. Instead I found myself turning away.

But as the days passed the initial feeling of revulsion passed too. I stopped noticing that he looked odd, or perhaps I decided that the oddness was all in my imagination. The nurses seemed genuinely enthusiastic about him, so I began taking my cue from them.

The trouble really began when I took him home, to my mother's, and tried to feed him myself, as I had done with Anthony enjoyably enough. He was insatiable, and although I had plenty of milk I was soon making up a bottle for him as well. First half-strength, then full-strength. It didn't matter how much I gave him, he went on crying and looking for more. In the end I gave up trying to breast-feed and put him onto extra-strength powdered milk. Not that it made much difference, but it was less exhausting for me. In retrospect it seems to me that he didn't stop crying for the next five years or so, but I suppose memory is playing me false. He *must* have slept sometimes.

We called him Paul Christopher. Friends assured us that once he had passed his first birthday he was bound to improve; and we waited longingly for that scarcely-to-be-believed-in day. Meanwhile he cried so long and so hard that he ruptured himself. He was only ten weeks old when our doctor discovered a hernia and decided that an immediate operation was called for. In a way, in spite of our obvious anxiety, the crisis was something of a relief. We thought that perhaps the mystery of his crying had been solved: he had had the hernia all the time without our suspecting it. Now perhaps he would stop crying. But the crisis came and went. Paul came out of hospital crying as hard as ever.

All that crying did not seem to affect his growth, and he was putting on weight fast. The sagging pockets of flesh were filling out, and in the foolish way that parents have we rather gloated over the phenomenal growth-rate. He was well ahead of the other babies at the local clinic, tipping the scales at a rate that caused eyebrows to rise. My mother-in-law spiked our complacency by hinting that this might be a cause for alarm rather than pride, but though we were both irritated by her seeming lack of perception we did not let it worry us for long.

Paul's first birthday arrived, that magic day when the crying was to stop and peace be restored. Alas for our hope. On that day he excelled himself, bawling for the entire day and reducing us all to a frazzle. So much for the prophecies of our friends; we should have to go on waiting.

Memories become blurred. At some time during the year that followed, I suppose he must have improved, because I remember a brief happy period when he was large and cheerful, with big china-blue eyes and masses of golden curls. An attractive child, mistaken by almost everyone for a girl. But our friends were even then beginning to be uneasy; they were noticing what we were too close to see: that Paul's blue eyes lacked intelligence, his nose was without a bridge, and the fingers on his chubby hands were disconcertingly spatula-shaped. He had done most of the expected things at the normal time – sitting up, cutting teeth, crawling, but one thing he had not yet done was talk. Instead of talking he made bizarre noises, rough, meaningless sounds which could not possibly be mistaken for speech. Unwittingly we joked about it. Anthony by this time was very advanced for his age and was bursting to go to school. Paul, we laughed, without any sense of foreboding, was certain to grace the bottom end of the class rather than the top. Perhaps he'd be good at football instead. A visiting social worker hinted that he might be deaf and suggested a hearing-test. But deafness was an unthinkable stigma, and I would not entertain the possibility of it.

About three months before Paul was two, I discovered, to my horror, that I was pregnant again. After the last experience, I could hardly welcome the prospect of another baby, but as I would not have considered having an abortion I had to get used to the idea. I was worried, though. With a restless three-year-old Anthony, and with Paul, my hands and days were completely full. And as if to underline the awkwardness of my new state, a few days later Paul was once again whipped off into hospital – again with a strangulating hernia.

In 1957 we had moved from Derbyshire to Hale, in Cheshire, which was much nearer to St Helens. Packing Anthony off to his grandmother's, I was free to visit the hospital as often as I was allowed. But though I went down there each day, nobody was able to tell me what the programme was likely to be. Paul had a wheezy chest, and as long as this was in evidence, it was not likely that he would be given an anaesthetic. It began to look as though he would be sent home untouched by medical hand, strangulating hernia or not.

The night when everything fell apart was a Tuesday in February, 1958, and every detail is etched like poker-work into my mind. The previous evening, the Sister in charge of the children's ward had asked if I would come early, as the house doctor would like a word with me. Somehow I presumed that the operation must be off, and I would be asked to bring Paul in each day as an out-patient.

Frank, who at this time was a manager with the Associated Octel Company in Northwich, was bringing a French colleague home to dinner, and fitting in the 6.30 visit to the hospital was a bit difficult. I had a mad scurry round before leaving, and at six o'clock put some sort of casserole into the oven. When I came back I should have to serve the meal immediately, and I wasn't taking any chances. No instinct told me, as I closed the front door and stepped out into the chill February night, that the door was closing on everything I had been: that this night would mark a new and fearful beginning. It seemed a night like any other, except that I was worrying about the dinner-guest.

When I got to the hospital, I didn't go to the ward, but asked the girl at the reception-desk to tell the house-doctor that I had arrived. I was directed into a small waiting-room on the ground-floor. Within a few minutes a white-coated doctor walked in, a sheaf of papers in his hand. He was a man of about thirty or so, recently arrived from some Middle Eastern country, with no more than a sketchy idea of the English language, and none at all of the language of diplomacy.

'You are the mother of . . . -er, -er . . .' He rifled idly through the papers in his hand. 'Ah, yes, Paul Craig?' I nodded.

'Of course, you know he is not normal,' he continued, in the same tone as before. His voice didn't ask a question, it made a statement.

NOT NORMAL. I stared at him blankly, my world slowly dissolving, all reality crystallising into that one murderous phrase which a stranger had just uttered with such casual ease. Not normal, not normal. My mind struggled with this alien concept, but could not grasp it. I felt buffeted by meaningless words which were heavy with menace. The voice went on, as though the world was still the same; it was a voice that struggled with a language that wasn't its own; a voice that lacked warmth and understanding. 'He has Höhler's Syndrome, a rare disease. In English you call it . . . -er, gargoylism.'

Through the thickening fog in my head I heard him, and into my punch-drunk consciousness swam hideous figures, straight off the pages of *Notre Dame de Paris* — gargoyles. Monstrous creatures carved in stone, water gushing out of their leering mouths. Oh God, not that; anything but that. Not my son.

Like a drunk crazily determined to walk a straight line if it kills him, I managed to dredge up some words. Very slowly, and as though from an immense distance, I heard my own voice ask the question which was already tormenting me. 'Will he be all right? I mean . . . his mind. Mentally?' I can still see that doctor shrug away the question. It was more than his scanty English could cope with — and in any case, there was no answer. 'I do not know. You must wait and see,' he said impatiently. And walked out.

It seemed like hours that I sat there after he had gone, not even trying to collect my scattering wits. Then in a drug-like stupor I dragged myself to the telephone and rang Frank. I don't think I did more than ask him to come for me. I wouldn't have found words to tell him what had happened.

In a trance I walked up the stairs to the children's ward, where I sat looking at Paul, with a heavy boulder where my heart had been. The scales fell from my eyes then with brutal suddenness. Self-deception was no longer possible; and I could see beyond doubting that Paul would never be as other children were. The stubby fingers, the too-thick lips, the flattened, bridge-less nose, the empty eyes, all pointed to this hateful but inescapable truth which we had gone on hiding from ourselves.

Frank came and took me home. It must have been terrible for him, but I was overwhelmed by my own misery and had no room for his. We had to go through the farce of a dinner-party, since our guest was a Frenchman who had nowhere else to go while waiting for his return flight from Ringway Airport, which was about five miles from where we lived. He knew something awful had happened, but we couldn't trust ourselves to talk about it. There was a spectre at that feast, and both the food and the effort at conversation nearly choked us.

When he had gone, we packed a suitcase apiece, and drove silently to my mother's. She had alerted her own doctor, an old family friend, and he had left a sedative for me. I took it with relief. It was a new product, which was just finding its way onto the market, and, because it was effective that first night and was easily available over the counter in chemists' shops, Frank went and bought a new supply of tablets for me next day. I went on taking them for several weeks. It was not until nearly two years later that the name of this product, Distaval, came into a shocking prominence, as one of the names for thalidomide. I was two months' pregnant and I took the tablets for at least a month. My blood runs cold at the thought of our narrow escape on this occasion: Mark, the child born in the December of that year, was a perfect baby.

There is a mental blank where the next few weeks must have been. All I remember is that after the first night I could shed no tears; a great freeze had descended on my emotional system. I was not, as some people believed, 'being wonderfully brave'; I was merely in an extended state of shock, with all my capacity for feeling paralysed. Perhaps it was nature's own kind of anaesthetic.

What triggered the change I don't remember, but I can never forget the night when the anaesthesia wore off, and I was left to wrestle with my blinding, asphyxiating terrors in a foretaste of hell. Despair rolled through me in waves as I looked into the future I did not want to face, and found it full of grotesque images: of enlarged heads, swollen abdomens and drooling mouths. The dreadful word 'gargoyle' was working its evil in me, filling me with self-pity and panic. From now on, I felt sure, I would see myself and be seen as some kind of pariah, the mother of a monstrous child. Friends would avoid me, and Paul would be taken away. Oddly enough, in view of all this self-pity, the fear of Paul's being dragged off to an institution was the blackest one of all. However agonising it might be to look after him, I could not face the prospect of letting him go.

It was the mother of an old school-friend who brought some sanity into my exhausted brain. 'Look,' she said briskly, 'if you ever do come to send him away, you and Frank will have arrived at the decision yourselves. No-one is going to drag Paul away screaming. For Heaven's sake, stop worrying about something that may never happen!' I knew she was right, and tried to cheer up. As I got up to leave, she came out with one of those pious clichés which at certain moments have tremendous force. 'God makes the back for the burden,' she offered, by way of consolation. The phrase impressed me, simply because it seemed so unlikely. God had picked a loser this time, one whose back was near to breaking under the strain.

Frank and I were both Catholics, conventional enough without being particularly enthusiastic. It didn't bother us much one way or the other, and at this stage it would not have occurred to us to look for any comfort in God or our Catholic faith. But to the Lancashire Catholics among whom I grew up (especially those of my mother's generation) life was nothing if not religion, and there were conventional pieties to cover almost any contingency. When things went wrong, God would put them right, though it must be admitted that, in their experience, he had very rarely done so. Nothing troubled their faith that God was a kind and loving Father; and doubt was alien to them, a shameful thing. My mother, I am quite sure, had never allowed even a momentary doubt to cloud her faith. Her own life had contained almost an unfair share of tragedy — she too had had a handicapped son, her husband had died of killer pneumonia at the age of thirty-two, and as his body was brought from their home in Scotland by train to Leeds for burial in the family vault, her young son had fallen from the train and been killed. Father and son were buried on the same day, while she was six months' pregnant with her second child, myself. When the time came for me to be born, she had quite plainly decided that she would die, because she left instructions that I was to be called Dolorosa, 'child of grief'. (I had another narrow escape there.) But that was her only concession to despair, and she never doubted that God was a loving God. Still less did she doubt His existence. My mother went every morning to Mass, and was never happier than when she was in church. Religion was not only a consolation, it was her talisman against life. Say the right prayers, make the right Novena, speak to the right saint, and all would be well. It was a child-like, untroubled faith, shared by many of her friends; and though on many occasions it reduced me to fury, I think now that such calm certainty is to be envied.

When an uncle in Dublin offered to pay all expenses if we wanted to take Paul to Lourdes, my mother was sure that her prayers had been answered. She genuinely believed that it was only a matter of time before Paul would be cured, and she urged us to accept my uncle's offer with all speed. We, of course, were much less sanguine, but, for reasons which were not the same as my mother's, we decided that we would go to Lourdes with Paul. We saw it as a gesture of sorts, and some kind of gesture seemed to be called for. Some symbolic act which would underline the separation of past from future. Besides, though neither of us came within a million miles of my mother's faith, we did believe that Lourdes had something to offer us. It was not the spring-water or the hope of miracles which drew us, but the feeling that in such a place we might be able to put our own problem in perspective. If nothing else, we would have visible proof that we were not alone.

There is in fact no better cure for self-pity than Lourdes. Where the sick and the maimed seem to pour together to proclaim their hope and their faith, or even just to share their fears, it is no longer possible to believe that one's own pain is either unique or unbearable. The discovery holds at least a measure of comfort.

We pushed, pulled and heaved Paul in a wheel-chair up, down and around, missing nothing. We went to the torchlight procession in the evening, and as a matter of course joined the massive crowds in the afternoon for the ritual blessing of the sick. It had not occurred to me to ask if I could join the group of mothers of sick children who were in a special reserved area at the front, near the altar, and generally Frank and I, with Paul, were somewhere in the middle of the heaving throng. One afternoon we had gone there as usual, and, as the priest came by, the sacred monstrance raised in his hands for blessing, the crowd fell silent. And in that pin-dropping silence Paul began to laugh. It was the laugh of a mad creature, a spine-chilling cackle that froze me to the spot with horror and shame. Suddenly an old peasant woman in a black shawl elbowed her way to where we stood and, eyes streaming with tears, lifted Paul out of his wheel-chair and held him up in her arms for the priest to bless. Paul was so astonished that he stopped laughing. It was an agonised moment, the significance of which did not escape me even at the time. It was another woman who had wept for my child, and who had taken compassion on me. Instinctively she had done what the moment demanded.

The woman's action pulled me up short. From that moment I shook myself out of my stupor, and scraped together some scraps of courage. I can't claim to have been inspired by anything more noble than common-sense and the urge to self-preservation, but they were enough for a start. The alternatives stared me in the face: either I could go on wallowing, over-protecting myself from hurt, becoming more and more bitter each day as I played the insidious chorus of 'why-should-this-happen-to-me?' as the background music to my life. Or — I could face the fact that what had happened was not going to un-happen, and might as well be come to terms with. I had been drowning in self-pity for long enough now to see where it was likely to lead. There was no doubt in my mind that I needed to change course.

Anyway, I was beginning to look forward to the new baby. A number of people had expressed horror — 'Surely you're not going on with it?' Relatives and friends were full of forebodings and fears, but somehow I knew with absolute certainty that their fears would be confounded. The new baby would be a consolation, not a fresh disaster. For once I was right. The birth was easy; the child, John Mark, everything I could have hoped for. With Paul at home, and Anthony a restless, energetic four-year-old, the new baby had to be propped up with a bottle and left to get on with it. He seemed to know from the start that he couldn't expect anything better, and to the relief of us all, he seemed to thrive on the inevitable neglect.

CHAPTER 2

Paul

DURING THE FIRST four years of Paul's life, there was little relief. A local girl, Jean (who became a lifelong and invaluable friend), came in once a week to help with the cleaning; but, except that I went shopping when she was there, I was almost completely housebound and Paul-bound. Frank and I had no social life. In those four years, at least, we never went out in the evenings. Dinner-parties, theatres, cinemas, were things once known but long-forgotten.

Once I had thought of myself as a woman with intellectual interests, but now my life was focused entirely on Paul. The other children too, of course, but mainly Paul. There was so much to do for him. Doubly incontinent, he was always having to be changed or cleaned up; he had to be watched constantly because his actions were unpredictable; and he had to be fed, like a baby, by hand, every spoonful shovelled into his mouth, since he could hold neither spoon nor cup for himself. And as he would chew everything a hundred times over, with maddening slowness, the time for getting the next meal ready was almost in sight by the time he'd got to the end of the previous one. He was a round-the-clock full-time job.

When I look back now on those early years with Paul, they

float in a mist of unreality. Can I really have got up two, three, four times every night to put him back to bed when he was chasing round and round his room like one possessed? I know that I did, and I remember thinking hopelessly that it would never end, that I'd go on doing that for ever and ever, or until the accumulating exhaustion got me down. Paul wouldn't even have a rest in the middle of the day to make up for the sleep he lost at night. He seemed never to get tired.

At first, I think it was other people from whom we suffered most, because it takes time to learn how not to mind, and you have to work at it. 'Old fish-face', the children in the road called after us, when I took him out in his pram. Paul didn't hear, and if he had heard he would not have understood, so why should I mind so much? I don't know, but I did. Sometimes the children just ran away when they saw us coming, and I had to steel myself to pretend that I hadn't noticed that the street was suddenly empty. Once I took Paul on a bus into nearby Altrincham, and I froze when I heard a woman behind me say: 'Children like that shouldn't be allowed on public transport. It's not right.' At that moment, I remembered, with a sharp stab of anguish, how I had felt about poor spastic Margaret.

I'm sure that it's fear which deprives well-intentioned people of their normal sensitivity. Or it may be that the shock of horror is so strong as to oust all other, more generous, feelings. Whatever the reason, I seemed to spend my life nerving myself against the barbs of those who certainly meant no harm, but who couldn't have hurt more if they had put their minds to it. There was a doctor, for example, an old family friend, who passed me by in the street one morning without a word, and with barely a nod of recognition. Next day he came round to the house sweating with outrage. 'An animal,' he almost shouted at me, 'that's what he is, an animal. Why don't you have him put away?' He was working something out of his system, and he didn't seem to realise what his words were doing to me.

Poor Paul, so gentle he would never consciously have hurt anything or anybody, but so clumsy that he couldn't help doing so. He infuriated Anthony. The latter was keen on making models of ships and aeroplanes, but there was no way in which the finished models could be kept safe from Paul's marauding hands. He would trample on the other children's toys and chew the wheels off their miniature motor-cars. Worse, he swallowed not only the rubber tyres, but every nut, bolt and screw he could lay hands on. We worried constantly, but the strange diet didn't seem to affect his health.

Sometimes he played in the garden, usually in a small glossy red car, which was his pride and joy. He went on shunting himself around in it, even when he had long since outgrown it. Cars were his great love, and he was always happy when he was in one. Going for a ride in our elderly Ford Consul used to exhilarate him, and he would sit bolt upright on the back seat, with a seraphic grin plastered all over his face. He regarded everything that happened in the car as entertainment laid on specially for his benefit. Once Frank inadvertently backed into a lamp-post and swore colourfully. Paul thought it was a marvellous joke, and rocked with an appreciative belly-laugh which didn't improve his father's temper.

We both did what we could for him, but sadly there was no question of a loving relationship between us. For love you need some kind of basic communication, a reciprocity. With Paul there was nothing. If he knew us at all, it was only as a vaguely friendly presence; there was no real recognition in his awareness of us.

Try as we would, we could never teach him that some things are just not done. He was incapable of learning from his frequent mistakes. If he pulled out the cutlery drawer from its moorings and proceeded to hurl its contents on to the floor, as he regularly did, you could give him a smack and put back the knives and forks a thousand times, but he never related the smack to what he had done. Cause and effect had no meaning for him; and neither had right and wrong; or dangerous and not-dangerous. In the end it seemed safer to limit him to one room, away from any obvious danger, with a few comparatively harmless toys to play with.

I still shudder when I recall the endless visits to hospital clinics, the hours of waiting for the ambulance 'milk-round', the countless requests from medical practitioners of varying eminence who all wanted permission to view this child with the rare and fascinating text-book disease. So rare that few of the doctors had come across it before; and they were eager to remedy the deficiency. 'There are so few of these cases around,' they would explain eagerly, bursting with professional excitement. 'If you let us examine Paul, you will be making your contribution to scientific research into his disease.' So Paul and I trudged (I didn't drive in those days) to one clinic after another, meeting students who stood in awed or bored astonishment, while their tutors prodded and poked and pointed out Paul's salient symptoms, referring to me throughout as 'the mother', as though I were not actually present in the room at all. Paul would play to the gallery on these occasions, acting the circus clown; while I sat there, positively crunching my teeth and reminding myself at intervals not to get sour.

When Paul was about four, I met a Belgian professor from Louvain who offered to try and cure him. Research on the subject of Höhler's Syndrome was more advanced on the continent than in Britain, and it was this man's speciality.

It was the first time we had been given any hope. Full of excitement, we decided to take Paul to Louvain. We didn't have a particularly auspicious beginning; for some reason we decided it would be better to fly from Heathrow rather than from Ringway, which was near our home. But by the time we arrived at Heathrow, fog had grounded the planes at every airport in the country — except Ringway. We had a nightmarish wait of nine hours, in the airport lounge with an increasingly ebullient and noisy Paul.

When we eventually arrived at the Clinique St Raphaël, where Paul was to be investigated, we found that specialists from all over Belgium were coming to see him; radiologists, ENT surgeons, neurologists, pathologists and cardiac consultants. One neurologist we met was quite excited. This man had written a medical tract on 'la pathogénie du gargoylisme', and was regarded as an international authority on the subject. He took me on one side to tell me about the little girl he had once treated, who had been completely paralysed by the disease. When given the treatment he had recommended, she was able to sit up and play with her toys, feed herself and even run about. Paul, he assured us, was in far better shape than this other child had been. In fact, Paul was the 'best' case of gargoylism he had ever seen; and he had every confidence that a cure could be found for him. I could hardly contain my own excitement.

Frank had come over to Louvain with us, but he had had to return to work in England at the end of the week. So after that time I was in constant attendance on Paul, who did not like Louvain or any of the things that were happening to him there. He hated and feared all the tests, blood-counts, injections, throat-swabs etc, and he refused to drink any of the concoctions he was offered so enticingly. His fears boiled over one morning when he was summoned for a cardiograph. He kicked, fought and bit the poor young nurse who was vainly attempting to hold him still. Mysteriously, sedatives only served to excite him and make him more uncontrollable than ever. There was nothing for it but to bring in reinforcements; in the end, six people held down the struggling Paul, one on each limb and one on each end. He fought like a fury, but he could not win. He cheered up later on though, when he went to have his photograph taken: he loved the electronic flashes, and wanted more.

On arrival at the hospital, I had been asked if I would mind taking Paul along one day to meet a few students. No, I said, of course I didn't mind. The presence of half-a-dozen or so students every time Paul was examined was by now a commonplace of life. A few more would make no difference.

So, early one morning, an escort came for Paul and myself. We were led down endless corridors, and across a quadrangle into another building, where we were ushered through a small door — straight onto the stage of a lecture theatre. I almost reeled with the shock of it, for, crowding the theatre in their serried ranks were the 'few' students who had been invited to see Paul — about five hundred of them. I suspect that the professors had issued a three-line Whip to get them there!

I sat there mute and choking, while Paul, hyper-excited by the tension and the spotlight so obviously focused on him, played up, charging round in concentric circles, and laughing his zany idiot laugh. With clinical detachment the lecturer began to point out the tell-tale signs. 'Observe this child,' he invited his audience. 'The spatulate hands are typical of Höhler's Syndrome. Notice too the protruding abdomen, the curvature of the spine . . .' On and on he went; and Paul gurgled and lurched around, paying his unwitting dues to science. I forced myself to stay seated, to stay calm, when every instinct in me wanted to run and run, far from that terrible place. 'They need to know all they can find out about this disease,' I told myself sternly, 'so they need Paul. It's in the interests of science.' Science, science, what the hell did I care about science? They could have pinned a Nobel medal for services to medical knowledge to my chest, and I should not have cared. All I wanted was to be a thousand miles away from that vast concourse of young people, to whom I was being indifferently pointed out as 'the mother' of a monstrous son. It was my moment of utter humiliation and abandonment; and it left a scar which has never healed.

It was all in vain, anyway. All our hopes came to nothing. But when I left the Clinique St Raphaël I didn't know that. The doctors permitted themselves a cautious optimism. Paul, they had concluded, was suffering from over-stimulation of the pituitary gland, and they had a suitable treatment worked out. It would involve some risky radiation therapy, but it just might work.

There was nothing either cautious or qualified about my own reaction to the verdict. Disregarding the enormous ifs and buts which hedged it round, I soared from despair to riotous hope. Floating on air, after my final interview with the eminent professor H., I dashed upstairs to the room I shared with Paul and recorded in my diary, with a naïveté which makes me blush to re-read it, 'Wonderful, wonderful news. We are going to see Paul improving in every respect, growing slimmer and taller, with finer features, better hearing, less excitability, more responsiveness. In fact, it sounds as though within five or six months we shan't recognise him.' Poor silly fool, I had heard only what I wanted to hear, and had entirely missed the crucial point that the achievement of this miracle was no more than an odds-on chance. With near-manic enthusiasm, I was busy planning Paul's future, doubtless speculating on whether he would go to Oxford or Cambridge.

Back home in Hale, a little more cold realism took over. The treatment recommended, irradiation of the tiny pituitary gland, situated at the base of the brain, was a tricky one and virtually unknown in Britain. It could not be undertaken lightly, on the say-so of a European doctor, however pre-eminent in his specialist field. But we were fortunate to have the Christie Hospital and Holt Radium Institute nearby in Manchester, and the doctors there agreed to give the treatment a trial on the National Health system. But they warned us that the risks were great, and they were ours alone. We asked them to go ahead.

And so, except when Frank could be free to take us by car, Paul and I started the ambulance milk-round again. Whole days were swallowed up in endless waiting – for the ambulance to come, for other patients who had to be collected en route, for the doctor to arrive, for the treatment to be given, for the anaesthetic to wear off, for the ambulance to return. Six hours was what it usually took, each week, with hope slowly dwindling to vanishing-point as Paul's condition did not alter. After a few months of this, when there was not the faintest sign of improvement, the doctors were unwilling to subject Paul to further radiation. Reluctantly we had to face the fact that there had been no cure, no improvement, but possibly some deterioration. It is a fact that Paul lost the one phrase he had so far been able to master. After the treatment, we never again heard him say – 'Bye-bye'.

Life with Paul went on being traumatic, but by 1960 there was a welcome relief. My mother and my Aunt Betty both retired, my mother very unwillingly from her job as a much revered local headmistress, and President of most of the teachers' and head teachers' organisations in St Helens; my aunt much more enthusiastically from a strenuous post in industrial nursing. Both were now free, with time on their hands and plenty of energy to expend. They decided that I ought to be the main beneficiary, and were very anxious to help.

Betty was the practical one, and she was wonderful with Paul. She had no illusions about what he could or could not do, and she knew he would never be any different. She simply accepted him as he was and did everything in her power to make his life a happy one. My mother was good with him too, but she had never come to terms with the situation. She had taken refuge in a sort of fantasy world in which Paul was no more than 'delicate'; and she was quite happy with this version of the truth. Her own first child, my brother Tony, had been, as far as we were able to make out, very like Paul, but my mother had never accepted the truth about him either. He had died before I was born, and in my early years my mother constantly told me how good Tony was, how helpful, even how clever. Her fantasy even extended to the manner of his death. He had died, she said, of appendicitis. It was left to others to tell me that he had been severely sub-normal, and that he had been killed when falling out of a train. The various doctors who made a study of Paul and who asked about my family history, got no change out of my mother. I could tell them the little I knew or suspected, but it didn't amount to much. *She* would admit nothing.

Betty — or Beb — as the children have always called her — was not my aunt at all, or indeed any relation. She was the nursing-sister in charge of the maternity ward where I was born. My mother had gone into the hospital to await my arrival and what she hoped would be her own demise. Betty had sympathised, taken special care of her, and afterwards had come to visit her at home. She was glad to make a friend, since her own home was in Yorkshire, and she had only just come to St Helens. Years later, when Betty decided to leave hospital work and take a job in industry, she moved in with us as a temporary arrangement — and stayed. We were a rather fearsomely all-female household: my mother, Gertrude, the sister with whom she had gone to live when my father died, Betty and myself. (The only men who ever came near were an occasional uncle and the parish priest.) I was always fond of Betty and was closer to her than to my mother. She and I would talk and share secrets, something I never did with my mother, of whom I was always in awe. The discovery, when I was ten or so, that Betty was not a blood-relation, was one of the most miserable moments of my childhood. I felt betrayed.

My mother had not even told Betty the truth about her son, Tony: she too had been told how clever he was. Then one day she met an old doctor who asked her if she had known my mother when Tony was alive. She said she hadn't. 'It was such a mercy he died,' the old man said, 'he would have been a millstone around his mother's neck.' But when Betty reported this strange conversation, my mother refuted it hotly. She had quite convinced herself of Tony's normality.

So it was quite logical that she would see the Paul-situation through the same rose-tinted spectacles: she could not bear very much reality. But she loved Paul, and though she could not do for him what Betty could, she did her best. After their retirement, they both became frequent visitors to our house, though it was Betty who came more often. Betty, in fact, had offered to come for three days each week to look after Paul while I took a part-time job. The Headmistress of the school where Anthony was now in the kindergarten had asked if I could come and teach Latin in the senior school, and with Betty's heroic help I should be able to. It wasn't the teaching in itself that was so attractive. It was the opportunity it presented of escaping at least for a few hours from my own four walls. It was a way of preserving my sanity. Thank God for Betty.

CHAPTER 3

Despair

PAUL WAS GETTING on for five and in the normal way of things would have been going to school. One of the tortures inflicted on parents of mentally-handicapped children at that time was the ordeal by letter. A school doctor was sent to the house to investigate the child's suitability for normal schooling (in spite of his or her very obvious non-suitability), and then would follow a formal letter, stating explicitly that the child was sub-normal and therefore unable to benefit from normal education (the word they used was 'ineducable'). Everybody concerned was well aware of this fact before the process was set in motion, but for some reason it had to be spelled out, the i's dotted, the t's crossed, and the parents' noses thoroughly rubbed in the dirt. Most parents resented this official humiliation, but they could do nothing about it. When our turn came, and I was told to expect the arrival of a school doctor, I bowed to the inevitable. It was only a routine visit after all.

But it did not turn out quite as expected. I have often hoped that the school doctor who came to see Paul that day was not typical of her species. There she stood on the doorstep, a large, bouncy, tweedy woman whose burly torso positively heaved with excitement. We had not met before, but she absolved herself from the courtesy of introductions. I had barely got the front door open before she announced with breathless fervour: 'I can't wait to see this child. Do you think he might possibly be a cretin?'

Blind rage swept over me, and I would have given much to slam the door, or, better still, my clenched fist, in her jolly face. How does it happen that doctors, who presumably set out on their careers because they see themselves as healers, become so frequently insensitive to other people's pain? For years Paul and I were no more than objects to be examined under a microscope, two animate creatures of momentary interest to medicine. It never seemed to occur to anyone, or if it did it did not seem to matter, that we were also sentient human beings who could be badly hurt. It was difficult learning to be a non-person, but I was learning fast. Building up a hard shell within which to shelter was part of the process of learning. The only sure way to protect myself from hurt was by refusing to be hurt at all, refusing to notice, refusing to care. Ordinary human feelings were becoming a luxury I could not afford.

That doctor had almost penetrated my defences, but my public self-control was still armour-plated. So I forced a smile and asked her in, and we began, as one inevitably did, on the old, old questions. Who is he, what is he, why is he, when, how, where? The questions rolled off an endless cyclic conveyor belt, and were answered as mechanically as they were asked. If I had been better organised, I should have made out a list of questions and answers, and made photostats of them to hand out. They were always the same. We always began at the beginning, at pregnancy if not at conception, and worked right through. No-one ever came pre-armed with the relevant facts, there had never been any liaison with previous questioners (even when they came from the same hospital or local authority), no data bank of information was ever consulted, if indeed any existed. We always started with a *tabula rasa*. The game began on square one, and our opponents were always the victors, if one could judge by the flushed face and air of triumph they wore on departure.

Even with Betty's help, the strain was beginning to tell. I was getting to the end of my resources. The climax came one day when

I was alone in the house with Paul. I went into the room where he was playing and found that not only had he soiled himself, but he was cheerfully smearing the faeces all over the wall. Ours was a largish Edwardian house, with half-landings recessed into a sweeping staircase. Holding Paul under the armpits I began to drag him up the stairs towards the bathroom, paying no attention to his squawks of protest. We had reached the first half-landing when he began to cough. I stopped there, but the coughing fit grew worse. Suddenly, to my horror, his breathing became jerky, he began to choke, and his face went black. I was terrified, stuck as I was half-way up the stairs and nobody within earshot. With a strength born of desperation, I pushed and pulled him up the remaining stairs and inside the bathroom. Shutting the door on him, I fled downstairs to the telephone to order an ambulance. Then I rushed madly up again to try and get him cleaned up.

The ambulance came. Unfortunately, in my panic, I had given no details over the telephone. I had omitted to say that Paul was breathing only with difficulty; and the ambulance arrived without the vital cylinder of oxygen. The minutes seemed like hours as we waited for the second ambulance to arrive, and Paul's condition got worse with every breath he tried to take.

The oxygen arrived in the nick of time, and Paul was taken off to hospital to recover from the first of many bronchial convulsions. He came out within a week, fully restored and entirely cheerful. But my nerves were raw. The problem of Paul had me utterly beat.

In the summer of 1962, we took the family to the seaside. But I could not relax; the change of environment only made me more conscious that I had come to the end of the road in more ways than one. I had lost sight of myself as a person, I viewed the future with fear, and I realised with a shock that even my rather vague religion had deserted me. I no longer believed in God. What more was there to lose? Self-pity, always lurking in the background, came surging in on a flood-tide. Life was absurd and meaningless, was it not, a dirty-tricks department writ large? And the whole idea of a loving God was a hollow sham, a cosmic joke worthy only of Paul's crazy laughter. But there was no way out of the impasse, and I could only go on compounding the meaninglessness. Suicide, even if I had not been the devout coward I in fact was, would only have shifted the whole ghastly mess into someone else's court, and I was not far enough gone to accept that as an answer.

Frank suggested that I should go away on my own for a week. I jumped at the idea, but couldn't think where to go. I had always disliked holidays, and couldn't face the thought of one on my own, especially in the depressed state I was in. Perhaps I could go and make myself useful somewhere, offer my services to a charitable organisation, sink my own troubles in the contemplation of someone else's. But I had never been a very useful sort of person; apart from a flair for cooking, my domestic talents were almost non-existent. Still, I *could* cook, so I had something to offer. But to whom?

I don't really know why or how, but somehow that same evening I found myself alone in a church. Maybe I'd gone there to give the Almighty a last chance. Or maybe I'd just gone there for a good howl in private. Anyway, there was no-one else in the church, and it was a fine echo-ey building. As even when I'm quite alone I tend to be self-conscious, I didn't howl, but muttered a defiant if muddled: 'Damn you, you don't exist, but I hate you.' Then I burst into tears, and threw decorum to the winds. 'All right,' I heard myself shouting, 'if you do exist, show me a way out. For a start, what the hell am I to do next?' After this unbridled exhibition, I was startled by the noise I was making, and ran out of the church at top speed.

Frank was in an armchair reading when I got back to the house, still tear-stained. My mother and Betty had the children in another room, where they were watching television. We had, as we always did, brought with us enough books to withstand a siege, some of them selected from the local library by Frank. Idly I picked up one of these and looked at the title: *The Face of Victory* by Group Captain Leonard Cheshire VC. I could see that it was autobiographical, and I put it down again with a grimace. Cheshire, the bomber pilot VC, had had a lot of publicity during and after the Second World War, and I was always suspicious of popular heroes. Not content with what others had written about him, I thought scornfully, he was now writing about himself. What an egoist the man must be. Frank saw the look on my face and more or less read my thoughts. 'Don't just put it down,' he urged. 'I think it would interest you. At least, give it a try.'

I had picked the book up again, and was rifling through the pages as he was speaking. As we went on talking, I stood with my thumb on one page somewhere near the end. When I put the book down it came open at that page. I stared at it, and saw that it was full of addresses, of Cheshire Homes For The Sick, where voluntary help was required. Right at the bottom, one address stuck out; a Home run not by Leonard Cheshire but by his wife, Sue Ryder. Home For Concentration Camp Survivors, Cavendish, Suffolk, I read. As I stood looking down at it, I realised that one part of my prayer in the church had been answered. I had demanded to know what I was to do next, and now I knew. I was going to Suffolk.

CHAPTER 4

Cavendish

IT WAS NOT just an off-the-cuff decision to step into the unknown. As soon as I saw that address, I knew I had to go there; the way had already been prepared — when I was in Louvain.

The address took me back with a jolt to the Clinique St Raphaël, where I had spent so many interminable evenings after Paul had been put to bed. I couldn't go out and leave him, so I had taken to pacing the corridor outside our room, up and down aimlessly for hours on end, past the various wards and single rooms.

One night I saw a woman wheeled on a trolley into one of the emergency rooms, and was forcibly struck by her gaunt appearance and her sunken staring eyes. They were the eyes of a woman haunted by some appalling and unforgettable suffering. The next night I heard a woman scream, and knew who it must be. It was an unearthly screeching sound, unlike anything I had ever heard, a sort of banshee wail; and it filled me with an unbelievable dread.

The screaming continued for an eternity of ten minutes or so, then stopped as suddenly and as eerily as it had started, leaving behind a silence that was full of nameless horrors. A man who was pacing in the other direction must have seen the fear in my eyes, and he came to join me. 'She was in Ravensbrück,' he said quietly, with the air of one who has explained everything. 'Ravensbrück?' I asked blankly, as much in the dark as ever. The man looked taken aback by my obvious ignorance, and proceeded to tell me more. Ravensbrück, he explained, was the Nazi concentration camp north of Berlin, where women and children were sent. Many of these had been subjected to medical experimentation, and many thousands had died there. (The official figure was in fact 92,000.) This woman had been one of the guinea-pigs on whom experiments had been carried out. She was a sorry part of the human wreckage which had survived such camps, as much dead as alive. The hospital was as much her home as any other place, since she spent more time there than anywhere else.

His words sent ice-cold shivers coursing along my spine. I would have walked away if I could, but I didn't dare. Mentally I resisted him. Why did the man have to tell me such things? Couldn't he sense that I didn't want to hear them? The war had been over for fifteen years, its effects had been neatly tidied away. When it had come to an end, I was still a child, and the stories coming out of Belsen and other places of that kind had scarcely troubled me, so great was my relief that the war was over at last. I didn't want to listen to atrocity stories now. Hadn't I enough troubles of my own?

But my companion, a man of about forty-five from Arlon, had no intention of letting me off. For four years he too had suffered in a concentration camp, Neuengamme, where only the strongest had survived. In spite of myself, I had to listen horror-struck to his nightmare memories: of the barely-alive prisoners piling the dead each morning into trucks and throwing the corpses into a specially-prepared ditch; of the six ounces of bread and two frost-bitten potatoes on which the prisoners were forced to perform slave labour. Sometimes, my friend recalled, the SS cook would fling a crust into their midst, for the sadistic pleasure of seeing starving men scratch and claw at each other in the scramble to stay alive. Rather than starve, they had eaten filth, keeping themselves alive on their own excrement. My friend had come through, but at a price. In the fifteen years which had elapsed since the Liberation, he had continued to suffer from severe intestinal disorders which forced him to spend one month out of every four in this hospital.

When he eventually let me go, I went back to my room and wrote in my diary, 'I shall not go out there again to-morrow. If these things happened I prefer not to know about them.' I was as good as my own cowardly word; I did not see the man from Arlon again; but I found that he was not so easy to forget. What he had told me could not be untold, and against my will it had had its effect. Every word he had spoken came unbidden to mind as I stood gazing at that address in Suffolk. With an uncanny feeling that the course of my life was being directed by powerful forces, I sat down and wrote to whoever was in charge at the Home for Concentration Camp survivors in Suffolk, offering my services for a week as bed-maker, and mentioning that I could cook. In the circumstances, it was no surprise at all when the reply came by return: Come as soon as you can, we need you urgently.

Wearing my best suit and carrying a large suitcase bulging with clothes, I passed the village duck-pond, turned into the drive of the Sue Ryder Home, and caught my first glimpse of the idyllic, pink-washed sixteenth-century house which sheltered physically handicapped patients, others who had been mentally ill, and a handful of survivors of Nazi tyranny. It was to become my own spiritual home over the next four years. The September sun was shining, and I was filled with a vague euphoria not entirely free of self-congratulation. I had come to indulge in a bout of do-gooding, and was all dressed-up to play the role of lady bountiful.

Without warning, a female figure erupted out of a mullioned window on the ground floor of the house, and hurled itself at me. 'Thank God you've come,' said the girl fervently, casting a baffled glance at my enormous suitcase, before rushing on at the same breathless speed: 'You must be the new slave. Look, the bathroom in the extension is flooded, and the water's seeped into Edward's room, and the whole place is in a terrible mess. Would you mind frightfully going over there and seeing what you can do? Good. I'll go and get a bucket and mop.' And with that she was off, leaving me feeling as bewildered as Alice accosted by the White Rabbit. I looked down at my good suit, and suddenly saw how ridiculous I must look, standing there kitted out for the London Hilton rather than for flooding bathrooms in deepest Suffolk. The girl was now back with mop and bucket. Resignedly I dumped the suitcase on the gravel, and went off in the direction in which she had pointed, mop-handle tucked under Windsmoor jacket sleeve. 'By the way,' the girl shouted after me, 'I believe you can cook. Well, when you've finished cleaning up over there, do you think you could manage supper for seventy? We've got a whole group of survivors over from Poland on the Foundation's Holiday Scheme, as well as the Bods who are always here.'

That was my introduction to Cavendish (not untypical, as I later discovered). I was sorely tempted to turn right round and head for home. Instead I meekly went off to tackle the flood.

Two days, several hundredweight of peeled potatoes and many gallons of soup later, I felt I had been there all my life.

Cavendish is an unlikely backdrop to the lives of the people who have found refuge there. It is a peaceful, sleepy village which minds its own business and does not take all that kindly to foreigners. Sue Ryder's mother had lived in the converted farm-house for several years and was much loved in the village, but when Sue moved in with her patients, Mrs Ryder, amid general mourning, went to live in the near-by village of Clare.

Sue Ryder, a tiny bird-like woman who looks vulnerable but is about as fragile as granite, was an attractive girl in her late teens when the Second World War broke out. She joined the exclusive FANYs (First Aid Nursing Yeomanry) and through them was seconded to Special Operations Executive (SOE), the highly secret organisation responsible for training agents in the difficult techniques of armed resistance and sabotage. During parachute training Sue unfortunately injured her back, and, unable as a result to be dropped behind enemy lines, she had to be content with a less active role. For the most part she worked with young Poles of both sexes who had volunteered to return to their stricken country and fight the invader from within. These young men and women knew very well that they were volunteering for almost certain torture and death, but nothing could deter them. To the young Sue they were giants; and they taught her a lesson that she would never forget: that the individual human being can do the apparently impossible, if only he cares enough.

Long before the war was over, Sue had come to realise that its aftermath would be terrible – for the whole of Europe, and in particular for those countries of Central Europe which had been occupied. As early as 1942 she had made up her mind to do relief work when the fighting stopped. 'I couldn't see, with devastation on that scale,' she says, 'how it could ever be cleared up.' She was quite prepared to give the rest of her life to caring not only for those who survived the holocaust but for the sick and disabled of all age groups in those countries where the need was greatest. Her work, she determined, would provide a 'Living Memorial' to those who had died, many of them anonymously, in two World Wars.

In the years that followed the peace she worked in different parts of Europe with various international relief organisations – until their mandate ran out. And when it did, she stayed on. 'How could I go?' she asks. Some of those who still needed her help then were adults and children in Germany who could not return to their own countries because those countries had been annexed by the Soviet Union; and there were others elsewhere who, although not exiled from their homes, were desperately trying to clear away rubble and rebuild their shattered cities and towns, battling against heavy odds to reconstruct the ruins of their lives. Then there were the non-German prisoners adrift in Germany: these were young men who had been deported to Germany at an early age and who had known only violence, brutality and the ethic of the jungle. When the war was over and they were released from the concentration and labour camps in which they had been held, they emerged to face a hostile world. Unemployed (they had no work permits) and hungry, they took the law into their own hands and lived off their wits until they were caught.

Sue began a long and lonely struggle on their behalf, battling against the German authorities for residence permits, permissions to emigrate, for jobs, homes, compensation, hospitalisation and remission of prison sentences. Initially she had 1,200 prisoners in her care – 'Boys', she called them. She would visit them in prison, taking with her the essentials – drawing-paper and text books – which were denied them by the prison authorities. As a senior colleague of hers once told me, 'those boys weren't allowed any occupational activities at all, but that cut no ice with Sue. She took things in and out of the prisons the whole time!' The fact was that Sue wanted to help the prisoners become people again; and if red tape got in the way, she would cut it.

Sue had lived in the displaced persons' camps and had made their despair her own. She knew only too well that in the face of such bottomless misery, official charity was simply not enough, that what the stranded men and women in the camps needed above all was an acknowledgment that they were still human, and accepted as such by other human beings. Their lost self-respect could not be restored by official hand-outs, it was personal service that was needed. Having decided that that alone was what counted, the young Sue Ryder determined that, whatever the cost to herself, she would give that service. (And that the cost was high no one can doubt – there are all too many signs on her face.) And so, at the time when the various international relief organisations were packing up to return home, Sue began a punishing routine: visiting camps, hospitals, prisons in an area extending from the Danish border to Austria, she lived on apples and flasks of coffee, travelling over a thousand miles a week in a small, anonymously donated, Austin car which she nicknamed 'Alice'.

'She was absolutely right', comments Joyce Pearce who, like Sue, was working in Germany in those days. 'Everyone else seemed to think of the homeless as a mass problem to be dealt with by mass solutions. But Sue's personal approach was the only real way in which they could be helped.'

She called them 'Bods' — a name which falls strangely, even harshly, on our ears today, but which was meant as a mark of deepest respect. For it was as 'Bods' that the young wartime resistance agents had been affectionately known by those who had worked with them, and for Sue the name was tinged with heroism. Her 'Bods', homeless and disabled flotsam of the war, adrift in the country which had caused their troubles in the first place, needed now to be found a permanent home. Every time she returned to England, Sue searched for suitable places, but she could find nothing that she could afford. Then one day her mother, always a staunch ally, made the suggestion which had already half-occurred to her daughter: why not bring some of them to Cavendish?

They came. Marie, for example, who had lost both her arms when thrown from a moving train by her SS guards, yet who polished furniture with her feet and did fine embroidery with the needle held in her teeth; white-haired Pani Jozefa, in her early fifties yet looking like an old woman of eighty — in Auschwitz for more than three years, and sent out from there on a death march which few were meant to or did survive; Edward, a Polish lawyer of distinction, who had languished for six months in the infamous Pawiak prison in Warsaw, before being despatched to five years in Dachau and Flossenburg; Mr Bor who put his whole heart into making chicken-meal for the Cavendish hens, as he tried to blot out his past. Mr Bor had been imprisoned in the Warsaw Ghetto, from which he and a handful of others had managed to escape through a sewer. Joining the official underground, he became a vital link in an escape chain which smuggled Jewish children out of the Ghetto. But the Gestapo caught him, and sent him to Auschwitz.*

* See pp. 49–50.

Then there was Kasi, still a young man in his thirties, who had, in his teens, been beaten up by SS guards using rifle butts, so that he was now no more than an animated vegetable, mute and semi-paralysed. I remember vividly trying to feed him one night, putting a spoonful of fish into his mouth, while salty tears ran down my face into the spoon. All the ills of the world seemed to be concentrated here in Cavendish, massively ignored by the world outside. There were residents who suffered from epilepsy-type attacks, the result of earlier skull injuries; others with dissemin-ated sclerosis or psychiatric disorders: schizophrenia, paranoia or delusions great and small. These men and women had reached this quiet Suffolk back-water by way of some of the greatest hells ever devised on earth, Belsen, Buchenwald, Majdanek, Ravensbrück and Auschwitz, and, on the way, everything that had given their lives value and meaning had been stripped from them. There were others, too, who had come here after months and years in imper-sonal long-stay hospitals, where they had been 'blocking' the beds needed for short-term 'acute' patients; and some who, foreign nationals, had lived and worked in England since the war, before disablement or mental breakdown struck.

As long as I live, I shall never be able to forget that first visit to Cavendish, because it changed my whole life. It was all so unexpected and disturbing. In theory I knew that I was coming to a home for the disabled. In practice I had little idea of what that meant. I was mentally unprepared to discover, in this peaceful part of rural England, an island of pain, an enduring reminder of man's extreme brutality towards his fellow-man. And an even more forceful reminder of the outside world's capacity for for-getting what it does not want to remember — except in terms of harmless statistics. Cavendish was a place where statistics had become persons.

At first, as I peeled potatoes by the bucketful, sliced innumerable cabbages for the *bigos* beloved of Poles, and immersed myself elbow-deep in beetroots for the inevitable *barszcz* ('Are your arms always that colour?' asked Leonard Cheshire with interest, catching me at it in the kitchen), I was aware only of the terrible suffering which these people had endured, and of the limbo in in which they now only half-existed. The shock of the discovery was tremendous. But after a few days, I began to notice something else: I was actually singing as I peeled those eternal spuds. The amazing truth took some time to sink in: Cavendish, against all the odds, was a happy place. Its serenity was catching. It was good to be there.

Slowly I came to know the 'Bods'. I would watch them in the morning, at the start of another, for them painful, day. Mr Bor would be stirring up messes for his chicken-pails. Then along came Mr Crab, shuffling with difficulty on two sticks towards the dining-room for breakfast. 'Good morning, Sister,' he shouted cheerfully to Margaret, the resident nurse. 'A beautiful morning, Mr Crab,' she replied, using the nickname by which he was always known. 'Fanta-a-a-stic morning, ma-a-arvellous sunshine,' echoed 'Bubi', a Czech originally from Prague who was crippled with arthritis, but was noted for his sunny disposition. ('Bubi' played the piano like an angel, despite his crippled hands, and on these occasions he was accompanied by his great friend Ben, a Hungarian, on the trombone. Bubi's room looked out over the tree-fringed pond and what he called God's garden. 'There is my chapel, it is all that I need,' he would say, pointing to the garden. When he was well enough he would spend hours looking out at it, but when he was sad, or the pain was too acute, he turned his back on it, as though he could not bear to look on beauty. Bubi loved life in all its manifestations. 'A party,' he cried delightedly, when I turned up to see him at Cavendish shortly before he died, 'we must have a party to celebrate. Go quickly to the shop, Mary, and get some ham.' Laboriously he counted out the money for me. When I came back, he had magicked a couple of plates onto the bed. I could see that he was in pain, but nothing could have damped his spirits that afternoon, as he laughed and sang, and we ate our ham with dry biscuits, and toasted each other with Nescafé. It is my last memory of him, and one that I shall always treasure.)

Little Mr Szkoda followed Bubi into the dining-room, coming in whistling from the garden where he had been digging potatoes. 'Little man with a hoe' is how I remember him. And Kasi brought up the rear of the procession, shambling along awkwardly like an injured bear, winking surreptitiously at one of the pretty 'slaves' who was serving breakfast.

The 'slaves', as the helpers called themselves, were pretty remarkable too. They were all girls who were capable of holding down good jobs with an excellent salary. Yet they were working full-time (round the clock, in shifts, not nine-to-five) at Cavendish for nothing, or for a derisory two pounds a week pocket-money. They were there because they could not conceive of being anywhere else, because they believed in the value of what they were doing. There was something very special about Cavendish, its people and its atmosphere, which called forth this kind of special devotion.

As I talked to the 'Bods', I began to understand that what I had stumbled on at Cavendish was a kind of miracle. These people had, as it were, walked into the valley of death, and out the other side, with their courage and their sense of humour intact. They were rich human beings, with no bitterness left in them. For years they had walked with starvation, torture, cold, loneliness and agonising loss. Yet they seemed to be beyond hatred. To me it was bewildering.

In fact I was being shaken up and turned inside out. Suddenly it seemed as though my whole life had been leading up to this one time and this one place, to which I had been sent (I was entirely sure of it) in order to come to terms with the problem of suffering in my own life. Somewhere here there was a key, and I must set myself to find it. I had gone to Cavendish to get away from my own troubles, to sort myself out by offering help to someone else, doubtless in the pious hope that such undeniable signs of virtue would bring their own reward. But all I had been doing was looking for a place to hide. What had I imagined I could possibly give these people, when there was nothing in me to give? Hadn't I been systematically surrounding myself with impregnable defences, protecting myself from hurt? I hadn't overcome self-pity, I'd merely been keeping it at bay; it was lying low just outside my defences, biding its time, gathering strength for the next, more vicious attack.

The survivors showed me another possibility: that one could live with pain precisely by not fighting it; by not denying its existence, by taking it into oneself, seeing it for what it was, using it, going beyond it. Precisely how I could not yet see; but I knew it could be done. I had tangible proof. If men could laugh after Auschwitz, then surely there was hope. My cure had not yet got under weigh, but by great good fortune I had found both the right doctor and the only possible medicine.

What happened to Mr Bor a few years later is worth the telling, if only to show that fairy-tales still happen. Stefan Bor, left an orphan at a very early age, had been brought up in the family of a friend, and in his teens had fallen in love with Zofia, the daughter of the house. Before they could marry, they were overtaken by the war and the Occupation; both of them joined the Resistance; both were arrested. They were sent to different camps and they never saw each other again.

Or at least they hadn't, when I first went to Cavendish. Mr Bor looked after his ducks and hens, and from time to time he spoke about Zofia, who was, he said, his sister. One day, he added, when he had acquired British nationality, he would go to Poland and look for her. An old man's dream, we thought.

But that is exactly what he did. When he was nearly seventy, Stefan Bor became Stephen Burton, and went to Poland in search of his lost love. Against all the odds he found her; and against longer odds still, she had waited for him, sure that he would come.

When he returned to Cavendish, he revealed to an astonished Sue Ryder that Zofia was not his sister but was now his fiancée, and that she was coming to England to marry him. Zofia too was nearly seventy when she left home to make the historic journey. Landing alone at Harwich, she walked towards her waiting husband-to-be, scattering handfuls of the Polish soil she had brought with her for the purpose, enacting a typically Polish bit of symbolism. 'Your country, she is now my country,' she announced with pride.

On 31st October 1967, almost thirty years late, Zofia and Stephen Burton were married in the timbered chapel of Clare Priory in Suffolk, a long way from Auschwitz. No couple ever approached the altar with greater faith in their future together; they had already proved their total steadfastness.

They were together for seven years – that is, until Stefan/ Stephen died in 1974. His widow is still living at the Sue Ryder Home in Cavendish.

CHAPTER 5

Paul Goes to Poland

THE JOURNEY HOME from Cavendish after that first visit passed as though in a dream. I was high — on memories. The links I had forged in that one short week, the friendships I had made, would be impossible to break. Among others, I had got to know Leonard Cheshire, who was at home recuperating from a serious illness; and my earlier suspicion that he was nothing more than a glamorous play-boy had given way to an enduring affection and admiration.

But although I had seen much less of his wife, Sue Ryder, during that week, she was the one for whom I wanted to work. I wanted to tell the world about her and what she was doing for that handful of people from a forgotten world. Frank came to meet me at the station, and as we drove home I began to try and explain. But I stopped in mid-stream because of the hopelessness of conveying the enormity of what I felt. 'So you've found your life's work,' he commented with a smile. I interrupted him sharply, near to tears, 'Please don't laugh. It's very important.' 'Who's laughing?' he asked. 'I can see something has happened to you. Tell me about it, and I'll try to help.' He really meant it, and his words were a tremendous relief.

From then on, I became a one-track bore, and it is amazing

that friends did not desert me in droves. All conversations led to Sue Ryder and the people at Cavendish. It became a matter of extreme urgency to let everyone know about them. An initial trickle of invitations to speak became a flood, and soon I found myself talking to most of the local organisations in Cheshire and Lancashire — Rotary Clubs, Inner Wheels, Townswomen's Guilds, Ladies' Circles, Round Tables, Women's Institutes. Fortunately I discovered a hitherto unsuspected talent for public speaking, and for getting across to people — it must have been because I cared about the subject so deeply. But, however much I cared, I could have got nowhere without the enthusiastic support and continuing commitment of the people to whom I was speaking. Slowly a network of support groups came into being, first in the Manchester area and then beyond, all of them intent on raising funds for Sue Ryder, not only for the Home at Cavendish, but for the sister-Home at Hickleton Hall near Doncaster, which had the advantage of being almost on the doorstep, and for Sue's work in Poland and Yugoslavia as well. Girls from the school where I taught (and from others where I gave talks) went in groups to help out at Cavendish or Hickleton in the holidays, and a few of them became as addicted as I was, going back again and again. One girl decided to train to be a nurse, and eventually returned to Hickleton as a nursing sister.

At first the support-groups held the usual coffee mornings, bazaars and lunches, until in 1963 we opened our first second-hand shop. To-day charity shops dot the High Streets of Britain like measles, but at that time they were relatively unknown. Sue Ryder had always been keen on the idea, and on the day that she was offered rent-free premises in Manchester she rang me up. 'Do take it, Mary,' she urged. 'We could make anything from £7–£10 a week, and we can't afford to turn away that kind of money.' Our marvellous Manchester supporters, led by Bessie Galpin and Eileen Ruhemann, leaped at the chance, organised themselves into relays, and within a short while had opened a shop in Rusholme (Manchester). This was almost immediately followed by three more in the Manchester area and eventually by dozens more throughout the country. We sold out everything we had on the first afternoon, but it didn't seem to matter. Miraculously we had found an ever-lasting fountain. Goods to sell, and volunteers eager and willing to help kept coming, and in that first week we made not £7 but nearly £100 — mainly on junk. That was fifteen years ago. Since then the Rusholme shop and others like and unlike it — in wealthy areas as well as poor — selling new articles as well as second-hand — have become the mainstay of the Sue Ryder Foundation. They are very different from each other in scope and merchandise but they have one thing in common. All of them make money for the relief of suffering.

But the shops were not my forte. Leaving them to others more capable, and with more stamina, I went on with the talks. Nervous as a kitten beforehand, I felt sick to the pit of my stomach, at least until I began to speak. Whether it was an audience of hundreds in Manchester's Free Trade Hall or a huddle of two on a foggy night in somebody's shed, I was equally nervous. But the warmth of response made up for the agony of nerves.

Some knew what I had come for, others did not, and in the beginning could not care less. 'It is my privilege to introduce Mrs Craig, a . . . er . . . star of stage, screen and radio,' announced one headmistress, realising too late that she hadn't a clue who I was (or was not). The stolid ranks of pupils looked surprised, to say the least. But I was not always up-graded like that. One Chairwoman gestured at me with her hand: 'We have with us to-night Miss -er, Mrs -er er-, who is going to tell us about — er, well, she'll tell you all about it herself, and I'm sure you'll all enjoy it.' The audience applauded this masterly introduction, though some of them were halfway through a row of knitting, and some were to all appearances asleep. One of them came to talk to me afterwards. 'We were ever so surprised,' she confessed. 'We thought you were going to talk about family planning. We must have got the weeks mixed up.' Doubtless the ladies were disappointed on that occasion; but perhaps not so much as the group to whom I was announced as 'the well-known superinten-dent of concentration camps'.

For six years I kept up the pace, and maintained the split personality; one week being the special 'weren't-we-lucky-to-get-hold-of-her' guest-speaker at an annual rally or exclusive luncheon club, and the next being mistaken for last week's Flower Arrangement, or being rung by a harassed Secretary at the eleventh hour because 'Mrs Jones was going to show us her colour slides of Bermuda, but she's got flu, and would you come instead?' On one such occasion a woman accosted me on the way out. 'I was looking forward to Mrs Jones's colour-slides,' she said accusingly. 'If I'd realised she wasn't going to be here, I shouldn't have come.' She was very indignant.

All this time, things were coming together for me. The more I talked to people about the survivors, and came to identify with them, understanding more and more about their lives, the more I found that I was helping myself to understand my own situation. The lesson I was learning was that though pain has the capacity to destroy it may also be creative. Just how much I was to owe to the survivors, as yet I fortunately did not know. For the time was not far off when I would identify with them even more closely.

For a while, perhaps a year, Paul went daily to a Junior Training Centre in Altrincham. He loved it, and loved being surrounded by other children, but the staff found it very hard to cope with his disastrous incontinence. He was one person's job, and, in a school which at that time was as short of staff as it was of facilities, he was more than they could handle. Nowadays schools for the mentally handicapped are better equipped to deal with children like Paul (there are special-care units for the more difficult and more disabled children), but fifteen years ago things were different. On one or two occasions, when visitors were expected at the Centre, the Superintendent asked us to keep Paul at home. It was the thin end of the wedge, as we were well aware. From there it was a short step to asking us to keep him at home altogether. The Superintendent saw this as a perfectly reasonable request, and while the Training Centres were still under the aegis of the Ministry of Health rather than of Education, she was quite within her rights. When, a few years later, they passed into the control of the Ministry of Education, children like Paul were given security of tenure. Paul was unlucky. His 'schooldays' were brief, but they had been happy.

Paul had no speech, no means of communication, no powers of retention, no ability to concentrate. The hardest thing of all was that he didn't know us, and couldn't become a member of the family in any really positive sense. He stayed marooned in the playroom downstairs, a lonely little figure, face permanently squashed against the window-pane, uttering strange, incomprehensible sounds.

Several times he almost died. During a tonsillectomy he began to haemorrhage badly, but in spite of a heavy loss of blood, he pulled through. The bronchitis that he had suffered from since babyhood never relinquished its hold, and twice he was rushed off to hospital black in the face. One night he had fifteen bronchial convulsions. I was advised to spend the night at the hospital, and at about midnight the doctor came in to see me. 'It looks like the end,' he said, 'you'd better be prepared.' 'I always am,' I answered. But by daybreak Paul had thumbed his nose at death once again and lay sleeping peacefully.

In spite of our disappointment over the earlier treatment, we were still prepared to try anything or go anywhere that offered any hope. I don't think it was a question of believing that anything could be done, so much as the feeling that making some sort of move was preferable to standing still.

It was Sue Ryder who precipitated the next move. We had become friends, and she had often spoken of a Polish friend of hers, a neuropsychiatrist, who had achieved some astounding successes in the treatment of mentally-handicapped children. 'If only Dr W. could see Paul,' she kept saying, 'I know he would try to help him. He's the one man in the world who could.' One evening she telephoned. Dr W. was in England for a Conference on mental health, and he had come to see her. Delighted as she was, she had promptly put him on a train for Manchester, and he was at that moment on his way to us. I thanked her for the kind thought, but couldn't think how he could help. But Sue does nothing by halves, and she had another bolt to shoot. 'One more thing, Mary,' she said, as if it were an afterthought. 'If Dr W. suggests Paul going to him in Poland, do let him go.' Then she rang off in a rush, before I could get my breath back.

The idea was preposterous, unthinkable, and I was quite sure
that Sue had taken leave of her senses. Taking Paul to Louvain
was one thing. Abandoning him in Central Europe was something
else. Impossible. Or that was the way it seemed before we met
Dr W. He was different from all the others, even the Belgians.
He didn't treat Paul as just another interesting case, but as a
person; and he didn't itemise the clinical symptoms as though Paul
were an inanimate object, but singled out a few limited areas
where there might be some hope. He not only examined Paul
minutely, but he won his trust and confidence, and, in so far as
it was possible, his affection too. He stayed with us for two days,
after which he was quite clear in his mind that he would like to
take the matter further. With Sue's last words still ringing in my
ears (and they no longer sounded quite so fantastic) I was not
altogether surprised when he asked us if Paul could go to him in
Poland for a year or so. There was a hope, a very slender one,
but a hope just the same, that he could bring about an improvement in Paul's condition, and he was very anxious to try.

What decided us in the end to let Paul go was not so much
the prospect of some great improvement as the fact of his present
isolation. Now that he was excluded from the Training Centre
and was at home all the time, he no longer had the company of
other children. He was eight years old and had loved being with
the others. It was tragic now to see his lonely face pressed
all daylong against the playroom window. If he went to Dr
W.'s children's sanatorium, he would have all the company he
needed.

Sue was delighted and set about making the arrangements. Dr
W. had come to us in November, and Sue wrote from Poland
in the following February to say that everything was fixed up.
It was better than we could have hoped for. The Polish Ministry
of Health had turned down our offer of maintenance payment
and were prepared, in consideration of my own (extremely
limited) services to the work of the Sue Ryder Trust in Poland,
to take Paul for two years free of charge. We could hardly believe
in our good fortune.

In September of the same year, Paul and I set off for Warsaw.

Once again I was hopeful, but I was keeping in mind the caution-
ary letter Leonard Cheshire had sent me just before I left: 'Something inside me makes me want to say to you, don't count on it
too much,' he wrote. 'Dr W. is an outstanding man, and we all
pray that he really can do what he hopes to do for Paul. But
please, Mary, don't raise your hopes too high.'

The sanatorium, which housed four hundred children, was
about an hour and a half's drive outside of Warsaw, on the road
to Lublin. The village which housed it was poor, and the place
itself had been an old barracks, ugly and ramshackle from the
outside. Inside the grounds, however, newer, handsomer buildings
were springing up, and in one of the annexes Paul was to be
lodged, sharing a room with Richard, a boy of about the same
age from Chicago.

One place was the same as another to Paul, and he was quite
happy to go off with a woman doctor as soon as we arrived. When
later I was taken on a guided tour of the hospital and came across
him, he showed no sign of recognition. He was wandering round
a playground with a young nurse, and when I approached he
looked straight through me. The Chicago boy, Richard, was
there too, and he, not Paul, gave me a kiss. One thing I could
be quite sure of, I was not going to be missed.

I left there a week later. My last sight of Paul was sitting at a
table with some little spastic children, being helped to ring sausage
and dill pickles. English food, Polish food, it was all one to him, so
long as it was food. There was an expression of pure bliss on his
face. I was crying as I bent over to kiss him, but his only response
was one of his deep chortles.

As I left the hospital with Dr W., a number of children seemed
to appear from nowhere to join us, drawn by his undeniably
magnetic presence. I thought of him then, as often later, as a kind
of Hans Andersen figure, irresistible to children of any age. I knew
I could not be leaving Paul in better hands, but that didn't prevent
me feeling tearful. But I had only my own feelings to worry about,
not Paul's. It was one occasion when I could be thankful that Paul
didn't know one place, or one person, from another.

In many ways, I felt relief as I boarded the plane at Okecie

Airport outside Warsaw: a new baby was expected in January. With Paul in safe keeping for a year or two, I could look forward to enjoying the baby without having my hands impossibly full, and my attention inevitably elsewhere.

CHAPTER 6

Nicholas

SUE RYDER WAS going to be godmother. I had told her about the baby as soon as I knew that I was pregnant. On the phone I was gloomy. 'What if the baby shouldn't be alright?' I speculated. She brushed away such unprofitable fears. 'Of course it'll be alright,' she said. 'You really mustn't start getting morbid.'

On the night of January 18th 1965 I went into the nursing-home in Bowdon, near where we lived. The matron was the friend of a friend of mine, and she had taken a special interest in me. Nothing, she said, must be allowed to go wrong, and she would make a point of attending to me herself.

It was the usual sort of labour, the familiar mixture of intolerable and merely awful; there were no special problems. I don't remember the actual moment of birth, but I have a painfully clear memory of hearing two nurses talking in the labour ward afterwards, while I was still no more than semi-conscious. 'Oh no, not another boy,' said one, 'what a disappointment for her.' I recall the slight stab of disappointment, because both of us had badly wanted a girl. Then the other one replied: 'Another boy! Dear God, if that were all she had to worry about!' That was all. Half-under though I was, the meaning of the words reached me, and I was touched with nightmare dread.

When I came to, I was in a small, two-bedded ward with another young mother. 'Hello, are you alright?' she asked, as I opened my eyes. I looked at her. 'I'm not sure,' I said, 'I think there's something wrong with the baby.' 'Oh no,' she said reassuringly, 'you must have had a bad dream.' Well, maybe she was right, I thought. But just then a young nurse came into the room. She scurried around doing whatever it was she'd come in to do, and whisked out again like a frightened rabbit who'd glimpsed a stoat. I had opened my mouth to ask her a question, but she avoided meeting my eye. That was the moment when I knew, beyond any possible doubting, that what I had dreaded most had actually happened.

It seemed like an eternity later when my doctor, Joe, came in. He was half-Italian and very emotional. At this moment he was tense and unhappy, obviously nerving himself for an ordeal. He sat down by the bed.

'I don't know how to tell you, Mary,' he began.

'I think I already know,' I told him.

'What do you mean? How can you know? I don't know what you're talking about.'

'There's something wrong with the baby, that's all I know. You'd better tell me and get it over with.'

Joe looked at me, opened his mouth to say something, then put his head in his hands and cried silently. Afterwards he recovered himself sufficiently to tell me that the child was a mongol. Not a very bad case, a hairline case, I think he said. But a mongol nonetheless. Not like Paul. There seemed to be absolutely no connection between the two cases. The odds against this sort of thing happening were several hundred thousand to one. Astronomical odds which had defied probability and caught us. If nothing else, we had made medical history.

When Joe had gone, I tried to shut out all thought, because all thoughts led back to the same intolerable one: we now had two mentally handicapped sons, not one. I was screaming inside.

When Frank came to see me that afternoon, he couldn't trust himself to speak, any more than I could. He held my hand, while we both stayed silent, frightened by the enormity of the blow and the collapse of our hopes. Even now, years later, we have never told each other what we felt when we first heard the news. There are feelings too deep for sharing.

The prospect of the long night hours ahead filled me with dread. I didn't see how I could get through them without being destroyed by the fear, anger, panic and shame that were raging inside me. Everything was falling to pieces. The tender shoot of understanding, the fragile hold I had got on the meaning of suffering were swallowed up in the whirlpool in which I was now drowning. Prayer? Not likely. I'd finished with that. I'd tried it, and look where it had got me.

And so the night came on, and I slipped further and further into the abyss. Past fears mingled with future terrors, and I thought I was losing my reason. As the fears grew more monstrous, my own descent to darkness accelerated. I was spinning in an endlessly twisting spiral.

It was when I had given up hope of ever reaching the bottom, that some words I had once read flashed into my mind with brilliant clarity: 'Our tragedy is not that we suffer, but that we waste suffering. We waste the opportunity of growing into compassion.' The words leaped out at me, acting like a brake on my despair, dramatically halting my slide into madness.

What happened at that moment was the only mystical experience I have ever known, and there are no words to describe its intensity. It seemed to me that suddenly I was held firm, safe from further falling, and a voice inside me was saying: 'there is a way through this, but you must find it outside of yourself. Remember I am here, in the darkness. You are never alone.'

The words from the prayer-book were still there, weaving themselves into my consciousness. Somehow mixed up with them I could see a group of people — the 'Bods', those survivors of disaster far worse than this, who had pointed a way through for me once before. I was linked to them by a fine thread, and I understood that now I had become one of them. Others joined them, and then others, and though they drifted in a mist of anonymity I knew that they were all linked together by common suffering. And, on the horizon, a Cross, radiating light over the entire assembly. In accepting the symbolism, that the love which triumphed from the Cross could alone save men from themselves, I would find the promise of peace.

Next morning, the flowers began to arrive, bringing with them an almost tangible awareness of supportive love and grief. The first to arrive were from colleagues at the Loreto Convent where I had been a part-time teacher, and the accompanying message was sad and uncomprehending. Without further thought, I reached for paper and pen, and wrote to console them, trying to put what had happened into perspective for them. Suddenly I realised that my 'vision' had borne fruit. In some mysterious way, it was my friends who needed comforting more than I, and I wanted to reach out to them and help them to understand.

Congratulations cards were conspicuous by their absence, but in their place came letters. No-one in their right mind could say that they were happy for us, but almost everyone I had ever known, even only slightly, felt impelled to write, to express deep feelings, or even to apologise for the fact that they did not know how to. One letter which moved me to tears said simply: 'We just don't know what to say, except that you have our love and prayers.' The letters formed a solid wall of affection – some of them were blotchy with tears – which was a far more powerful support than their writers could have realised. The awareness that barriers were down, reserves dropped, differences forgotten, was profoundly healing. People who were normally inarticulate strove to pour out on paper what they had felt on hearing the news. Many said, 'Talking to you would be easier,' but they were mistaken. The letters, representing as they did, so much human feeling, so much anguished groping for words, said more than the spoken word ever could. They could be looked at over and over again, they had a strength out of all proportion to their actual stumbling content, and I still have them all. Had they offered glib religious consolation, or pious hopes of a better world to come, they would have been difficult to take. It was the sheer floundering incoherence of so many of them that made them important and precious. I felt I was being upheld by a genuine human response, and it seemed to me the most powerful force in all the world. Those letters did not take the place of prayer, they *were* prayer.

A French friend who lived nearby in Bowdon, underlined for me what I was feeling very strongly, that even this latest hammer-blow had meaning and purpose. She sent some lines of a French poem which summed it up exactly:

Et crois-tu donc distrait le Dieu qui t'a frappé?
L'homme est un apprenti, la douleur est son maître,
Et nul ne se connaît tant qu'il n'a pas souffert.

(Do you imagine that it is in a fit of absent-mindedness that God has afflicted you? We have so much to learn, and grief must be our master. It is only through suffering that we can hope to come to self-knowledge.)

Buoyed up though I was with all this affection, I couldn't help but be aware of the handful of friends who had not written, among them two who were closest to me. I fretted about their silence, and did not realise that it might reflect the intensity of their grief rather than indifference. One of them wrote later, 'I refused to let myself write to you at the time, because I didn't want to intrude upon whatever little privacy you had. I know that there are moments when one simply wants to hide away from everybody.' No, I hadn't felt like that, but I should have known that she would see things that way. That is the way she would have wanted it in similar circumstances. As for the other friend, I did not know till years later that she had rung my mother to see if the baby had arrived, and on receiving the news had fled to her room, locked herself in, and cried for two days. Months after I came out of hospital, I met her briefly. 'Why couldn't you have written?' I asked bitterly. 'Even just a line to show that you cared.' My own fretting had turned into hostility, and she lacked the courage to explain that she had made several attempts to write but had given them up. Thirteen years passed before we saw each other again, and renewed our friendship as strongly as before. She told me then that ever since that time she had always written immediately to anyone she knew to be in any kind of trouble. 'I had never realised how important it was until then,' she said. I regretted the hostility I had felt, and I had learned something I should have known: that silence does not always mean indifference.

CHAPTER 7

Breaking the Shell

THE BABY WAS called Nicholas Peter, and he was exactly a month old when I first saw him. The Matron at the nursing-home was unwilling to disturb me further for the first day or so, and I have to admit that, in spite of my resolve to accept the situation and use it for good in some way, I was in no hurry to take the first practical step — that of holding the baby in my arms and loving him. For the moment I had to face the simple fact that I was no less a coward than I had always been.

Then matters were taken out of my hands. Complications were discovered. The baby had been born without a rectum, and within half an hour of the discovery had been transferred to a large Children's Hospital in Central Manchester. There he was hurriedly baptised and an emergency operation was carried out.

When they told me, all my noble resolution evaporated into an unworthy hope that he would die. It was a fifty-fifty chance: he was very young to undergo such a serious operation. Shamelessly, I wanted those odds to lessen. I wanted a way out. At this stage, Nicholas was no more than an unfortunate happening, and now there was a distinct hope that the misfortune might be blotted out. God, how I wanted that to happen.

Nicky, of course, survived — so there was no way out. One

day in early February Frank and I went over to the hospital to
see him. When we were taken to his cot, a chill struck both
of us. He hardly looked like a baby at all. A pathetic little object
strapped to the cot, with tubes sticking out of every aperture. I
felt a disbelieving sense of nightmare, a horror undiluted by any
tender feelings. I can't pretend that I felt any love for that tiny child.
Pity, yes, but most of all horror, because this was my child, and
very soon now he would be coming home to me. I hoped more
than ever that he would die.

A few weeks later Nicky came home. The tubes were gone,
but he had a colostomy, an opening on the abdomen instead of
the normal rectum. In a year's time he was to return to the
hospital to have the colostomy closed up and a false rectum
provided. Meanwhile we should have to learn to adapt to the
colostomy.

He was the most pathetic waif I had ever seen; and there was
so much wrong with him. Something happened to all of us that
first evening; we all became his devoted slaves. Perhaps it was his
helplessness, I don't know. What I do know is that before that
first evening was out, we loved him, and there was no more
wishing that he would die. From then on the struggle was to
keep him alive.

We began to look for the positive elements of life with Nicky.
He was lovable and loving, and he would always need us. The
paediatrician had told us that he would make limited progress,
and that what little there was would be in spurts, so that there
would be vast acreages of time in which nothing would seem to
happen. So we set our sights low. If we didn't expect much, we
could not be disappointed. It was amazing what a difference this
readjustment of attitude made. Instead of looking for signs of progress and fretting if they did not appear, we were now delighted
by the least thing. Our hopes for Nicky stood in no danger
of being thwarted, because we had none. This second disappointment must have been a cruel blow to Frank, but he did not say
so, and he never complained. As a support he was like a rock.

The first few times I went out shopping with Nicky in the
pram, I was well aware that a few people were discreetly crossing

the road to avoid the embarrassment of meeting me. I knew enough now to realise that there was no malice or scorn in this, only fear and inadequacy: they were bereft of words to fit the occasion. Not being able to coo over the new baby, they would be transfixed by anxiety about what to say. Better to dodge the issue by avoiding a meeting. I learned to make the first move myself to avoid this kind of stalemate. Giving a cheerful greeting and a smile, were ways of ensuring that they could come to terms with their lack of savoir-faire. If I came face to face with someone who quite obviously wished she was a hundred miles away, and desperately talked about the weather, I would bring up the tabu subject myself and strip its terrors away by talking about it naturally. Slowly the neighbours relaxed, and people would come and talk to Nicky in his pram with as little embarrassment as they talked to normal babies.

When I finally stopped feeling sorry for myself, I found myself beginning to think deeply about the whole problem of grief and suffering in our lives. More and more I was convinced that, though suffering was itself negative, it could very easily destroy. On the other hand it could be used positively, for growth. It was, in fact, the only means of emotional growth, the route from winter to spring. 'Your pain,' wrote Kahlil Gibran, in 'The Prophet', 'is the breaking of the shell that encloses your understanding. Even as the stone of the fruit must break, that its heart may stand in the sun, so must you know pain.' That seemed to me to reach the heart of the matter. I knew that, in my own case, however hard I had been trying to come to terms with the tragedy I had in effect been shutting out the pain, trying to deaden my awareness of it, allowing a rock-hard shell to form and insulate me from it. The mother of a school-friend had written: 'I realise that some people have interpreted your courage as hardness, but that is often the only possible way to counter such a devastating blow.' Was it? Perhaps for a time it was. Building up the shell *was* an answer, but in the end it was a rotten answer; and until that shell could be smashed, there was no hope of personal growth.

Nicky's birth was giving me a second chance, smashing that

hard shell with hammer-blows. I was left vulnerable, and when one is vulnerable one has the humility to learn.

It was all a question now of learning to take this new pain into myself so that it could become creative. To do that, I should have to face the facts head on, hiding nothing, neither exaggerating nor playing down. To see my situation exactly as it was, to go forward from there, that was the secret.

Inevitably that could only be a beginning, but it was a good one. A calm, clear appraisal of reality is the crossing of the Rubicon in a situation of this sort. There is no going back, but the land ahead is unknown, and the roads are all uncharted. 'Here be dragons' a-plenty, but the worst enemy, that composite of self-delusion and self-pity, has been identified, and at least some of its power to destroy has gone.

CHAPTER 8

Journey to Poland

IN THE SUMMER of 1965, leaving Nicky in the capable hands of Betty and my mother, I went to Poland with Sue Ryder, to see Paul, and to see something of her work among the chronic sick in that country. It was more than a journey, it was a spiritual odyssey, and it set the seal on everything I had been thinking over the last few months.

In the many talks I had given about the work of Sue Ryder, I had often described the situation in Poland in post-war years, although I had no first-hand experience of it. Poland had suffered more than any other European country from the war and the Nazi occupation; and Warsaw suffered more devastation than any other capital city. Heavily bombarded in 1939, it experienced two further catastrophes before the war was over. The first was the total destruction by the Germans of the Warsaw Ghetto, almost every inhabitant of which had been murdered or deported to concentration camps by 1943. The second was the 1944 Rising, when the SS killed or maimed the Resistance forces with unimaginable ferocity, and Hitler sent a personal telegram to the General in charge of the operation, ordering him to raze Warsaw to the ground. By 1945 the death toll in the city was about eight hundred thousand, and, when rebuilding began, about a quarter of a million bodies were found under the debris and in the city's sewers. An estimated 90% of Warsaw's buildings were destroyed: on the left bank of the Vistula there was scarcely one left undamaged. Destruction was systematic, apocalyptic: homes, schools, hospitals, churches, were, if not obliterated, open to the sky. Men and women returning from the death camps of Auschwitz or Lublin — and indeed from all over Europe — were forced to live in ruined shells, without gas, electricity, running water, transport, telephones, and with very little food. In an economy that was struggling to drag itself out of chaos (with no outside aid), the chronic sick stood little chance. And yet, thanks to the war, the number of chronic sick was multiplying and many of them lived in incalculable poverty and distress.

During her war-service with SOE, working mainly in the Polish section, Sue had admired the tremendous courage of the young Polish agents, and she felt a deep sorrow for the ruin which had befallen their country during the Nazi occupation. The war over, she wanted to help repair that ruin in any way she could; and on her first visit to Warsaw, after meeting with ministers, doctors, nurses and social workers, that way stood clear before her. She would provide Homes for the many categories of chronic sick, particularly for those suffering from cancer. In post-war Poland thousands were dying of cancer each year, without hope of hospitalisation, drugs to relieve the pain or even, frequently, running water.

The Sue Ryder Foundation and the Polish Ministry of Health came to an agreement. If the Foundation would provide buildings, the Poles would make themselves responsible for the maintenance and staffing of each Home. And so the first of many Sue Ryder Homes came into being, and for some years teams of tradesmen belonging to the Foundation were sent to Poland, for periods varying from six months to three years, to erect new Homes and renovate the older ones.

Sue never forgot that what she had set out to provide was personal service, the kind of which no State institution is capable. She took it on herself to visit all the Homes regularly, to chat with the occupants, get to know their personal stories, discover their hidden as well as their obvious needs. She also spread the word around that whenever she came to Poland she would be available for anybody who wanted to see her, particularly for the many people, sick in either mind or body, for whom no place could be found in a Sue Ryder Home.

All this I knew, but somehow, when I came to experience the reality it was more poignant.

We set off from Cavendish early one morning. I had arrived the previous evening to find the driveway humming with industry. At the centre of the fuss, standing solidly in the golden evening sunlight, was Elijah, the giant Austin van, latest of a line of Biblical prophets, successor to Daniel, Jeremiah and Joshua. It was obvious that loading had been going on for days; 'Bods' and 'slaves' were clambering in and out and on top of Elijah, off-loading into him what seemed like the entire contents of the Home. I watched open-mouthed (and not in the least disposed to join in), as the cargo mounted: provisions, sheets, mattresses, blankets, winter clothing, bed-jackets, second-hand fur coats, wedding dresses (dozens of them), wheel-chairs, sewing-machines, hot-water bottles with hand-knitted covers, bedpans, medical samples, jars of coffee, oranges and home-made cakes. It was an incredible sight, and I felt bemused watching the endless procession of boxes, cartons, bales and tins of every possible size, shape and description, all carefully labelled for their precise destinations. All these things were now being hauled on to the top of Elijah as his innards would accept no more.

A sudden thought struck me, and I ventured forward and took a look inside the driving-compartment. Apart from a few feet of space around the driving-wheel, I could detect no other sign of a vacuum into which I, the passenger, might squeeze. 'Where,' I asked with a sinking feeling, 'am I supposed to sit?' 'There, of course,' said Sue briefly, raising an impatient eyebrow at the silliness of the question, and indicating a stack of pillows, bed-jackets, petrol cans, thermos flasks and a kettle, waiting to be loaded onto what had once been a seat. 'You'll have to sit on those.' I could see it would be futile to pursue the matter – she would probably have decided to leave me behind if I'd started to argue. Better to go and get a night's sleep, or practise sitting with knees drawn up to chin. Elijah was putting on weight by the minute, and by now he was twice his original height. How was anyone, particularly anyone as small as Sue, going to be able to drive him?

We left shortly after dawn. In the discreet lanes of Mercedes and Bentleys queueing for embarkation at Dover, Elijah stood out like a vulgar defiance, and entire car-loads passed us by, gawping freely. We sat tight, ignoring the scrutiny, or returning stare for stare as the fancy took us. We had no option but to stay there, as we could not go aboard until the last because of our huge, unwieldy shape. I began to think the port authorities might refuse to take us. In fact, I was already so uncomfortable that I rather hoped they would.

With our arrival at Ostend, the relatively normal part of the journey was over. After that we drove almost non-stop through Belgium and Germany till we seemed to come to a halt at the German-Czech frontier. The Czechs did not respect our haste, nor were they impressed by Elijah. They were distinctly suspicious of his monstrous bulk, in spite of our presenting a sheaf of imposing letters with big red seals from the Polish and other Embassies in London, authorising us to proceed. We were left to cool our heels while the border guards decided what to do with us, or until they had received instructions from on high. What caused their change of heart we never discovered, but suddenly they were all round us, wreathed in smiles and urging us forward with benedictions. They did, however, take the precaution of sealing up the van at the back, forbidding us to open it again while in transit through their country.

Elijah, liberated, began to eat up the miles to Prague. As I remember only too well, that was the only eating that was done, apart from a lone banana on the shores of a lake where we stopped to wash off the grime. As we drew near the outskirts of Prague, I promised myself that as soon as we reached the city, we'd be stopping for a meal. No such luck. As we drove out of Prague again, I began to be obsessed by the idea of food. Mile by mile I dwelt on the prospect, sighting possible restaurants with hope, sighing as we left them behind. At last, halleluia, we stopped at an inn of some kind, went inside, and found that it sold only sausage. That was fine by me, but I had forgotten it was Friday, still at that time a day when Catholics were forbidden to eat meat. Sue wouldn't stay, and I, to whom the sausage seemed more desirable just then than Lobster Thermidor, and who would have agreed to burn in hell for the chance of a plateful, followed her sulkily outside. It must have been about two hours later, when night had already fallen, that we stopped outside a village tavern. By that time I was past hunger, and could manage only a bowl of soup.

We drove on towards Poland, then, when we were not far from the frontier, we slept for a little while, propped up in the van, with an alarm clock placed between us, ticking its way to zero hour. My rebellious stomach protested throughout the night like an erupting volcano, and sleep was fitful. By morning my ankles had developed acute elephantiasis. Sue was unsympathetic. 'You ought to be with me in winter', was her only comment. She has crossed mountain passes in fierce blizzards and force-nine gales, and she has come within centimetres of death on ice-bound roads. The summer, she could not help implying, was only for softies. This particular 140lb weakling was obviously being tried and found wanting.

We crossed into Poland at dawn – a beautiful crimson dawn rising over the Beskids in Southern Silesia, and for a few perfect moments we stopped to enjoy it. We ate a banana each (I was beginning to loathe bananas) and brewed Nescafé from a kettle plugged into a socket specially installed on the dashboard. The interlude was short-lived. Not for us the long, restful contemplation of a roseate dawn. We had a deadline to meet in Wroclaw.

Wroclaw was not always Wroclaw. Once it belonged to Germany and was known as Breslau: it was part of the hotly-disputed Oder-Neisse territories taken from Germany and given to Poland after the war. Feelings still ran high, and rivers of ink continued to flow, but we were not concerned just then with international politics. Our immediate destination was a Home for Incurables, run by Polish nuns, for terminal patients with cancer.

As we drove into the courtyard of the Home, we were hot,

sticky, dusty, cramped, tired and famished. A young woman of twenty or so detached herself from the crowd of people waiting to greet us. She ran towards Elijah with arms flung wide, and, as Sue alighted, enfolded her in a massive bear hug, her face a broad beam of delight. Greetings over, she proceeded to a commando-type assault on Elijah, almost leaping onto his roof to strip it of parcels, boxes and trunks single-handed. Her energy was exhausting to watch.

'My God,' I thought sourly, 'what it is to be young and full of energy. *She* hasn't been travelling hundreds of miles, wedged into that black hole of a van for three days, with nothing but bananas to feed on.'

Quite right. She hadn't. Sue told me her story later. Her name was Malgosia (Margaret), and she was one amongst approximately one hundred and fifty six children who survived Auschwitz. She knows that she was born in Lwow and that her father was a regular soldier in the Polish army. She thinks she was a twin but she is not sure. When she was about three she and her mother were transported by cattle truck to Auschwitz. (She believes that her mother was caught helping Jewish children to escape.) When they arrived at the camp, her mother was immediately liquidated, but the three-year-old child was 'selected' for medical experiments by the SS doctors in the camp. Petrol was injected into her legs to induce osteomyelitis (a favoured treatment for the women prisoners) and, for reasons forever unknown, her internal organs were removed and put back in different positions. She survived, and when Auschwitz was liberated she was rescued by the Polish Red Cross and removed to a children's home.

When she entered the home, Malgosia was incontinent, suffered from a heart complaint, was unable to concentrate on anything at all, and had no interest in living. Her life was an unending series of long illnesses culminating in unsuccessful operations. A teacher who knew Malgosia at that time remembers what she was like: 'She had no-one, she couldn't even speak a word of Polish. She was just an unhappy scrap of a child who belonged nowhere.'

Sue Ryder had discovered her on one of her earliest visits to Poland, and immediately arranged for her to have medical treatment in London. She had already undergone surgery in Poland, but her condition was unchanged. Doctors at a London hospital agreed to have a look at her, and when they did so they agreed that Sue had not exaggerated her case. They operated on Malgosia without much hope, but the story had a happy ending. Almost incredibly, after three major operations, Malgosia was no longer incontinent, no longer bed-ridden, no longer apathetic. She was, in fact, on the way to becoming the noisy, strapping young woman I had so envied that morning. 'I was one of the lucky ones,' she says, without a hint of irony.

The more I saw of Malgosia, the more I marvelled. She wouldn't have had time for bitterness even if she'd been disposed to feel it. She had no energy to spare for recriminations or hatred. Although she lived alone in a tiny garret up four flights of stairs (no lift) in an ancient apartment block in Wroclaw, she was actually, positively, shiningly happy. Her health allowed her to work for only a few hours a day, but she made the most of those few hours. She helped the nuns in the Caritas Home where we had met her, and quite clearly she was not only deeply loved but indispensable there; and on two days a week she became a social worker, for ZBOVID, a survivors' organisation, looking after children in a crèche. 'I must be with children,' she said. In her spare time, she did not take a well-deserved rest. She helped the Sue Ryder Foundation, collecting lost and stray survivors and finding out their needs — a deaf-aid, a bedpan, a wheel-chair, or perhaps a holiday. There was something very special about Malgosia, to which everyone she met seemed to respond.

The nuns who welcomed us at the Caritas Home took it for granted that we had had lunch (well, we had — two days ago) so they just gave us coffee. It was not till much later, when Sue was getting ready to drive off into the dusk, and I was beginning to think I'd never see food again, that Mother Superior walked in on our preparations, and invited us to supper. I could have thrown my arms around her neck. But Sue is made of sterner stuff, and hates taking food out of people's mouths. She began to protest that we could not stay. Hunger gave me the strength to resist her. More influenced by the thought of those blackening bananas awaiting us in the van than by the black looks Sue was giving me, I thanked the nun warmly and accepted her kind invitation. Now, at last I could let imagination run riot, savouring the taste of culinary delights to come. At supper-time I almost ran into the refectory — only to see a solitary boiled egg on each plate. 'It is such a pity that we cannot offer you more,' smiled the Mother Superior regretfully, 'but you see, today is the Vigil of the Feast of the Assumption of Our Lady, and it is a fast-day.' I might have known there'd be a catch. I could have wept.

We stayed in the Home that night, sleeping like logs on makeshift couches in the surgery, out for the count as soon as we hit the pillow. It was wonderful.

As we returned to Elijah next morning, I could see my square foot of seat was already occupied. 'Meet Pan Kowalski, a survivor of Buchenwald,' explained Sue. 'He's coming with us to help unload at the other end.'

'All the way?' I asked, looking a question at her.

'All the way,' she agreed cheerfully, climbing aboard. 'Well, don't just stand there, Mary, for heaven's sake. You can sit on a cushion between us, over the engine.'

We drove the one hundred and fifty kilometres to Zielona Gora like that, with me sitting on the hump, getting black and blue. Pan Kowalski was merely the harbinger. He was followed by scores of others. That square foot of plastic seat, which I had thought inadequate at the start of the journey, became a desirable luxury, mine by default when it wasn't taken over by an assortment of survivors of every camp under the sun. But bumping about between the gears and the hand-brake, I threw English stuffiness to the winds, and began to enjoy myself. Meeting these people, hearing their appalling stories, marvelling at their courage, I was lifted into a new world. What I had found at Cavendish had been no fluke. These people were characterised not only by courage and lack of bitterness, but also by an infectious gaiety and a child-like fun. Laughing with them, enjoying the absurdities of life with them, I was being given living proof that the human spirit was indestructible.

CHAPTER 9

Sue, Paul and a Party

As WE DREW up alongside a pavement in a side street in the centre of Warsaw, someone tapped on Elijah's window. When I opened it, a hand thrust in a bunch of flowers. Sue had prepared me; the Poles shower her with gifts: flowers (sometimes complete with vase and water), Polish chocolates, young trees, live chickens, and sundry other offerings. Once there had even been a large turkey. I blanched at the thought of sharing my metal perch with a furious barnyard fowl.

Within seconds, it seemed, the grapevine had got to work and borne fruit, and the whole of Warsaw knew that Sue had arrived. Survivors (and others, of all ages) appeared to come from nowhere, out of nooks, crannies or holes in the ground, like children answering the call of the Pied Piper. It was all beginning for Sue, and, for a few days, finishing for me. For her the coming week would hold an unending flurry of meetings with the Minister of Health, with the British Ambassador, with architects, painters, all manner of officials and local authority workers. There would be visits to the Sue Ryder Homes and to the local hospitals, and to housebound people, too sick to come to her.

For me, there was Paul.

He looked right through me, without the faintest idea of who

I was, though he was quite willing for me to hold his hand. On first glance he was not any different from when I had last seen him, but when I got used to seeing him again, it was obvious that he was a little taller, a little thinner, a little straighter. Best of all, he was a lot calmer, no longer dashing around like an aimless spinning-top. Dr W. was pleased with him. The adaptation period was now over, he said, and everything had gone as he had hoped. Even the chronic bronchial trouble seemed to have cleared up, and Paul was not wheezing any more. As he sat and watched the other children play ball, an angelic smile lighting up his face, I thought I had never seen him so happy.

It was a time for clutching at straws. 'A day to remember,' exults my diary for Friday, August 20th. On that day, I had again gone to the sanatorium outside Warsaw, this time with Basia, the friend with whom I was staying, and who was bilingual in Polish and English. (Her mother was an Englishwoman who had come to Poland after World War One.) Until then, language had been a problem. I spoke French fluently, but my German was halting and fractured, as well as inadequate. As few people at the hospital seemed to know French, our conversations were usually conducted in a bastard mixture of English, German, Latin and Polish. The result was that I was short on hard facts. With Basia present, I could at last hope for some real answers to my questions.

When we arrived, Paul was sitting on a bench in the sun with several other little boys, one of whom had an arm draped affectionately round him. Tears stung my eyes at the normality of it. It was the first time since the Training Centre days I had seen a child (apart from his brothers) go near Paul, let alone put an arm round him. The nurse in charge saw that the scene had affected me. Yes, she said, the other children were fond of Paul. 'He is a very lovable little boy,' she added. It was sweet music to my ears. Paul, said the nurse, knew the other children and responded to them. Whenever he heard the sound of their games outside his room, he would dash out, in his lumbering, bear-like way, to join in. I could scarcely believe it; it was more than I had ever dared hope for.

Watching the children have their mid-day meal, I was given

another welcome shock. Paul, whom we had always had to feed, spoonful by dreary spoonful, was now happily helping himself to gherkins, and later to apples and cake. He still couldn't manage the softer food, but his fingers could pick up and put down the more solid items. 'If he drops a piece of cake on the floor,' the nurse smiled, 'he picks it up and puts it in his mouth.' Hygiene be blowed, I was delighted to hear it. When he was at home, he would have been unaware of the dropped bits, and would simply have walked on them.

It was marvellous to see him adapting so well, and so patently happy. He was brown and fit too; the climate was suiting him. The fact that he did not know me from Eve, nor respond in any way to my voice, was something I had long ago trained myself to accept, as all of us at home had had to. What you have not had, and are not likely ever to have, is not worth sighing over. Not even communication with your own child.

Paul had come through the settling-in stage with flying colours. But what of the future? Dr W. was fairly sure that he could teach Paul to feed himself properly and even to overcome the chronic incontinence. But when I spoke to some of the medical staff later, they were much less sanguine. Paul, one of the doctors told me, was one of the most difficult cases in the whole sanatorium; he and his colleagues doubted that any more progress was possible.

For the time being, I was content to bask in Dr W.'s optimism, and to go and see one of his training programmes in practice. He had pioneered a summer camp not far from the hospital, persuading the Government to give him some land which had belonged to a former collective. (The policy of collectivisation met with little success among the fiercely independent Poles). It was rich farm land, bounded by a forest on one side and a river on the other, and on it Dr W. already had sixteen cows, one hundred pigs, and enough farm-produce to make the sanatorium self-supporting.

A group of children was under canvas when I arrived. They were all at the 'training' stage, children who had been brought to the hospital a year or so earlier, unable to talk, walk, or even sit up in a chair. Now they were doing all three. The week they were spending at the camp represented Dr W.'s desire to bring them into close contact with nature and the simple life. On the previous night, someone had lit a bonfire. The children had never seen fire before, and their immediate response was to shout and sing and dance up and down with delight. None of them showed the slightest sign of fear.

Living in the open, learning about the elements at close hand, taking their turn in the queue leading to the communal cooking-pot, they were being taught essential lessons about life, in the most natural way possible. In an atmosphere like that, they could not fail to improve.

Nearby, on the same terrain, a new building was going up. Here the better-adapted among the children would spend an entire year, working on the farm or in the fields, gardening or doing simple carpentry, any jobs to which their small talents might be stretched. And, at the end of it all, the pot of gold at the end of the rainbow, the only reward that Dr W. dreamed of – the possible return of his children to a normal life within the community.

That evening, when I got back to Warsaw (a two-hour journey by bus), I found a message waiting from Sue. We were invited to a party. The Poles love parties, and any excuse will do. They don't need alcohol, they can get stoned on good will and high spirits. Sue Ryder's visit was an opportunity not-to-be-missed, and a gala night had been planned. Nothing loth, I found my way to the address I'd been given, and walked into a scene of chattering festivity, in which I was seized, greeted and smothered with sandwiches and questions. The guests were all women, dressed in their best clothes; and about half of them wore tattoos on their fore-arms. I knew that that meant Auschwitz. The others, I soon discovered, were survivors of Buchenwald and Ravensbrück, and the party was being given by the Survivors' clubs of those camps. For a moment, the evening took on a hint of the macabre, as I looked over that sea of young-old faces, every one of which had supped full with horror. It was grotesque, and I wasn't sure that I wanted to stay. Then there was a rustling and a sighing. Sue had arrived ('Mamusia', they call her, which means Mama). The faces glowed with anticipation. The evening could now begin.

It began, as did so much else, with flowers. Flowers for Sue, presents for her and even for myself, presented with much giggling and shuffling and hugs. Someone made a very Polish speech to the effect that we were welcome, not once, not twice, not three times, but a thousand and a hundred thousand times. Everyone cheered and then they burst into that rousing 'May you live a hundred years' song ('Sto Lat'), which is their equivalent of 'For she's a jolly good fellow', and without which no Polish gathering is complete. Poles always break into song, given the least chance, and they sing with a marvellous blend of melancholy and passion, which is tremendously moving.

One song led to another, and soon they were well away. Between singing and dancing and ruby-red barszcz, mushroom patties and tiny wild strawberries, the evening passed like a dream. There was much laughter. The astonishing thing was that a few of them could even talk about their experiences in the camps and laugh about them. On this evening at least, memories were not allowed to dim their gaiety.

Maria, a survivor of Ravensbrück, for example, told me in a matter-of-fact way about sleeping conditions at Ravensbrück camp – hundreds of women crammed into wooden bunks, stacked on top of each other. 'I dreamed the same dreams every night,' she said, 'I dreamed of having a pillow, and of being by myself in a room of my own.' In all the filth and human misery, she had clung to her two dreams, longing for the privacy that might one day be hers. 'And, do you know,' she said with a smile, 'it never happened.' She got the pillow but the rest of the dream couldn't come true, because when at last she was released, her health had collapsed and she was unable to work. She lived with some distant relations, who provided for her basic needs; but they were so poor that they all had to sleep in the same room.

One woman at that party seemed to be hovering on the fringes, not joining in. She was the stranger at the feast, I thought, the only obviously unhappy person present. I was curious, and moved closer to her. She was eager enough to talk. She had come along because she wanted to meet Sue Ryder, from whom she wanted a favour for a friend. So far she hadn't been able to get near, because of the crush, but she hadn't given up hope. Then, without warning, she seemed to crumple. 'I wasn't there, you see,' she said, with real anguish in her voice. I looked at her in surprise, not understanding at all. 'I wasn't there,' she repeated heavily. 'Not in Auschwitz, not in Majdanek, not in Buchenwald, nor in any of those places. But I wish to God I *had* been. I'm on the outside. Can you understand?' The pain in her voice shook me.

Suddenly I knew exactly what she meant. The other women in the room were linked together indissolubly by a common bond of suffering, and by a mutual compassion. Somewhere in the depths of the hells they had lived through, bonds had been formed which could never be broken. They had been compelled to draw out of themselves almost impossible reserves of moral courage, and they had discovered an inner strength of such power that no amount of physical hardship or deprivation could touch it. Their humanity had been stripped of everything that was not essential to it; and they had found its rich distilled essence. They were special. If I had been Polish, I think I might have felt as this woman felt.

As it was, I could only marvel at their present happiness. As Sue and I left, they sang one of their heart-tearing songs by way of farewell. My own heart went out to them. I already knew what a lot I owed them.

CHAPTER 10

Wanda, Hanka and Others

IT IS DIFFICULT, and even invidious, to single out a few stories from among so many, but Wanda, Hanka and Professor Reicher will serve.

Wanda was a Girl Guide in Lublin during the Nazi occupation. She helped look after sick people, and from time to time she took secret messages to members of the Polish Resistance. One day, just after her seventeenth birthday, the Gestapo came to the house and arrested her. They took her to their headquarters in Lublin where she was beaten mercilessly. But they got no information from her. Then they threw her into a prison with prostitutes and criminals, a terrifying experience for a middle-class Girl Guide with a sheltered upbringing.

Much worse was to come. Before long, she was sent from there to Ravensbrück, the concentration camp for women, north of Berlin. She will never forget that long train journey, on which the women sang to keep up their spirits, and a strange comradeship sprang up among them. In the Polish part of the journey, villagers would throw scraps of food into the train as they passed. One of them threw a forlorn bunch of heather.

At Ravensbrück, Wanda discovered to what extent luck had deserted her, when she was sent to the medical experiment block.

Her legs were injected with petrol, and diseased bacilli were introduced into the bone marrow. Samples of muscle and bone tissue were taken away. All these details she discovered later. At the time, like the other terrified women in the block, she lay in fever for days, without any kind of post-operative care, not knowing what had been done to her or why. Some of the 'guinea-pigs' died. Wanda did not.

As the Liberating armies drew near, Ravensbrück's numbers were swollen to bursting point by an influx from other camps which had been hastily evacuated. Large numbers of men and women, for example, had been driven out of Auschwitz, on 'death marches' to other camps, to prevent discovery by the Russians who were approaching the camp. Only the very sick and the half-alive (many of them children) were left behind, as it was presumed that they would be dead by the time the Russians arrived. Of those sent on the death marches, many thousands perished; but some survived, to straggle into camps like Ravensbrück and add to the chaos already reigning there.

In Ravensbrück too the SS had laid their plans: the 'guinea-pigs' were to be liquidated, so that they would tell no tales. But there was an 'underground' movement within the camp, and in the prevailing chaos, they moved into action, their top priority being to save the 'guinea-pigs'. Wanda was among those constantly shifted from one dark underground bunker to another, hidden from the hourly searches made by the camp Gestapo.

One night she found herself lying side by side with a gipsy-girl of about fourteen. Even as she turned to look at her, the girl died.

When she saw this, Wanda was convinced that she too was dying, and thought how strange it was that this child of fourteen should have died before her, now an old woman of twenty-one. Suddenly she realised that she was past caring. The only thing that could touch her now was death, and that would be welcome. Even if the Gestapo caught her now, what could they do to her that they had not already done? Except kill her?

But strangely, as fear left her and she began to accept death as imminent, the conviction grew in her that she would not die. She would survive, because there was so much for her to do, when sanity returned to the world; and she fell to wondering what freedom would bring for those many women in the camp whose sanity had snapped under the intolerable pressures. And in the new calm which had possessed her, she determined that if she came out alive she would train to become a psychiatrist and strive to heal the minds that had been unhinged by a surfeit of suffering.

She was as good as her vow. Though she is frequently ill herself, and her legs bear the scars of those ghastly experiments, she has put her entire experience to good use. She works now as a psychiatrist in the south of Poland, among the endless streams of mentally ill survivors, many of them unfortunately turned criminal. 'With her direct gaze and piercing blue eyes,' says a friend, 'Wanda was made for the work she is doing. She's the sort of person who can look at another and know what is going on in that other's mind.'

Wanda has worked with great compassion and understanding among the children who survived Auschwitz (even children who survived other camps were known generically as 'the Auschwitz children'), charting their development as they grew into adulthood, trying to counter the nervous instability and lack of trust which characterised so many of them. A few years ago, she published a book of short stories based on her experience of these children. In one of these haunting stories, a little boy, Antek, was fostered by loving 'parents' but remained withdrawn, secretive, never known to laugh. They played games with him, gave him toys, told him stories, but they could never raise so much as a smile. Then one day he went to sit with an old man, a neighbour, who was dying. Faithfully, he went back day after day. He seemed very fond of the old man. Then the old man died, and suddenly the boy began to laugh. The mother glanced in astonishment at him. 'Perhaps he is abnormal after all,' she thought.

The boy sat staring in wonder at the old man. His mother tried to lead him outside, but the boy pulled her towards the bed where the old man lay. He stood beside it smiling. It was the first time she had seen him smile. She was astonished and embarrassed and tried to pull him away.

But the little one suddenly turned to her and said in an excited, breathless, childish whisper: 'Tell me, tell me, is it true, can somebody really die like that? Just ordinarily like that? Can someone really die without being killed?'

When she told me the story many years later, the woman still had tears in her eyes. She added: 'From then on, he started to laugh.'*

Hanka, a tireless worker for the Sue Ryder Foundation, whom everyone I knew seemed to call Pani (i.e. Mrs) Hanka, was married, with a two-year-old son, and living in Warsaw when the Germans overran the country. Her sister, but not Hanka herself, joined the Polish Resistance, and eventually came under suspicion. When the Gestapo came to make an arrest, Hanka, who was living in the house at the time, passed herself off as her sister, believing that, as she obviously knew nothing of any value, the Gestapo would soon let her go. It was a naïve hope.

She was taken to the Aleja Szucha, the dreaded Gestapo HQ in the centre of Warsaw. Even to-day, Poles can't walk past the building without a shudder although the name of the street has been changed. On the wall of one of the underground cells one can still read the words scratched by a wretched captive: 'It is easy to talk about Poland. It is harder to work for her, harder still to die for her, but hardest of all to suffer for her.'

Hanka was incarcerated underground in the Aleja Szucha for six months, and during that time was subjected to constant interrogation and beatings. When the Gestapo could get nothing out of her, they sent her to the infamous camp at Majdanek, where she became a block 'mother', renowned for her kindness and practicality. Those who were in the camp with her still talk with admiration of the help she gave them. She was the practical one, to whom they all turned.

But Hanka's own memories are more sinister. For a time, she was made to separate the newly-arrived mothers from their chil-

* From a collection of true short stories, *Stare Rachunki* by Wanda Poltawska. Published in Poland and translated (unpublished) by Jessica Gatty.

dren, under threat that, if she refused, the guard dogs would be let loose to do the job more thoroughly. As it was, the children, she knew, would go straight to their deaths, the mothers later, when they had outlived their usefulness. 'All I could do,' she says, her face ashen at the recollection, 'was try and inject some humanity into the agonising task, but no amount of kindness could make any difference. How could it have? The faces of those poor children, their screams of terror, the anguish of the mothers, will haunt me to the grave. I wake every night, sweating and screaming, and the nightmare is always the same one.'

Poland is hag-ridden with memories of that sort, images of horror that refuse to go away. It is surprising that mental illness is not rife, the fruit of experiences which no words could describe. My own friend, Basia, is still haunted by the memory of an old Jew bending down in the street to fasten a shoe-lace, and being hauled to his feet by a passing SS man who proceeded to beat the old man's brains out against a lamp-post.

But most people do their best to put memories like that behind them and to live in the present. Like the woman I saw in a Home for terminal cancer patients just outside Warsaw. I have a photo-graph of her, but even without this constant reminder, I would be unable to forget her. She was sitting up in bed wearing an old-fashioned, buttoned-up-to-the-neck, snowy-white night-gown, with a white kerchief on her head. Her eyes were button-bright. Her husband, she told me, had disappeared in Auschwitz, her sons had been killed in the Warsaw Rising. She and her daughter had survived the siege, but during it the daughter had become severely crippled. They had scraped along as best they could since the war, but now she was dying of cancer. 'I am so lucky,' she kept saying. 'I have a room to myself, and it has curtains at the windows. Look how pretty the curtains are. And I have food brought to me three times a day. I think I am already in Heaven.'

I grew used to meeting people like her. In the Sue Ryder Home in Gdynia (which has since become a treatment-centre for men, women and children with cancer), I met three women with terminal cancer. They knew they had not long to live, but the agony of that knowledge had been offset by their joy at being given a place in this Home. A weight had been miraculously lifted from them, they said. 'I shall be able to die in peace now,' one of them said quite calmly. 'I feel so very happy.' Her companions nodded agreement. 'It's the English mattresses,' said one of them, by way of explaining the inexplicable. 'You cannot imagine what a difference they make.'

Professor Eleanora Reicher was Jewish. She was one of the handful of men and women who survived the liquidation of the Jewish community in Poland. Throughout the Nazi occupation she remained hidden in a Catholic convent, but she never stopped working as a doctor. She was one of Sue's earliest contacts in Warsaw, and she shared with the young English-woman her own dream of setting up a Home for the large numbers of post-war children, born with rheumatic arthritis and living in difficult conditions all over the country. With Sue Ryder's help, Dr Reicher's dream came true. Fourteen miles out of Warsaw, in the health-resort of Konstancin, two simple Homes were built by the Sue Ryder Foundation amid the pine forests. Here in these near-idyllic surroundings fifty or sixty severely crippled girls were admitted, not only to receive medical attention, but also to study for examinations, a possibility not open to them in the conditions in which they had been living at home. Of all the Homes she has established in Poland, this one in particular is home to Sue on her journeys. Konstancin is the Polish equivalent of Cavendish, the place where she feels most completely at home, and where she is always assured of a most ecstatic welcome. As soon as her van is sighted, girls of all ages set off walking or hobbling on crutches towards it, putting all they have into the effort. Amid the excitement and the expectant laughter, it is easy to forget for a moment that the girls are often in great pain, and that many of them will be disabled for the rest of their lives. But then, that sort of thing always seems secondary in Poland.

CHAPTER II

The End of the Journey

NOT ALL THE Sue Ryder Homes were conveniently near to Warsaw. Many of them were far away. Homes and Centres for the dying and the chronic sick merged indistinguishably in my consciousness during the long drives to the north, south, east and west of Poland. Fleeting images remain: passing hay-carts, waddling ducks and gaggles of slow-moving geese in the sunshine one day, and the next nearly skidding over a dead cow lying across a wet road in the eastern forests; pitying the unfortunate peasants huddled under sheets of newspaper or sodden tarpaulins while their animals wandered dispiritedly all over the road; crossing the Vistula one night on a slippery, makeshift bridge; and being diverted one dark evening through a forest in central Poland, watching Elijah's headlights illuminate the trunks of ageless trees, to the magical accompaniment of Bruch's No. 1 Violin Concerto on the radio. From Poznan in the west, south to Cracow and the Carpathian mountains, to Radom in the centre, over the flat Warsaw plain, east to Bialystok, then north to the lake-land of Masuria and what had once been Eastern Prussia. Night and day blurred into one, and I could not remember that far-distant time when I did not spend every night sleeping upright in an Austin van.

Hospitality was frequently offered us by friendly villagers and farmers, but we always refused because of lack of time. Sue would drive until she felt tired and then stop. (She had been driving for too long not to realise the stupidity of continuing to do so in a state of exhaustion.) When that moment arrived, she would bow to the inevitable and get out her small alarm clock. 'Three hours then,' she would say, somewhere in night's blackness when I had long been bleary with sleep. Down went the clock between us, ticking away inexorably, while we wriggled and turned and vainly counted sheep. No sooner did we drop asleep than the alarm dragged us relentlessly awake, to rub the sleep from our eyes and be on our way once more.

Some places are unforgettable. Treblinka, for example. It was a glorious day, the sky was a radiant blue, and it was hard to believe that in this peaceful setting over eight hundred thousand Jews and other victims had been murdered. Treblinka was not even a labour camp; it existed for one purpose only — extermination. Suddenly to come upon the memorial to the dead at Treblinka is a heart-piercing experience. I don't know what I was expecting. Perhaps a vast imposing sculpture and a flood of propaganda. The reality was a simple mound of stones surmounted by a fresco, while all around great jagged rocks thrust upwards as if in supplication, each bearing the names of towns or villages throughout Poland whose sons and daughters had ended their lives in this place. I was glad of the awesome silence, the solitude, the almost tangible need for prayer. A place of pilgrimage indeed.

Not far from Treblinka, we stopped at a rambling convent where a small band of devoted Benedictine nuns looked after eighty mentally-handicapped boys, without benefit of running water. They worked on a rota system, drawing the water they needed for drinking, cooking and washing from a nearby well. Knowing only too well the washing problems inherent in the care of the mentally handicapped, I was aghast at the difficulties under which the nuns were labouring.

And there was Radom, a town in central Poland where Sue was hoping to build a Home for men and women suffering from different disabilities. Many of these were single, and although until recently they had been able to work, they could do so no longer; others had lost their entire families and had nobody to care for them. Sue's Home was to be built as an annexe to an already-existing one, run by Sisters of Charity and over-crowded. I imagine Bedlam to have been something like it. Outside in the sunlight a woman was knitting — with one arm. The other hung, withered and useless, by her side. An impossible feat, but there she was, performing it with great skill and dexterity. When we had finished admiring her work, Sue went off to talk to the patients on the ground floor, suggesting that I might do likewise with those upstairs. I did my best, but it was her they wanted, not me. Apart from that fact, language was a terrible obstacle; I had to summon every word of Polish in my scanty vocabulary, and strain to catch at least the gist of what was being said. In the end some sort of rapport must have been established, as I have a vivid recollection of an old blind woman bursting into tears and throwing herself into my arms. And when that happens you don't need words.

On the night before we were due to leave for England, the streams of people arriving to make last-minute requests to Sue stretched on towards dawn and beyond. Next morning about thirty of the 'Bods' were on her doorstep to say goodbye, armed with biscuits, flowers, chocolates, sandwiches, vitamin pills, medical prescriptions, good advice and tears. They are always quite sure that if they don't provision her she will die of starvation on the way home. Remembering our own outward journey, they could well be right.

We could not leave immediately though. Sue had to get some more sleep before she could contemplate the long return journey — even though she almost knew it by heart. At 2 am the following day, she came to collect me from Basia's flat, and we slipped quietly away towards Katowice.

The name didn't really register at first, amid so many strange Polish names that I had grown used to. We were nearly there when I remembered. Katowice was near neighbour to Oswiecim, and Oswiecim was better known as Auschwitz. I wasn't sure that I could take Auschwitz, but I was quite sure Sue would make me try. She did.

Pan Tadeusz Szymanski, the curator of Auschwitz, and Pani Odi, his assistant, were both survivors of the camp who went on living there (in what was now a museum) because they believed they had a sacred duty to do so! Sue left me in their charge, while she drove off to visit a Home some miles away. Mr Szymanski, I learned, spent most of his spare time trying to unite the former child-prisoners of Auschwitz with their parents. A few weeks earlier he had managed to reunite a Russian boy, now aged twenty-eight, with his mother in Russia. A happy ending? Not entirely. The boy (after years of living in Poland) could speak no Russian, and the mother no Polish. There were many grave problems of that kind in Mr Szymanski's self-imposed task; the long hoped-for reunion often caused more problems than it solved. But he still felt he had to go on working to reunite parents with their long-lost children.

It is surely not possible to visit Auschwitz and be unaware of evil. Viscous and fetid, it is everywhere. It seeps into the pores, it is part of the air you have to breathe. From the moment I walked through those gates whose cynical legend still boasts: Arbeit Macht Frei (work sets you free), I was almost overcome with nausea. Standing in the museum with its vast glass cases filled with the macabre evidence of the wholesale slaughter of the innocents, I was near to fainting. It was unbearable to see the mountain of shorn human hair, the piles of false teeth, spectacles, clothing; the pathetic heaps of human trivia which the victims had brought with them, believing they were going to a resettlement camp: suitcases, cooking utensils, chamber-pots, walking-sticks, shopping-bags. Most poignant of all — the wooden legs, children's teddy-bears and family photographs. The intolerable pathos of little things. And in the main hall the flags of forty different countries recalled the homelands of the four million who came to this infamous place to die.

Auschwitz is a silent place where words are not only unnecessary but impossible. You do not speak here, you choke back the tears. You stand and look at the innocuous railway-siding, remembering the cattle-loads of human beings that once were shunted there, to be disgorged with shouts and kicks. Nearby, the remains of the crematoria, hastily but not completely destroyed in the last days of the camp, still bear a mute, appalling witness. And beyond, the fields, the unhealthy tracts of marshland where the ashes of four million human persons were scattered. Kneel down and pick up a handful of earth, and as the wet mud silts away, see the tiny, unmistakable fragments of human bone.

Words could never convey the effect of Auschwitz. It is a searing of the soul. It leaves you stricken, bewildered, convulsed with anger, terror, pity, grief, and a violent desire to be sick. Mentally and physically I felt pulverised, and the sense of nightmare was increased when I was led to a former SS cell, where Sue and I had been given beds for the night. But Sue did not come. The minutes became hours, and still there was no sign of her. I was convinced that she had met with a fatal accident, and wondered in a panic how to word the telegram I should have to send to Leonard, if that were indeed the case. In the event I was very nearly right. Just before midnight, she arrived, pale and exhausted. Short of time, she had decided to ignore one of the ubiquitous Diversion signs (these often meant a detour of up to forty miles, nearly drove us berserk with irritation and usually seemed quite unnecessary). Suddenly she had found herself teetering on the edge of a precipice. By some miracle, she had righted herself, but she was badly shaken. 'Funny thing,' she said, before flaking out like a light, 'when I thought I was going to die, all I could think of was that I wished you were with me.'

We had a couple of hours' sleep in that grisly cell, and at just after 2 am we were on the road once again. As the Warsaw 'Bods' had done, Mr Szymanski sent us off well provided with flowers, sandwiches and flasks of tea. Mercifully, nobody gave us bananas. But then, that would have been impossible, since there were none to be had in Poland.

Auschwitz wasn't quite the end of the journey. There was work to be done on the return journey through Czechoslovakia, visiting the relatives of men who were still imprisoned in Germany, surely the most forgotten men in the world, and the most hopeless. Deported to slave labour and other camps in Germany at the outset of war, they had survived, half-starved and desperate. Released from the camps, they found themselves in a chaotic alien world, which held no place for them. Perhaps in a desire for revenge, or perhaps merely in order to stay alive, they had committed various crimes, ranging from petty theft to murder. Retribution was swift and certain, the sentences savage and, middle-aged now, they had not seen their families for more than twenty years. (Some of the men, of course, no longer had any family.)

I knew that Sue spent a great deal of her time visiting prisons in Germany, but it was only now that I realised the full poignancy of the situation. Meeting wives, mothers, and even grandmothers, I could understand at last, as never before, the full horror of a war which, twenty years after it had officially ended, was still casting its dark shadow of suffering.

Most of the women we saw were in Prague, but not all. On our last night, we drove to a small village outside Pilsen, had a brief sleep in the van, and set about looking for the final address on our list. At the inhuman hour of three in the morning we were prowling around looking and feeling like burglars. Hopefully Sue shone a torch on a lighted window, and I cringed, waiting for a torrent of abuse or a bucketful of cold water. But the face which appeared at the window was friendly and we got the directions we needed. We drove on and a few minutes later Sue

was parking Elijah outside a large apartment block where everything was dark apart from one lighted window. I sat back, prepared to wait. Sue looked at the window speculatively, then at
me. 'Well?' she asked.

'Well, what?' I already half-suspected what was coming next.

'What about you going up there? Someone's bound to know
the woman we're looking for.'

'Please,' she added. She knew I'd have to do it.

Unnerved at the thought of the hour, the strangeness, my own
inability to say so much as hello in Czech, I was even more unnerved by the prospect of being called chicken if I refused. So,
taking a deep breath and muttering a fervent prayer, I uncurled
myself from Elijah and entered the dark apartment house. I went
on climbing the stairs until I saw a shaft of light underneath a
door, and then nervously pressed the bell. If whoever answered
my summons had turned nasty, I was quite prepared to run, but,
to my amazement, I was greeted without surprise and with
polite friendliness. My garbled German managed to elicit the information we wanted, and with a sigh of relief I fled down the
stairs reflecting on the probable reception I'd have met in England
if paying social calls at such an uncivil hour.

All was well in the end. We found the woman we were looking
for, and she was so excited and happy with the messages we
brought from her prisoner-son that I realised how little it mattered that the hour was unsuitable. She made us welcome, and
hope shone in her eyes as she looked at Sue and listened to news
about a sad middle-aged man in Germany whom she had last
seen twenty-five years before, when he was nineteen. Always
she hoped that one day he would come home.

After that, we did a hell-for-leather dash for Ostend, almost
non-stop for eight hundred miles. Towards the end of this mara-
thon stint, even Sue was flagging. 'Can't you sing or tell me a
funny story or something?' she asked irritably. As I didn't deign
to reply (I was far too tired), she looked at me suspiciously. 'You're
not going to grumble, Mary, are you?' she pleaded. 'I couldn't
bear it.' I asked her what she usually did when she reached
exhaustion-point. 'Oh, I go into a field and scream my head off,'

she replied, 'but there's no time for that to-night.' As for the reason why she went on putting up with the discomforts of journeys like this, I knew the answer to that one. She had, in fact, once told me, but I hadn't needed to be told, because it was the only possible explanation. 'I think of the survivors and what they endured. I could never have stood that, but somehow one has to try and measure up to their courage.'

Sue had set herself a lifetime's task. 'As long as I am alive, my work is to try and relieve suffering,' she had once said. And in the prayer which she and Leonard had composed, and which hung in the chapel at Cavendish, lay the secret of what guided them both:

> ... Grant peace and eternal rest to all the departed, but especially to the millions known and unknown who died as prisoners in many lands, victims of the hatred and cruelty of man. May the example of their suffering and courage draw us closer to Thee through Thine own agony and passion, and thus strengthen us in our desire to serve Thee in the sick, the unwanted and the dying wherever we may find them. Give us the grace so to spend ourselves for those who are still alive, that we may prove most truly that we have not forgotten those who died.

When the young Sue Ryder had first arrived in Poland, she was caught up in the struggles of the Polish people to rebuild their shattered country. The English girl's selfless determination to help galvanised many of those who had been standing on the sidelines. My friend, Basia, one of Sue's earliest helpers, was one of these. Basia was no stranger to suffering. Her husband, Ryszard, had been arrested and sent to a concentration camp in Germany a few weeks after their marriage; and in the first year of the Occupation her young brother Tadeusz was shot dead in one of the frequent sporadic street round-ups. (When the news of Tadeusz's death was broken to his mother, she burst into tears and said 'I suppose I must thank God he cannot now be sent to Auschwitz.') When the war was over and Ryszard had returned, Basia had preferred to close her eyes to the misery all around her. 'Before Sue came,' she said, 'there were many of us who knew all about the problems of the chronic sick and their terrible struggle to survive. But there were so *many* problems. In every city and town people were clearing away rubble with their bare hands before rebuilding could start. With so much destruction and misery everywhere we turned, some of us felt paralysed. It was Sue who made the difference. She was full of compassion and afraid of no-one. Somehow she showed us what could be done. She opened our eyes, and that was when we found our courage again.'

It was two-way traffic, of course. The miracle was that the survivors, in being helped, gave so much in return. They had learned lessons about human values which only those who had lived with death could have learned. They had gained an extra dimension because they had learned what was important in life and what was not, and because, in their own daily lives, they were passing on that lesson. Perhaps, in the world's terms, they were abject failures, every one of them — sick, poor, unable to work, with a life that was going nowhere. But as I left Poland, I knew that they were rich beyond measure. And I envied their wholeness, if not the paths by which they had come to it.

CHAPTER 12

A Death in the Family

I HAD NOT been home very long when I received a long letter from an Auschwitz survivor called Stefan. Stefan's wife, who had been in Ravensbrück, had died after the birth of her second child in 1952. Stefan's own health was failing rapidly, and he was trying not to think about the day when he would be forced to stop working. Most Poles in those days took two jobs in order to make ends meet. If Stefan lost his one and only job, he would be in serious trouble.

The letter told me that the blow had fallen. His health had given up. For years he had dreaded this moment, and he knew just how bleak his future prospects were. 'I worry most of all,' said the letter, 'about the children. What will they become?' Having written those words, he must have stopped to reflect on what he had written, for he crossed out the last sentence and wrote: 'No, I must not worry about them. They are in God's hands, and there is only one important thing for them. I hope they will learn to have compassion for others.'

The reflection knocked me sideways, and years later it still does. Suddenly all the accepted ambitions that parents have for their offspring, and that I had for Anthony and Mark, were reduced to size. Health, wealth, reputation, success, fame – where did these stand on any eternal scale of values? Stefan had stumbled on the pearl of great price. He had, as his wife had, suffered at the hands of men and women without compassion, and the effects of their cruelties would be with him till he died from them. Yet, in spite of it, or perhaps because of it, he had learned a secret of inestimable importance: that the strongest force in the world was love, and that to share this knowledge with one's children was the most precious gift one could make to them. In the concentration camps, when all other qualities went to the wall, only loving-kindness had counted. Cleverness, rank, talent were of no account. What kept the spark of humanity alive was compassion – one wounded, stricken human being reaching out to another.

Somehow Stefan's letter epitomised everything that the 'Bods' had come to stand for, at least in my eyes. Because they had lived with death, they had understood what was essential to life. Their values were the right way up.

I think this came home to me most clearly when I returned to England after my visit to Poland with Sue Ryder. We had been, for the space of a few weeks, with men and women who were materially poor, if not down-right poverty-stricken, and whose condition was unlikely to improve. Yet one was aware of them as a community bound together by past suffering and present caring. They helped each other, shared what little they had, laughed together, wept together. They wore their humanity like a blazon, proud, triumphant and unconquerable. Then we found ourselves back in the land of plenty, where every man was an island entire unto himself, where false gods multiplied, the rat race was the general goal, and no-one knew how to talk to anyone else, let alone share his loneliness and pain. Becoming aware of the fear and dissatisfaction underlying the prosperity was like being hit in the face with a wet sponge. 'I want to do my own thing' had the status of divine revelation; success, keeping-up-with-the-Joneses, seemed to occupy the nation exclusively. Big was beautiful, 'getting it made' was all that mattered. Failure was out of fashion, and inadequacy had to be swept under the carpet. Who cared?

Well, that was the way it seemed, and I honestly had not been thinking of making comparisons until they reared up and hit me. And when they did I felt an overpowering nostalgia for what we had lost, somewhere on the road to full and plenty. At what point did material plenty (desirable in itself) become a surfeit? At what point did it cease to promote human happiness, and begin to destroy it? I'd have given a lot to know.

All the same, I did not suspect that before a year was out I should be back in Poland.

Paul was not going to get better. In spite of his earlier optimism, Dr W. had hinted as much just before I left Poland. And in March of the following year, Sue had written to me from India: 'I had a long talk with Dr W. when I was in Warsaw. He feels you should know that there will never be any real improvement in Paul's condition, in spite of all his efforts.'

It was a disappointment, but hardly a very great surprise.

The telegram arrived one bitterly cold December afternoon, an unremarkable English-looking telegram in the customary buff envelope, with no outward sign that it had started out in Warsaw. At first I could hardly take it in. It read simply: CHILD DESPER-ATELY ILL. COME IMMEDIATELY.

The Polish Embassy in London arranged for me to collect a visa the following morning. By the next night I was in East Berlin, where our Warsaw-bound plane was grounded for twenty-four hours due to fog and ice. Fully two days after receiving the telegram, I rushed breathlessly into the sanatorium where Paul lay critically ill.

It was his ancient enemy, bronchitis. He lay there, breathing stertorously, a cylinder of oxygen by his bed in case of emergency. The immediate crisis had passed, and I was reminded of all the other crises which had come and gone before he came out to Poland. But a closer glance at Paul made me realise that this time would be different. He had gone into an obvious decline, and the shadow of death seemed to lie over him.

I knew that, if he was pronounced fit to travel, I should have to bring him back to England with me, even if it was only in order that he might die there. In any case, he had already used up his time in Poland. Two years was all he had gone for, and he had already exceeded that time.

For the next two days I shuttled between the Polish Ministry of Health, the British Embassy and the Lot airlines office, making arrangements for our journey back. Within a week it was all fixed. Paul was coming home, and God alone knew how we would manage.

Because I was terrified of what might happen to Paul in mid-flight, the return journey was a nightmare, although everybody concerned made it as easy as possible for us. Paul was a dead weight; and there was always the sheer physical difficulty of coping with his incontinence on a journey. The ambulance which brought us from the sanatorium was allowed onto the tarmac, right up to the plane steps. Paul was lifted out on a stretcher and, as the plane was less than half-full, we had a row of seats to ourselves. On one of these an oxygen cylinder lay ready. At Heathrow, where we made a brief stop, an ambulance took us to a private room where a nurse was waiting. And when we reached our home airport of Ringway, Frank was allowed to bring his car out to the plane.

So next morning, there they both were, Paul and Nicky, together under the same roof for the first time, and neither of them aware, even now, of the other's existence. We kept Paul downstairs, turning one of the reception rooms of our Edwardian house into a temporary bedroom. Although he was only ten, he no longer seemed like a child; he had become a chronic invalid, his heavy body no longer supported by his puny legs. He would never again be able to walk, and there was something in his eyes which suggested that life had become intolerable to him. Poor Paul, condemned for the rest of his life to a bed, and, even within that small confine, unable to move without help. It was a herculean task which confronted us.

We held a family conclave. My mother and Betty had come to stay for a while, knowing that Paul was coming home. Betty was a skilled nurse, but she was getting on for seventy, and Paul was a heavy nursing case, unable to help himself in any way. She would not be able to cope for long, however skilful she was. Then there were the other children. Had we the right to inflict this double burden on them? Anthony was twelve, Mark eight; they both had friends whom they wanted to bring home from school. The presence of Paul and the problems he presented would inevitably make a big difference to their lives, and might well prove insupportable. When our doctor came to see us, he did not mince words.

'You can't keep him at home,' he said. 'It wouldn't be fair to any of you.'

Agreeing with him, we arranged for Paul to go into a hospital about twenty miles away. But when the time came for him to go, we found that we simply couldn't bring ourselves to send him. It was as though we were sending him out to grass, to settle into being an animated cabbage in some vast general hospital. However little awareness of his surroundings Paul had, we felt sure that he would know he had been abandoned.

So yet another agonised discussion followed. We all felt sure that he was going to die, but had no means of knowing whether it would be sooner rather than later. If sooner, then we needn't hesitate. If later . . . It could have been a matter of days or weeks; it could also have been one of months or years. And we were not sure of our physical strength.

In the end, Betty and I worked things out between us, on a three-month trial basis. She would come over from St Helens each week from Monday to Friday, leaving me free to get out of the house and concentrate on part-time teaching, and the public speaking I was doing on behalf of the Sue Ryder Trust. On Friday she would go home, and I would take over. I had no experience of 'heavy' nursing, and I was scared to death. But I didn't like the alternative, so I had to set about learning.

Frank and I got through that first week-end by trial and error, emerging bloody but unbowed, with a mixture of relief and sadness. It was only too obvious that Paul was suffering. When I turned him over onto his side, sat him upright, dressed or undressed him, washed him, changed his pads, he whimpered. Sores were forming, his body was a burden to him. It seemed more than ever tragic that we were unable to communicate with him in any way, or provide him with any means of temporary escape. He couldn't talk, play, read, and he was too deaf to listen to music.

Nevertheless, when Betty came back on the Monday, I felt almost happy. A hurdle had been crossed. Next time would be easier, because I would have more confidence. We would manage somehow.

There was no next time. The following Friday morning, 10th February, we found Paul dead — on the floor by the side of his bed. The irony was that it was not the arch-enemy, bronchitis, which had done for him. He had fallen out of bed, and suffered a heart-attack. He was ten years old.

Before grief, before tears, before any real understanding took over, I was conscious of the one, solid thought: 'Thank God we did not send him away to die among strangers.' If we had sent him, just one week earlier, as we had intended, we should have been tormented with regret. It was bad enough as it was. He had died alone, in the dark, while the rest of the household slept. We could only hope that he had died quickly and mercifully.

I was in a vacuum of feeling. Shocked, numb, distressed, incredulous, emotionally worn-out, I went through the motions that Friday like a zombie. Mechanically answering the questions of doctor, undertaker, parish priest, I just as mechanically went into the kitchen and prepared a Cordon Bleu lunch. I have often looked back on this item of behaviour, and found it inexplicable. With the world falling about my ears, and for no reason that I have ever been able to fathom, I set about meticulously chopping herbs and choosing spices, making a wine sauce, and generally concocting a banquet for which none of us had the least appetite. Perhaps we all do unaccountable things when under stress.

What did we really feel when Paul died—this child of ours who had never even recognised us? I can only speak for myself, and admit to a confused complexity of emotions. I knew that Paul's death was a release for all of us, and there is no denying that I felt a deep thankfulness that this phase of my life was over. But I felt grief too, most probably for the loss of the child he might have been; and there was the even greater pain of believing that I had failed him. A kind of desolation swamped me for a time, and for nights on end I could do nothing but cry. It was a crying which had no rationale except in remorse, and in some odd way I felt I was not entitled to genuine grief. Our friends were so sure that Paul's death was an unqualified blessing that I felt guilty about the grief I felt for him. I knew that what hurt most in the general rejoicing was the assumption that Paul's life had been a useless irrelevance, a disaster best forgotten.

To me it did not seem like that. Yes, I was glad he was dead. But at the same time, I owed him an incalculable debt. If our value as human beings lies in what we do for each other, Paul had done a very great deal: he had, at the very least, opened the eyes of his mother to the suffering that was in the world, and had brought her to understand something of the redemptive force it was capable of generating. I had been broken, but I had been put together again, and I had met many who bore far more inspiring witness than I to the strength inherent in the mending process. What Paul had done for me was to challenge me to face up to the reality of my own situation; and he had handed me a key to unlock reserves buried so deep I hadn't suspected their existence.

Self-knowledge comes to us only in the dark times, when we are stripped of illusion and naked to truth. If Paul had helped me towards even a little understanding, how could I agree that he had lived to no purpose? He had taught me a lesson, quite unwittingly, and now that he was no longer there, I owed it to him not to forget.

CHAPTER 13

A Year-round
Christmas Gift

IT WAS FEBRUARY 1967 when Paul died and Anthony and Mark were thirteen and nine respectively. They were both bright, intelligent boys, who were very different from each other in temperament and skills. Anthony at that time was more withdrawn and academic, Mark much more of a carefree extrovert. Anthony was a potential mathematician almost from the cradle. To him Maths wasn't so much a school subject, it was a language, a philosophy, even a poetry. There was never any doubt about what he would become. In fact he eventually read for an Honours Degree in Mathematics and Computer Science and now, at twenty-four, works for a large international computer organisation. Even as a small boy, he read widely, particularly in history which, together with armchair sport, was an abiding interest.

Mark was much less keen on reading, except for books about wild animals, particularly snakes. Reptiles have been a life-long passion and he is at present spending six months working on a Snake Park and Crocodile Bank in Southern India, before going on to the university to read for a science degree in Psychology. Mark is a clever boy, but he has always felt in the shadow of his more academic older brother. He is much more of an all-rounder: good at languages and music and all kinds of sport. In his last year at school he became Captain of Rugby Football as well as being a very popular Head Boy.

Neither of them remembers very much about Paul or what it was like when he was at home all the time. Anthony was ten and Mark six when he went away to Poland. They were good to him, but like everybody else they found it impossible to have a real relationship with him or to get through to him at all. Mark was the more patient of the two, but then I always felt that the situation was much harder for Anthony, because he was older. Paul had been part of Mark's world from the beginning, but he had come into Anthony's world and disrupted it. And how could a small boy understand that? There is no way of knowing the damage Paul's presence may have done to Anthony. Certainly it meant that he couldn't or wouldn't invite his friends to the house. I think that he came to feel that, because of Paul, he was different from other boys, and in time he began to resent it. Perhaps for him Paul went away in the nick of time.

But Nicky, for both boys, was a very different matter. They worshipped him from the start. From the first moment he came home to us, Nicky was able to draw out reserves of patience, tolerance and actual unselfishness in them both. As he grew older, they often got mad with him, because he could be infuriating, but on the whole they were phenomenally patient and understanding, drawing him into whatever they were doing, teaching him new words, games, songs, playing cricket with him. Nowadays when they go away they send him picture postcards almost daily, and spend hours choosing a toy that will be within his limited scope. Whatever the drawbacks and difficulties, and in spite of the regrets that he is not like other children, the presence of Nicky among us has always brought out the very best in his two brothers.

'Don't expect too much too quickly,' warned the paediatrician, when Nicky was a small baby. 'He'll make progress, but it will be at his own speed, not yours.' Neither Frank nor I minded much about that, because something else this doctor had said had filled us with hope. There was no reason, he had said, why Nicky should not be able to talk. Perhaps not clearly nor very fluently, but there was nothing to stop him talking, in his own good time.

We both felt a tremendous relief at that welcome news, and we didn't mind how long we had to wait. Nicky had got off to a very slow start, having spent most of his first year in and out of hospital, and we should just have to wait for him to start catching up. We could afford to be patient. After our experience with Paul, Nicky's disabilities, severe as they were, seemed comparatively minor. It wouldn't be difficult to keep our sights low; for Paul they had had to be set even lower.

The first big break-through came when he was four. Until then he neither walked nor talked. But by the time he was four and a half, he was staggering around drunkenly on matchstick legs that were only just strong enough to support his weight. And his vocabulary was growing in great leaps. My mother used to spend hours (and so did I) singing nursery rhymes to him, and now we got our reward. Although he did not and does not have the faintest idea of tune, he started reciting them all, jumbled and garbled but quite recognisable. Baa baa black sheep was the all-time favourite, with Oh dear, what can the matter be? and something which always came out like ' 'ere we go ram the mummy push'. By the time he went to school (a special school for the mentally handicapped), he had such a large repertoire and was so proficient that he was selected to star in their Christmas concert for the parents. He was dressed as John Bull, in top hat, black suit and a Union Jack, and he sang Rool Bittamya with great gusto — until, like a fool, I stood up to take a flash photograph of him.

He recognised me, stopped in mid-phrase, and could not be persuaded to continue. I have never felt more like kicking myself.

He was less of a star at the school sports days when he usually either sat down when the whistle blew, or staggered off in the wrong direction. As he was given a balloon or some other toy as a consolation prize, he saw no need to make any great effort. In any case, he hadn't the slightest idea of what was expected of him. But success didn't matter to Nicky. He was blissfully happy at school, singing, dancing, playing with sand and water, making grey, sweaty pastry and banging the triangle in the percussion band.

We had moved from Hale to South London when Nicky was three. The move meant that Betty and my mother now lived far away, and I missed their help sorely. Obviously I was no longer free to go out and teach (which I was not really sorry about), or to continue giving talks for the Sue Ryder Foundation (which I regretted much more). Most meetings are held in the afternoon or evening, and I was once again house-bound at those times.

As I didn't see myself as either earth-mother or house-slave, I looked for something I could do in the mornings after all the boys had gone to school. The answer, surprisingly enough, was easy to find. I turned to free-lance journalism, and beyond it, to broadcasting — something I had always wanted to do, ever since I had first left university. I was lucky enough at this late stage to find an entrée. Interviewing, book-reviewing, feature-writing, mainly for the BBC's religious broadcasting department, but also quite often for magazine programmes such as *Woman's Hour* and *You and Yours*, I could fit in the dizzy whirl between 10 am and 2 pm, at which hour, like Cinderella, I had to leave the fun and make for home, in order to meet Nicky's school-bus at the end of our road.

It was a new world and I revelled in it. The restricted hours didn't really bother me, but all the same I was delighted when a group of nuns, Sisters of St Joseph, who lived in a small convent opposite us, offered to meet Nicky off the school bus on two days a week, and take him home for tea. Nicky adored them and quickly made them his abject slaves. He couldn't manage their real names, which were a bit difficult — Columcille, Regina, Ita, Reverend Mother. To him they were Colum, Jinga, Tar and Miller, while his beloved Sister Raymond, who made him special jellies and chicken sandwiches for his tea, became known to us all as Sister Ray Jelly. (The local parish priest who dropped in from time to time was Father God). The nuns kept tins of sweets and biscuits especially for him, turned on his favourite television programmes, and begged or borrowed children's records for him to listen to. He had his own place at their refectory table, and he knew the rules about meals. He would not let them forget about Grace, and when once he'd grasped that they often listened to readings from a selected book during mealtimes, he would go and get the current book out of the cupboard before the meal started and present it to Reverend Mother (Miller) saying: ' 'Ere's Jesus book. Read.'

From the moment he could walk, he proved to be as full of mischief as any normal toddler, hiding everything within reach. I would find apples in the washing-machine, screw-drivers in tea-pots, socks inside pillow-cases and the kettle-lid in the fridge. He was an opportunist. If I paused in the bed-time songs I used to sing after he was tucked up, he would open his eyes and ask hopefully: 'cuppa tea, cake?' And when once I dozed off in mid-song, he seized his chance, slipped out of bed and went to join the rest of the family round the television set. 'Richard Baker — nooz' he explained helpfully when I rushed downstairs to retrieve him.

Nowadays we live in the country, in a village in Berkshire, and he has had to make new friends. The children here find him a bit strange, and he's too shy and clumsy to join in their games. But he's happy to stay on the fringes and watch. The children are patient with him and keep an eye on him; and if they see him wandering too far they bring him back. We live in a U-shaped Close, and the neighbours have become used to periodic, unsolicited visits from Nicky. None of them seems to object. Nicky bestows his affections liberally on everyone he meets. One Sunday when we took him for a walk along the Kennet and Avon Canal, he ran up to every stranger like an exuberant puppy, saying hello and giving them a hug. His victims looked startled for a moment but they soon thawed under the unexpected onslaught and hugged him back.

Country life has few charms for Nicky, a born townee and lazy to boot. On the rare occasions when I take him for a walk through the woods at the back of our house, and over the adjoining common, he protests loudly and makes a great nuisance of himself, darting off down overgrown paths which lead nowhere, and having to be retrieved like an errant dog. ('I've been pickled,' he announces indignantly, picking the thorns out of his knees). It gets wearing. I gave up trying to make the walks educational after one occasion when I had been faithfully pointing out flora and fauna as we went along. We sloshed through thick mud in our wellington boots, trying to avoid the 'pickles', with Nicky trailing along ever more mutinously. Eventually we saw a horse in a field, and went to talk to it (or rather *I* did). In another corner of the same field were four donkeys. 'Look, darling, donkeys,' I enthused. Nicky ignored the donkeys and glowered at me. 'Bloody donkeys,' he muttered, 'bloody horse, bloody mud, bloody trees, bloody flowers.' Then he gave me a glare to end all glares — 'and bloody RICE PUDDING,' he thundered furiously. Having got all that off his chest, he recovered his good humour and was quite cheerful for the rest of the way home.

Not long ago we went on a touring holiday in the English Lake District. All attempts to interest Nicky in either new-born lambs or age-old mountains failing lamentably, we settled for the petrol stations which seemed to interest him much more. Though he resists anything which he feels might tax his brain, we taught him to identify them, and by the time we were homeward-bound he was an expert shouting out the names of Shell, Esso, Texaco, Burmah, BP and National before we had spotted the signs ourselves. Not much, as intellectual achievements go, but he was immensely proud of himself. 'Orl bah m'self,' he crowed, every time he scored a hit. Success even made him better disposed towards the cows and sheep in the fields, and he deigned to give them the odd glance as we passed. 'Cows give petrol,' he suggested with a glint in his eye. 'Sure, Nicky, remind me to give you a nice glass of petrol when we get home.' 'Na-ow,' he gurgled, doubled up at his own wit, and suddenly knowledgeable. 'Cows don't give petrol, cows give milk an' butter an' cheese an' meat.' But the possibility of a game had occurred to him. 'Pigs give eggs, an' hens give elephants', he chanted hopefully, giving us variations on this theme for the next few miles. It made a change from petrol stations.

Later, when this palled, he thought of something else. 'Mumps in me ear,' he said firmly, and looked at me for approval.

'What did you say? Come again.'

'Mumps in me ear, MUMPS IN ME EAR.' He was getting frustrated and irritable because he couldn't make me understand. It was only when he started: janulary, febually, march, that I realised he meant 'months of the year'. Then I knew what to expect. All such catalogues lead to 'Nobember' and Guy Fawkes Day (he doesn't bother with December, in spite of Christmas). 'NOBEMBER,' he yells in triumph, 'NOBEMBER THE PIFTH — farworks. Wockets.' He suits actions to words, and his joined hands shoot skywards in a great whoosh. Every year as Bonfire Night approaches his excitement grows, and we get more and more anxious-because the truth is that he hates fireworks. Two years ago we took him to a fireworks party, and as soon as he got there he covered his eyes and ears and asked when we were going home. Last year we tried having a few at home, with Frank and Mark setting them off, and Nicky watching from the sun-house. He kept pretending to cheer, but his terror was obvious. At intervals he would tell himself consolingly: 'Nebber mind. Soon be over. Better soon. Won't hurt,' — like a doctor trying to reassure a nervous patient.

Nicky is instantly at home anywhere and with anyone. 'Whass-your name? I'm Nicky,' he asks. He is completely trusting, believing that everyone he meets is a friend. No-one has ever given him reason to think otherwise, as he is a great charmer. When we had the outside of the house painted recently, he was a confounded nuisance to the painters, but they became firm friends. He adopted one of their phrases: 'Cheers, mite,' he greeted them each morning, with thumb extended from closed fist, and with a knowing wink.

But even though he takes universal good will for granted, he knows when appreciation is due. He and I were once invited to have lunch with an Earl at the House of Lords. Halfway through the meal (unimpressed by his august surroundings he had firmly ordered fish and chips and ice cream), he leaned forward and touched our noble host on the sleeve. 'Marbellous meal,' he murmured politely, 'nice, kind gentleman.' As we left, the peer fished in his pocket and gave Nicky a fifty-pence piece. 'Good lad, L——,' said Nicky, in tones of awed admiration. Though most of the time he is a thirteen-year-old scruff, his manners are impeccable when the occasion arises.

The big moments in his life are when he is allowed on to an escalator or into a lift. 'Escalator' was one of the first words to enter his vocabulary, and he never once got it wrong. When he went to Lourdes some years ago with a party of handicapped children, he went missing, and was eventually discovered happily going up and down in the hotel lift. ('What did you do in Lourdes, Nicky?' 'Went in lift.' 'And then what?' 'Got smacked.') Once when I was in hospital he was brought to see me, and was so excited by the lift that he hardly noticed me. 'Went to hoptible. Saw lift,' he replied when asked where he'd spent the afternoon.

His Saturday afternoon treat, which he talks about all week, is a visit with Frank to Newbury's one and only biggish store, where there is an up but not a down escalator. All the shop assistants in the store know him, and they wait for his gap-toothed grin to appear. When he gets to the top, he has to work his way through the shop, across the underwear department, and down some stairs. The first time he did this, as he walked amid the frilly things, his eye caught some objects familiar from his television viewing. 'Look', he exclaimed, in high excitement, and in a very loud voice, 'Playtex Cross-Your-Heart Bra, FOR A BETTER FIGURE.'

The television commercials have the attraction of constant repetition. He knows most of them by heart, repeating the text along with the voice-over, delivering the punch-line with all the hamminess of which he is capable, which is a great deal. Through them he has learned to read the brand names on grocery products, and he swoops on my shopping bag to identify them. 'BOVRIL', he announces happily, 'full of beefy goodness'. Or 'Oil of Oo-lay – makes my skin so nice and smooth'. He pats his cheek and drops his voice to an ecstatic whisper. His memory is excellent, and he does not forget what he has seen. 'Fly the flag,' he shouted excitedly, when we were on the motorway near Heathrow Airport. When I looked puzzled, he jumped up and down impatiently and pointed to a British Airways van just in front of us. 'Look. Fly The Flag,' he explained, adding with a smirk, in case I hadn't recognised the commercial, 'We Take Better Care Of You.'

Nicky is an out-and-out television fanatic. What he does at school (where he is very happy) is shrouded in mystery. When we ask him what he's been doing there, he says, 'Tomato pie and custard' or 'Carrots and ice cream' or even 'Mahnd yown bizness'. It's no use hoping that he'll wax more informative, because as soon as he reaches home, television is all he cares about. He sets about his hobby with considerable thoroughness. Every morning at breakfast he produces the Radio Times and TV Times and has two days' worth of programmes read to him. (If they can't be found, we have a crisis on our hands. He goes into a fearsome sulk, refuses all food, and is inconsolable. He can never be brought to understand that the loss is minor and temporary. To him it is major and devastating. Little things like this upset his equilibrium completely.) He listens carefully, assimilates what he has heard, and from then on he knows exactly who's on, what's on, where and when. And though he still cannot tell the time, except for the hour, he appears to have a built-in timepiece which tells him when to switch from one channel to another. (And if the colour on the set goes wrong, or the picture is otherwise distorted, he knows which button to press to put it to rights.) He likes most programmes, though he has his pet hates: Stars on Sunday, the early evening News summary, and Jackanory, during which he stalks outside the room and stands outside the door waiting for it to be over. He is passionately addicted to soap operas like Crossroads and Coronation Street; cartoons, especially Scooby Doo, have him rolling about the floor; and one year he sat through the entire Labour Party Conference with every sign of rapt attention.

Life with Nicky has its bitter moments — for one thing, he has
had a lot of pain over the years — but it is a lot of fun too. He
has the enviable gift of living in the present. When he's hurt or
miserable, he howls or yells or sulks furiously. But he comes out
of the misery with an engaging grin, like sunshine after storm,
and all is completely forgotten. He has his own world of make-
believe, a limited world which borrows its reality from others'
actual experience. 'Right, I'll be off then,' he remarks purposefully
donning anorak and shoes with great determination. 'Where are
you going?' 'To the pub for a beer — to a party — to the folk-club
— to a rehearsal — to play rugby — to the farm to see cows — to
watch cricket,' he replies, according to his mood, in studied
imitation of his brothers. (Once, in a burst of one-upmanship, he
answered: 'to the House of Lords'). 'See you later,' he says
breezily, and goes out by the front door, slamming it behind him.
A minute later, he comes in again, by the back door. 'I'm back',
he shouts, as though he's been gone for hours. We used to worry
that he really would go off somewhere (and if ever he attempted
to cross the main road at the top of the Close, he'd go right under
a bus. He has not the faintest glimmering of road sense). But we
now know that it is all a game, very necessary to his self-esteem
and his own sense of identity. It doesn't seem to matter that none
of it has any substance, that all of it is fantasy. He takes off his
anorak, changes back into his slippers, and starts a long, highly
realistic conversation on a toy telephone; or 'presents' a TV show,
('To-night, we are lucky enough to have . . .'); or runs through
a DJ act, doing a count-down just like Tom Brown on Pick of
the Pops, the only radio programme he ever listens to. He can
always fill you in on the latest pop songs (as long as you can
understand what he's telling you). As soon as he hears the first
bar, he'll tell you the name of the song and the group singing
it.

Although he is far from pious (despite an inexplicable and
short-lived urge to sit at the piano each day, reciting the Lord's
Prayer) Nicky rather enjoys going to church. Or rather, he likes
the energetic bits, like going up to the Communion rail and
singing hymns. When the time approaches for the Sign of Peace

to be given, he gets quite excited, and as soon as he gets the go-ahead, he rushes round wringing the hand of everyone he can reach, with a beaming, 'Peace be with you, Mr Happy... Mr Bouncy... Mr Sneezy' after the pattern of one of his favourite TV programmes, Mr Men. 'Nicky's idea of the Sign of Peace,' commented a friend recently, 'is nearer the truth of it than that of most theologians.'

And when Mass is finished, he has been known to finish the recessional hymn with a resounding Boom, Boom; and most weeks he brings proceedings to a close with a discreet, sotto voce, 'That's it. That's all for this week, folks. Join us again next Sunday, same time, same place. Till then, cheerio.' He gabbles all this like an incantation, a mysterious ritual with which he cannot dispense.

The other great enthusiasm of Nicky's life is cricket. During the season he sits glued to the television set, refusing to come away even for meals. Avidly he follows every stroke, and when play is finished for the day, he solemnly collects his own bat, ball, wicket and stumps, and drags whoever is available out into the garden to play. He does a serious run-up with the ball, pausing to polish it professionally on his trousers, obviously lost in a Walter Mitty world, in which he is Gary Sobers and Ray Illingworth rolled into one. When he's batting, his ambitions change: he is far more interested in hitting the ball over the garage roof or over the fence next door than in hitting a six.

Betty came to live with us when my mother died six years ago, and she is now an extraordinarily active eighty-four-year-old. Nicky adores her, regarding her as his own private property, a point of view which she is happy to share. The two of them live in a private world of mutual devotion, in the sort of harmony that exists between the very old and the very young. They share jokes and silly catch-phrases from her Yorkshire childhood which make them both giggle. Nicky teases her, calling her 'lovely man', 'nice boy', and occasionally he pulls a beret down on his face and does a Frank Spencer act. 'Mmmmm, Be-e-tty,' he spoofs, and they both fall about with delight. She is the heartbeat of Nicky's world, and when she goes away, even for just a weekend, he is bereft. He hates her to go out of his sight, and she is quite content that it should be so. 'Where she gone?' he demands, knowing very well that she's escaped upstairs to play a game of Patience. We are all very close to Nicky, but Betty is closest of all, since she is entirely his.

The future is hazy, and we cannot confront it yet. The biggest problem is likely to be Nicky's continuing incontinence. If it cannot be brought under control (and we do not see how it can be, unless he reverts to having a colostomy), we may find doors closed to him. And though none of us can bear the thought of being without him, sooner or later, for his own sake, we want to try and get him into some sort of community. A farming community, perhaps, such as those run by the Camphill Village Trust, or Care, or L'Arche — where he can learn to do simple, undemanding tasks while living in a fully supportive environment. If he goes on living with us at home as a mentally handicapped adult there will be the shadow which hangs over all parents of such people. What happens if one or the other parent dies? If both die? Rather than face the logic of that question we would prefer to ease him into a caring community, where he can build up other enduring ties of affection. It will be heart-breaking for us to make a decision about his future, but we shall have to decide what is best for *him*, long term, rather than take the short-term view, for ourselves.

Perhaps by the time we have to do our heart-searching, society will have come up with a few more answers to the eternal problem of the mentally-handicapped adult in its midst. Sheltered hostels would be the ideal. Nicky is blithely unaware that a question-mark overhangs his future. Though he is now a tall and apparently strong thirteen-year-old, in many ways he is still a baby, with a baby's need of protection.

We've kept our sights low, and Nicky's mental age does not seem all that important to us. What *is* important is the joy that he has brought us. He is the focal point of the family, the most beloved of every one of us. Not long ago a priest-journalist who is a close friend made him the subject of a Christmas reflection in the *Tablet*. Musing on the happiness and open affection which characterise so many handicapped children, he wrote:

No outsider like myself is in a position to dictate where the limits of love lie, or to criticise those who find caring for the handicapped an impossible burden. But it is astonishing how often they draw out from others, especially their parents, hidden reserves of patience and affection. How we treat them seems to be in some wise our own and society's acid test. In them, as in the Child of Bethlehem, we see, uncamouflaged, the native value of humanity itself, helpless, vulnerable, possessing nothing. And they have much else to teach. They are fearless: they have no enemies. They are trusting: their world includes no villains. They are loving: they do not doubt themselves. They are the ghosts of our lost innocence. Nicky will never build a car, or fly an aeroplane, or balance a set of accounts. But he never stops producing joy and love wherever he goes. He is a year-round Christmas gift, however crumpled his wrapping.*

'I'm *glad* there was a Paul and a Nicky,' a friend of mine suddenly burst out, a few weeks ago.

By and large, I think I am glad too.

*John Harriott: 'Periscope': *The Tablet* 18/25 December 1976.

CHAPTER 14

What Makes the Desert Beautiful . . .

ONE DAY, ABOUT a year after Paul's death, I was asked to give a talk to a group of women about Suffering. I had to sit down and try and work out what I really did believe, try and impose some order on the jumbled rag-bag of ideas I had been assembling. It seemed impossible, but late one evening I suddenly found everything taking shape and assuming a coherence; and I rushed for a pen so as to capture the moment before it escaped me. I wrote far into the night, and was almost surprised next morning, when I read through what I had written, to find that it was as nearly authentic a summary as I would ever achieve, given my necessarily limited understanding. Everyone has to make his or her own terms with the suffering in his life. I had made mine.

The talk went down well. The women to whom I spoke obviously felt that here was something to which they could respond. The warmth of their response left me in no doubt that my conviction of the redemptive power of suffering was not something I had whistled out of the wind. It was a genuine human response, one which most people could illustrate from their own experience of life.

That was the first of many talks, articles, broadcasts. Too many for my peace of mind. I began to find it increasingly difficult. It wasn't so much the pain of remembering, but the fact of telling my experience over and over again began to empty it of significance, made it seem trite and commonplace. Also, in my determination to say only what I knew to be authentic and to avoid all hint of romanticism or self-pity, I was being emotionally drained.

I was feeling like this when the publishers asked me to write this book. Painful though it has been to write (and parts of it were so painful that if I hadn't forced myself to write them quickly I should never have written them at all) I've encouraged myself with the thought of the many people who have found the things I have previously said or written helpful. Perhaps this book will help a few others. Inevitably, though, it will offend those who deny that life has a pattern, and those who believe that to bring two children such as mine into the world is a heinous crime. (I have had one or two letters to that effect.)

In any case, I have reached the end, and what I have written here is intended as a post-lude to what has gone before, my final word on this subject. I shall give no more talks.

It is immensely difficult to say anything useful about a subject — suffering — which is at once so private and so painful. Even the lessons we learn can be learned only for a time, and then have to be learned all over again. Each fresh onslaught reduces us to jelly, and we have to wait for time to show us some kind of perspective. It's the same for all of us. One way or another, being broken up and put together again is the universal experience, the never-ending central drama of life. ('Man is born broken', wrote Eugene O'Neill, 'he lives by mending; the grace of God is glue') No-one can talk his way out of that basic fact about life, no-one can offer once-for-all solutions. There aren't any. My only excuse for wielding the pen in this delicate area is as one very ordinary human being who has discovered what many others have also discovered: that suffering can teach ordinary people some extra-ordinary things.

In the teeth of the evidence, I do not believe that any suffering is ultimately absurd or pointless. But it is often difficult to go on convincing oneself. When someone we love dies or meets with a violent accident, when a child is brutally murdered or dies of cancer, when a deep relationship is broken up, or when any disappointment or upheaval strikes, despair may set in. We are marooned in misery. Shaking our fists, pounding the air, we ask that despairing and futile question, why. Why, why, why? Most of all, why ME? What have I done to deserve it? If I were God, I wouldn't allow such awful things to happen. How can there be a God of love when the world is full of suffering? The very idea is a mockery. So we give ourselves two frightful alternatives: either God is cruel, unjust, without mercy, a super-being who delights in the affliction of his creatures; or there is no God and we are adrift in total absurdity, in uncharted and unchartable seas. It's a classic double-bind, a Catch-22 situation. Heads nobody wins, tails we all lose.

It's not really surprising, in a world which spawned Auschwitz, Hiroshima and Vietnam, and which seems now hell-bent on self-destruction, that so many have turned away from the mere idea of God, and from the possibility that life has a meaning and an underlying purpose. Job's 'I cry to you and you give me no answer; I stand before you but you take no notice' is not a cry for today, in the sense that there is no 'you', and the universe is believed to be empty. But today's cry is just as despairing, if not more so because there is nobody there to hear it. Any idea that good may come out of the evil we see, and that it may have a redemptive force we do not as yet comprehend, is a matter for scorn and derision, the pathetic bleating of a fool or a religious maniac.

Yet, isn't it at least possible that in the course of time all things do work together for good? In the concentration camp of Ravensbrück, that graveyard of so many human hopes and desires, an unknown prisoner wrote this prayer on a torn scrap of wrapping-paper, and left it by the body of a dead child:

> O Lord, remember not only the men and women of good will, but also those of ill-will. But do not remember all the suffering they have inflicted on us; remember the fruits we have bought, thanks to this suffering – our comradeship, our loyalty, our humility, our courage, our generosity, the greatness of heart which has grown out of all this, and when

they come to judgement, let all the fruits which we have borne be their forgiveness.

That prayer, with its white-hot humanity, seems to me to proclaim and affirm the presence of God in the heart of the dark. And if we dislike or are embarrassed by the word 'God', as so many are, we can substitute another word or phrase — Love, perhaps, or 'the one who *is*'. For myself, I had always clung to Søren Kierkegaard's definition of the deity as 'the beyond in the midst', but the playwright, Dennis Potter, has given an even more satisfying one: '(God is) . . . someone present in the quick of being . . ., in existence as it exists, in the fibre, in the pulse of the world.'*

But if 'God' is the ultimate reality behind our world, it is men who have been given the task of creating that world, inch by inch, generation by generation, confronting the task every day of their lives. We have been free — free to choose evil courses as well as good. Free will, which is our glory, distinguishing us from the animals, has also caused our sorrow. We needed no divine interference to turn our world upside down, to destroy our own harmony and rhythmic at-one-ness with that world, to sow the seeds of dissonance and discord. We could do it, did it, and continue to do it ourselves through our greed, pride, ambition, envy, blindness, stupidity and through the ignorance which we can only gradually overcome. There is a fatal flaw in man which makes his affairs go awry. (Theologians have called it original sin, but the phrase is not a popular one to-day.) It is not God but men who have made wars and devised ever more devastating weapons of destruction or enslavement. Why should we blame God for the concentration camps, or for the new and terrifying concept of megadeath by radiation?

If God is present in our situation, surely it is as a guarantee of continuing hope, of an eventual end to darkness, as the promise that, in spite of present appearances, all will finally be well. It is

* The Other Side Of The Dark—Lent Talk by Dennis Potter, Radio 4, March 1978.

precisely that hope that Christians find in Christ. The very heart and core of the Christian faith is a man dying in pain and confusion and shame, after his life has collapsed around him in total failure; a man who cried out in genuine anguish a few moments before he died on the Cross, 'My God, my God, why have you forsaken me?' It has always seemed to me that, at that moment more than at any other, Jesus was one with all the men and women who have ever existed or ever will exist, sharing with them that sense of abandonment, the desolating fear that their lives are without meaning.

Yet Jesus's death on Calvary showed that despair, anguish, emptiness and darkness were not the end of the story. What was to all appearances a shameful death (that of a common felon), the epitome of muddle and failed hopes, brought a new, confident hope which rapidly spread throughout the world. Good Friday is always followed by Easter Day, as surely as spring always follows winter; and we continue to call it Good. The joy of Easter is compounded of suffering and death *and* resurrection, each element a vital one: despair followed by hope followed by assurance.

To me the death of Jesus on the Cross demonstrates that self-offering love is the only force in the world strong enough to overcome death. Calvary is the greatest act of love the world has ever witnessed, because it was a pledge of new hope and new life from within the crucible of despair. 'If you refuse to love,' we read in St John's Gospel, 'you will remain dead.' 'Caring is the greatest thing', wrote the philosopher von Hügel, 'caring matters most.'

But it is no use thinking that faith in the redemptive power of the Cross is some sort of easy, comforting placebo. We shall not find there a hole in which to shelter, a pious refuge from the harsh onslaughts of reality. The Cross will not protect us from pain, it will face us with it. Calvary challenges us (as does our own personal suffering) to see ourselves as we are, in the situation which is ours. It offers us the present moment in which to search out and find the unsuspected reserves buried deep inside us. As Léon Bloy once wrote, 'There are places in man's heart which do not yet exist, and into them enters suffering, so that they may have existence.' Suffering is a key to the discovery of what we are, and what we have in us to become, if only we can summon the strength. 'What makes the desert beautiful,' reflected Saint-Exupéry's *Little Prince*, 'is that somewhere, far below its surface, it holds a spring of fresh water.'

The men and women I met at Cavendish and in Poland had discovered that life-giving spring. I don't need anyone to tell me that hopelessness and despair reigned in the concentration camps (just as they must reign in similar places today), that men suffered and died there without hope, that many were turned into raging beasts. Hatred and greed and the law of the jungle flourished. But everywhere there were the undeniable signs of grace – in the countless examples of self-sacrifice and compassion. There were heroes like Janusz Korczak, the Polish-Jewish doctor who refused all offers of a safe-conduct for himself and shepherded his orphanage children from the Warsaw Ghetto to the extermination camp at Treblinka, singing all the way; the Orthodox nun, Maria Skobtsova from Yugoslavia and the Polish priest Maximilian Kolbe, both of whom gave their own life as the price of another's; and Betsie ten Boom from Holland, who spread love around her in Ravensbrück, refusing to hate even the guards who beat her, and whose dying words to her sister Corrie were: 'We must tell people what we have learned here. We must tell them that there is no pit so deep that He is not deeper still.' *

Evil as they were, the Nazi concentration camps bore powerful witness to the human truth that, when the chips are well and truly down, the only thing that matters is the spirit. When the pressures were removed, the lesson was almost too painful to go on applying. In *The Real Enemy*, a moving account of his experiences in Buchenwald, Pierre d'Harcourt wrote with rare understanding:

> All I know is that when it became hardest of all for men to behave like decent human beings they spread their wings and rose to great heights; and when the strains and temptations were removed, they sank into the mud.

* *The Hiding Place*: Corrie ten Boom, Hodder and Stoughton.

In their heart of hearts they may have felt, as I did, that, in its way, it was the life of the camp that was the true life, the life that bore witness to what really counted in humanity, the Spirit . . .

This for me is the first lesson of the camp — that it made beasts of some men and saints of others. And the second lesson is that it is hard to predict who will be the saint and who the beast when the time of trial comes. Only one thing prevailed — strength of character. Cleverness, creativeness, learning, all went down; only real goodness survived.*

So the possibility persists that my friends, the survivors, have so much to teach us, *because* of what they endured rather than in spite of it. The value of suffering does not lie in the pain of it, which is morally neutral — but in what the sufferer makes of it. Two persons can go through the same painful experience, one be destroyed by it, the other achieve an extra dimension. The real tragedy of suffering is the wasted opportunity.

When disaster first makes its unwelcome appearance into our lives, self-pity is the first, unavoidable, normal and probably right reaction. Courage flies out at the window, the world seems all of a sudden hostile and menacing, an alien place where we are no longer at home. We feel as though we are falling apart, and are deaf to everything but the shriek of our own misery. In the early stages I don't see how it is possible to fight self-pity. We only exhaust ourselves in trying to keep it at bay. But there is a time limit, and we alone can fix it. I believe it is possible to recognise the point of no return, the moment when self-pity threatens to become malignant. And that is when we have to stand firm, for if once we allow it to get a real hold we are doomed. Self-pity is a cancer which erodes not only our courage and our will to happiness, but also our humanity and our capacity to love. It destroys us, and it destroys the friends who love us and who want to help. After all, if we come to see ourselves as the

* *The Real Enemy*: Pierre d'Harcourt, Longmans.

ill-used victims of outrageous fate, all our actions and thoughts will be governed by bitterness, rancour and sour envy.

It is like the moment that Jesus faced in the Garden of Geth-semane. With the sweat of fear pouring down his brow, he knelt in prayer and begged to be let off the grinding agony that lay in wait for him. But he added the words, 'Father, if it be possible', and, if it should not be possible, then 'Thy will be done'. He accepted that he would have to go through his ordeal to the bitter end, so that the work of redemption could be done. He may have uttered those words — 'thy will be done' — with diffi-culty, but they meant that he accepted and would be ready to face and to use whatever was in store for him. It was his spoken assurance that he would not run away, that generosity of soul would triumph over fear.

That moment in the Garden has always seemed to me a crucial one, the moment in which Jesus faced up to his own Passion, perhaps in doubt and fear of his own capacity to endure it, but in full acceptance of what had to be. That is a moment we all face at some time or other, when we can opt to run away (to drink? drugs? sexual licence?), to lose ourselves in fantasy or superstition, to submerge ourselves in self-pity; *or*, to look reality in the face, exactly as it is, with all its implications. If we refuse to face reality, we run away from ourselves and turn our backs on the possibility of wholeness. It is no good sinking ourselves in good works: if we are in flight from ourselves, we have nothing to offer other than our own emptiness.

However tempting the flight into unreality may be, there is no lasting comfort in it. Fantasy feeds on itself and turns into mad-ness, drug-taking becomes addiction, drinking easily leads to alcoholism. They are blind alleys. The only cure for suffering is to face it head-on, grasp it round the neck and use it.

Suffering is difficult to define. Basically, it is something (maybe quite minor) which happens against our will, is unpleasant, and blows our carefully-regulated lives asunder. We protest, kicking and screaming for the restoration of the *status quo ante*. If we can persuade ourselves to stop struggling and come to terms with the pain, adapt our natural rhythms to it, accept it as no better and no worse than it is, we may still be floundering in darkness, but the darkness may contain the promise of light. It is a paradox, but one that has been borne out again and again by individual experience, that it is *only* in the darkness, the emptiness and the hopelessness that we find our true selves.

A political prisoner, facing death, once wrote to his fiancée: 'I now realise why man, at certain times of his life, must descend into the depths. First, that he may learn to call upon and cry out to God; second, that he may recognise his own failings; and third, that he may undergo a change of heart.'* C. S. Lewis said the same thing in different words. 'Pain', he wrote, 'is God's megaphone to arouse a deaf world.'† In the normal rush and hullabaloo of life, we have neither time nor mind for personal stock-taking. It is only when we are brought up short, when we are afraid or bewildered or disoriented, that we turn to God with an uncomprehending, frequently agnostic, cry for help. The bubble of our self-esteem has been pricked, our complacency has gone, and we are totally vulnerable. Then and only then can grace begin to operate in us, when we begin to take stock of ourselves, and to listen to our inner voices.

Is it really paradoxical that when we are distressed we turn to the friend who knows what distress can be like? We don't quite know why, but there doesn't seem much point in going for sympathy, the deep-down, understanding kind, to those other friends whose paths have always been smooth. It is as though human beings lack a whole dimension and cannot come to maturity until they have faced sorrow. There is an old Arab proverb which says: 'Too much sunshine makes a desert' and the human heart is very often a desert. But sorrow irrigates the desert. A few years ago a friend of mine, a poet, stricken by the death of a close friend, wrote:

* *Dying We Live*: Collins/Fontana.
† *The Problem of Pain*: C. S. Lewis

> Shall I complain
> How swift you passed?
> Could I regret the widened heart?
> Could I complain of it at all?

It is told of Elgar that he once sat and listened admiringly to a young singer with a beautiful voice and faultless technique. She was good, he said, but not great. 'But she will be *great*,' he went on to suggest, 'when something happens to break her heart.' The same holds good for most, if not all, creative artists. There are truths which only sorrow can teach, and it is the source of the most important discoveries about life It is in sorrow that we discover the things which really matter; in sorrow that we discover ourselves. As Ernest Hemingway is said to have written to Scott Fitzgerald, 'When you get the damned hurt use it. Use it and don't cheat.'

When it's our turn to be broken on the wheel, we are aware only of the breaking. The wounds are bleeding and raw, and the pain is so great that it seems impossible to survive it. We are so often beset, not only by the pain of loss or unfulfilled dreams, but by our own personal demons of jealousy or anger or bitterness as well. If we wrestle with the demons we exhaust what little energy we have, and place ourselves even more at their mercy. If any well-meaning fool were to suggest, at such a time, that everything was really for the best, we should be justified in heaving a well-aimed brick. We are not ourselves, our identity is confused, our self-esteem in tatters.

Yet we cannot run away from our own battles without losing ourselves in the process. In the midst of chaos and confusion we catch an occasional glimpse of the calm, still centre of our being, the essence of our true selves, waiting to be discovered,

> and the end of our exploring
> will be to arrive where we started
> and know the place for the first time.*

* *Four Quartets*: T.S. Eliot, Faber and Faber.

If we can stand still and let the storm do its worst, we may still summon the strength to move forward when its bitterest force is spent.

> Blunt the sharpness;
> Untangle the knots,
> Soften the glare.*

The words are from the *Tao Te Ching*, but their meaning is universal. Human beings have a deep need for stillness and harmony. In the standing still, in the acceptance of the unavoidable moment in all its bleakness, lies the possibility of salvation and growth for ourselves and for others. We can say to whatever deity we pray to, 'For what it's worth, here it is. Take it and use it. Use it for the hungry, the homeless, the lonely; for the man down the road who's lost both his job and his wife; for the friend whose little girl has been killed. Use it to help me understand, to be less self-centred, more loving.'

Heaven knows, we may be feeling so wretched that we have to do violence to ourselves to utter such a prayer. We may do so through clenched teeth. But if we even hope one day to mean what we say, we are expressing a trust that one day, though not yet, all will again be well; and all will finally be well. On that day we shall at last 'arrive where we started' and know what it is to be whole.

---

* *Tao Te Ching*: Lao Tzu, Penguin Classics.